FAKE HISTORY

FAKE HISTORY

Ten Great Lies and
How They Shaped
the World

OTTO
ENGLISH

WELBECK

Published by Welbeck
An imprint of Welbeck Non-Fiction Limited,
part of Welbeck Publishing Group.
20 Mortimer Street,
London W1T 3JW

First published by Welbeck in 2021

A CIP catalogue record for this book is
available from the British Library

ISBN
Hardback – 9781787396395
Trade Paperback – 9781787396401
eBook – 9781787396418

Typeset in Sabon by seagulls.net
Printed and bound in the UK

10 9 8 7 6 5 4 3 2 1

www.welbeckpublishing.com

For Helen, James and Sophia.

CONTENTS

THE PAWNS OF HISTORY

Through nothing more than sheer longevity, my grandparents became time travellers from another age.

When I knew them, in their declining years in the late 1970s and early 1980s, they were living in the same place they always had – a two-bedroom Victorian house halfway down the one street of the Staffordshire pit village where they had both been born in the previous century.

Their home was a portal to another era. The front parlour was filled with wartime 1940s utility furniture that was kept for a best occasion that never seemed to happen. They dwelled instead in one gloomy back room, where the hearth always burned while the wind rattled at the windows that looked out to the garden and the valley beyond.

There was no telephone, no central heating, and for most of their lives no hot running water. They cooked on a tiny oil-burning stove in the kitchen and only had a bathroom fitted, at my aunts' insistence, in the early 1970s. Both, quite obviously, viewed the innovation with some considerable suspicion.

The silence of their days was broken by the sound of the front gate swinging, heralding the arrival of a neighbour or grandchild, or perhaps the district nurse, who would come every morning to visit my grandmother and dress her sores.

At some point in the late 1970s, my grandmother had lost the use of her legs and a gigantic hospital bed had been imported that filled up the tiny room. She would sit up in it and greet visitors, while all the while, she faded away.

They had few interests – my grandfather loved Norman Wisdom films and my grandmother loved to talk – but that was the extent of it.

They took the *Daily Express*, then still a broadsheet newspaper, but never seemed to read it, and I was too young to ever notice them talk about politics, if they ever talked about it at all.

In the corner of that dark back room stood a black and white television – their one nod to modernity – and beside it, two old wirelesses and a headset that had not seen action since the TV arrived. The detritus of the electronics of a passing century.

Several times a year my mother would drive me and my sister up there – and after the initial excitement of seeing my grandparents, boredom would swiftly set in. There was a small wall at the front that we could jump over. And that creaky gate that we liked to swing on. But that was the extent of the entertainment landscape, apart from the telly, which was rarely turned on.

Sometimes I'd sneak into that slightly creepy front parlour and read the encyclopaedias gathering dust in the corner. Once I came across my grandfather's teeth in a glass and, having never seen dentures before, assumed they were a novelty toy and waved them about until someone told me off.

The only truly fascinating thing in the house, at least to my 10-year-old boy's eyes, was the rifle. Parked behind the desk in the back room just beyond my reach – but never beyond my grandad's. I longed to be shown it properly, or better still hold it or be told what it was for – but whenever I asked, silence descended and the subject was changed.

Like many boys of the 1970s, I was obsessed with two things in childhood: *Star Wars* and real wars. In between playing with my toy guns and action figures, or pretending that my sister's hockey stick was a lightsaber, I'd read "soldier" comics like *Warlord* and *Commando*, both of which told dashing tales of British men fighting those evil Germans. I was proud that my own father had been in the Second World War and prouder still that my surviving grandfather had fought in the First.

So, when my obvious boredom could be placated no more my mother would encourage my grandfather to: "Tell him about the war, Dad!"

And Grandad would try to oblige. He would fetch down a picture of himself in uniform of kilt and cap; young and upright, he was very different to the 90-year-old man whose pipe sparks peppered his cardigan with holes as he tried to engage with his grandson.

Stirred to entertain me, he'd talk about how he'd joined up and marched off to war. He'd speak at length of the mud and the trenches, the noise and the friends he made. And sometimes he would take out a Bible in which he'd noted down the names of all the battles he'd been engaged in: Ypres, the Somme, Vimy Ridge. And all the friends he had lost.

And as he talked more, his voice would falter and his eyes would start to brim. Sooner or later – to my horror – he'd begin to cry, at which point my grandmother, observing things from her bed, would boom:

"Is he talking about the war again? He's a bloody warmonger. Shut up about the war, Martin! Nobody's interested." Or words to that effect.

And, after an awkward moment or two, I'd leave, while my own mother tried to calm things down between her parents and go off to swing on the gate out front with my sister and wonder what it was all about.

One thing was clear. His stories were nothing like the ones in the comics. None of this matched up to *Warlord*. And frankly, I was a bit disappointed. I didn't care about his chums and the mud and lice. I wanted to hear about the hand-to-hand combat stuff and all the times he had shot people or come face to face with people who might have been Adolf Hitler – you know – before he was famous.

Everyone knew it had all been tremendous fun in the wars, but when he talked about it, all he seemed to do was cry.

My grandmother died in the winter of 1985 and my grandfather a few short weeks after that. In time my parents bought the old house and did it up. They ripped out the partition wall between the two sitting rooms, put in a kitchen and central heating and added another bathroom upstairs. Soon, all that was left of my grandparents' home was the teak mantelpiece above the fireplace and a patch on the right, where the varnish had been worn away by 70-plus years of Grandad leaning on it.

Once they were gone, my aunts and uncle and even my mother began to open up about them. Grandad had, by all accounts, not always been the kindly old man I had taken him for. In his earlier life he had had a terrible temper and had once tied a local man to a tree after an argument.

Nobody had been brave enough to cut the poor fellow down and all through the night he could be heard whimpering:

"Martin, Martin, please let me go." It was a bizarre story and one that had clearly affected my mother, because she'd retell it over and over again.

He had also hated Germans with an almost unhinged frenzy. At the end of the Second World War, my then teenage aunts had befriended some German prisoners of war who were working on a nearby farm and when my grandfather had found out he had shaved off their hair.

"He could be a terrible man!" my aunt said once. "We were all scared of him."

It was unclear how he'd earned a living. Mum loved to tell a good story, but she wouldn't give much out about that. In her version of things, his father had owned a small farm but when my grandfather inherited it, he'd sold it for a pittance and frittered the money away. He had been a coal miner for a bit and then done nothing very much at all, apart from drinking in the pub and worrying about wars.

During the 1930s, he'd built an air raid shelter and long into the 1960s stocked it up with tins of food in case the Russians or Germans – or someone else – tried to invade.

The one source of enduring pride, which the whole family shared, was his war record. There was something gallant about that. The saga went that he had run away in the middle of the night, after an argument with his father, and joined the heroic Argyll and Sutherland Highlanders "through family connections". Then, after four years of living in the trenches he had made it back "on the last boat" and collapsed into his mother's arms on the doorstep of the farm.

Families, as we shall see later in this book, have a tendency to spin their own history and frequently exaggerate and make stuff up. An asker of awkward questions from an early age, over the years I'd pick holes in the story, much to my mother's irritation.

"Last boat in 1918? What last boat? The war was over. Why was there a last boat?"

* * *

Ten years ago, my own mother became ill and we were obliged to sell our family home. As I set about clearing out the letters and remnants of lives that filled the drawers of our house, I found a file compiled by my late uncle that detailed my grandfather's war. It had been tucked away by my mother unopened and unread. Inside it contained the truth of Grandad's war. It was much darker than the fairy tale of the handsome young farmer in a kilt going off to fight for King and country.

He had indeed been attached to the Argylls but he was never really a member of that illustrious Highland Regiment – with its long history and roll call of battle honours. He was in fact in the Machine Gun Corps, the butchers of the Western Front, who created orphans and widows and bereaved parents, as they gunned down men in the First World War.

Grandad, undoubtedly, would have killed a lot of people.

The Corps' main tool was the Vickers machine gun, a device that industrialised murder. The weapon could fire 500 rounds a minute over a range of 4,000 metres. Anyone advancing into it was cut into ribbons of flesh.

Known as "The Suicide Club", because of the high casualty rate they sustained, courtesy of the sniper bullets they attracted, my grandfather's corps were the most hated people on the Western Front – at least from the point of view of the enemy. They suffered some of the worst casualties of any unit. One in three were killed or seriously wounded. If they were captured at all they rarely made it to prisoner-of-war camps alive.

As I went through the record, it began to make more sense. The anger. The sorrow. The names of lost friends that he tried to pass on to a 10-year-old boy. The failure to ever amount to anything – because what was the point? His visceral hatred of Germans and his unwillingness to let his daughters go near them. The tying of people to trees – a common wartime punishment. The tears in front of the fireplace as he tried to tell his grandson the story he wanted to tell but the one that I, as a child, didn't want to hear.

Quite obviously, he had been suffering from Post-Traumatic Stress Disorder.

* * *

All of the adults who lived through the Great War have now gone. Nobody can remember first-hand the events that wrecked my grandfather's peace of mind and coloured the lives of those who knew him.

And yet even as the memory of the War becomes second-hand, there are those who were not there, who seek to attach themselves to it and shape the narrative further.

In the process, Grandad and millions like him are no longer ordinary people caught up in events. They are rendered as homogenous heroes or victims, and their lives and the scars they carried have been reduced, massaged and appropriated to fight a different battle long after they are gone.

At the same time many of "the big names" of history have had their roles greatly amplified. "Great men" narratives ensure that statues on plinths in European and American cities continue to shape the way that a good proportion of us perceive the past. Many a modern populist politician would like it to remain so. They insist that statues are "history" and that to question them is to seek to "erase" it – as if history itself was defined by lumps of brass and marble.

We will look at this curious conceit further on – but those twin elements of unquestioned acceptance and the false narratives they propagate are critical to the debunking of fake history and the theme of this book.

Statues are not harmless artifacts. They deliberately contrive to shore up narratives that attribute all of history and its deeds to a carefully selected group of mostly male individuals.

In the process, the vast majority of people are simply ignored and nowhere is that more apparent than in history's almost complete disregard for women.

I'm ashamed to admit that I never asked my grandmother Lizzie to tell me about her life. Back in childhood, I simply wasn't interested. She had been the mother to my own mother and the wife to my war veteran grandfather and that was enough. Her role was secondary and her life seemed somehow less important.

I never learned the names of her parents or what she had done before she met my grandad. I never learned anything about her at all.

And trying to find out, long after she has gone, is a challenge. The collective family memory draws a blank. The very few stories that tell us who she was are not properly curated. Like women throughout history, the events of Lizzie's life have been largely forgotten.

I know she worked as a scullery maid in a "big house" and that her family were very poor. But that's it. The rest is guesswork.

There are moments in this book where I have tried to draw out the stories of other women, only to be similarly set back. All too often, their lives have been eclipsed by those of the men who lived at the same time or excised from the narrative altogether. The further back we travel the more we see women reduced, almost entirely, to anonymous or even absent people. We know the name of Cleopatra's father* for example – but who her mother was remains a complete mystery.

Matters have not been helped by the fact that almost all of the most celebrated historians from antiquity onwards were men. Cutting women out has created a false impression that they "didn't do anything" of note. Among some male academics and historians that attitude still prevails.

Those women who are present, whether Queen Elizabeth I or Catherine the Great, the playwright Aphra Behn, Maya Angelou or even (dare I say it) Margaret Thatcher, had to be greater still than their male contemporaries to succeed and make their mark. And in the process of scrutiny, they inevitably attracted less "fake history" than those men who jostled so vigorously to carve their names for posterity.

The same issue presents itself in aspects of race and geography. Africa's past in particular has for too long been neglected by scholars and documentary makers – with interest only perking up when the Europeans arrive.

In short, the "dominant narrative" of history has, for the last thousand years at least, been dictated by "the dominant people" and that means that it has been written by white males, about white males, for white males.

---

* Ptolemy XII Auletes

Much of the "fake history" in the coming pages is therefore, inevitably, about those people and what they actually did rather than what we think they did – because challenging that is the reason I'm here.

I start with my grandparents because it's important to remember that the history of the world is not simply one of "great men" but of the very many more supposedly "ordinary people" too. The majority. The individuals whose lives got tangled up in the power games of politicians, emperors and kings. The nameless soldiers on the fields at Culloden or Waterloo. The victims of the Irish and Bengal famines. The Mongol horsemen in Genghis Khan's army.

I have dubbed them the "pawns of history". The people who have been reduced to extras in the "big events". The millions who throughout time were obliged to sweat, toil and suffer as a result of – or for – the ambitions of others.

By upending the great lies and lazy conceits of the past, we can better comprehend it, and by doing that we can elucidate our present. Fake history runs deep. This book's mission is to topple it from the plinth and lift up truth in its place.

In the process, we can come to understand our modern world better and make sense too, of why my grandad cried when I asked him to tell me about what he had done in the Great War.

CHAPTER ONE

WINSTON CHURCHILL WAS BRITAIN'S GREATEST PRIME MINISTER

How we deliberately misremember the past

The greatest challenge facing anyone writing a book that could theoretically cover the entire course of human history – is that there's an awful lot of history.

Trying to get a grip on everything that happened in the past would be like painting the Forth Bridge. You'd have to dedicate your entire life to the task. Although given that this is a book about *fake history*, I should perhaps clarify that the legend of that never-ending paint job is itself a myth. Never happened.

Most people get their "history" from dimly remembered lessons in school, the "things that happened to Grandad" or those generally agreed notions of what "we all accept to be true".

The subject is far more than a mere academic discipline. The events of the past are nowadays part of the entertainment landscape. The TV schedules and streaming services are clogged with documentaries about kings and queens, wars and empires, which for the most part, concentrate on recent events. There's a very good reason for that. Near history is accessible. There's something familiar about it. We feel we can almost reach back and touch it. It also makes for cheap telly, thanks to the vast wealth of archive material available.

There's audio of George VI stuttering his way through speeches, footage of suffragette Emily Wilding Davison throwing herself under a horse, and even a creepy snatch pic of Queen Victoria thanking people at a garden party; but we can't hear the tremble in Charles I's voice as he is sentenced to death for treason in 1649.

The cadaver of recent history is still warm. It doesn't need actors stumbling about on wobbly sets – the clothes are still in the family dressing-up box. Our grandparents were there.

And in much the same way we feel we know our favourite soap actors, the protagonists who occupied centre stage feel familiar and known to us.

In Britain, no figure from the last century looms larger than Sir Winston S. Churchill. He is a 20th-century icon every bit as big as Elvis, Dolly Parton or Marilyn Monroe. Signature cigar in hand, bow tie around the neck, his carefully crafted image still resonates five decades after his death. He is more than a statesman. He is Britain's most enduring celebrity – and a man whose story has become as mythologised as any still revered idol.

And so, inevitably perhaps, this book starts with him – or more specifically, with someone who worked for him – standing on an empty pavement, on a chilly winter's night in 1944, staring down at a bundle of documents marked "Top Secret" that were lying in the street.

Who exactly had dropped them is unknown, but the woman who found them, according to no less a source than Churchill's grandson Nicholas Soames, was a cleaning lady at the Ministry of Defence – who we shall call "Mrs Jones".

As it was the middle of the night and as the wartime blackout was still in full swing, it is something of a miracle that she managed to see anything at all. London in that winter of 1944 would have been almost imperceptible to the naked eye. On moonless nights, it would have been impossible to see your hand in front of your face and simply walking along the roads was fraught with danger. The blackout was meant to stop the Luftwaffe identifying targets on the ground, but it generated home-grown carnage all of its own.

In 1941, an astonishing 9,169 people were killed on Britain's roads, the highest traffic casualty toll in British history and almost 10 times higher than the annual figure today, despite the presence of considerably more cars.

Writing in the *British Medical Journal* in 1939, the King's Surgeon, Lancelot Barrington-Ward, suggested that thanks to blackout regulations, "the Luftwaffe [is] able to kill 600 British citizens a month without ever taking to the air."

The blackout was also a gift to muggers, thieves and pickpockets, who seized the opportunity to rob their fellow citizens, having clearly never heard of that famous Blitz Spirit.

It was therefore, no doubt with some trepidation, that Mrs Jones emerged into the streets of Whitehall late on that January night, and it was perhaps an acute over-awareness of the dangers, lurking there, that led her to spy the ribbon-bound documents lying in a puddle. Mrs Jones had been dusting the filing cabinets of Whitehall for years and she knew an important bundle when she saw one. This was obviously something that needed to be safeguarded, but Mrs Jones was no fool. She knew that if she turned back now there'd be a lot of awkward questions. So, fulfilling her patriotic duty, she scooped the file up in her coat, looked swiftly about her and hopped on the night bus home to the East End.

The previous year, the war had turned in Britain's favour. Hitler's invasion of the Soviet Union had left the German Wehrmacht on the back foot in the east and things were little better for him in the south. The Allies had pushed the German army across the Mediterranean and in September 1943 had begun advancing through Italy.

By the onset of winter in 1943 they had reached the Gustav Line and that is where the problems started. This was one of the many defensive lines that had been built across Italy by the Germans and Italians in anticipation of an Allied invasion and it was so effective that it ground the Allied advance to a halt.

In early December, Churchill flew to Tunisia to visit the troops in a morale boosting trip, but as soon as he landed, he fell gravely ill. According to his physician Lord Moran, on the night of 14th December the PM almost died from the combined effects of pneumonia and heart problems, although by the 16th, thanks to Moran's efforts, Churchill was on the mend. As he recuperated in bed, Churchill pored over plans that would break the stalemate in Italy, and it was those plans that Mrs Jones had now found in the street.

For a few brief hours, the course of the Allied campaign in Italy lay in the lap of a middle-aged woman from Wapping, with her weary feet up in front of the stove, enjoying a biscuit and a well-earned cup of tea.

And then the back door swung open and her son marched in fresh from the pub.

"What's that?" he asked, pointing at the folder, and when she told him, he declared: "I should probably take it back."

After some debate as to whether that was wise, what with all those people being killed by traffic, he jumped on his bike and hot-peddled it to Whitehall.

Not for the first time in British history, the young man's patriotism was to come up against the bureaucratic stiffs at the Ministry who told him to "leave them there and go". Taking umbrage, Jones Junior declared that he wouldn't hand them over to anyone less than an Admiral. Eventually some blimp* was dragged from his glass of brandy and took the documents away.

Shortly after that, the penny dropped.

The following morning, in a growing climate of panic, an emergency War Cabinet was called and the security breach assessed. Churchill flew into one of his rages. How had this happened? Who was to blame? Who should be sacked? His Chief Military Assistant, Hastings "Pug" Ismay, was quick to reassure him that no secrets had been compromised and then told his boss about the cleaning lady and her son. And as Ismay spoke, Churchill was so moved by the whole rambling bikes, blackouts and biscuits saga that he began to cry. The old man was a bit of a crier and it didn't take much to push him over the edge. Once the tale was over, he wiped his tears, blew his nose, banged the table and declared:

"She shall be made a Dame Commander of the British Empire! Make it so!"

So, the order was sent out that Mrs Jones, the MOD cleaning lady, should be given a damehood, but by the time the King's birthday honours came out it had been downgraded to a mere

---

* A pompous or irascible military figure who clings to an outdated ideology; the name comes from a British comic strip character created by David Low in the 1930s.

MBE. Churchill, who seems to have been keeping an unusually close eye on the awards lists, wasn't having that and was determined to make good on his promise. And sure enough, when his own resignation honours were published, Mrs Jones was fifth on the list with a DBE.

This is one of those fabulous Churchill stories. It illustrates the inherent decency and wisdom of the man. A politician, as concerned for the common charwoman as his commitment to defeat Hitler. Winston Churchill. Top bloke. Gong giver.

It's also completely made up.

The anecdote originates with a Churchill biographer by the name of Alexander Boris de Pfeffel Johnson, who was later to emulate his political hero by becoming Britain's 55th Prime Minister. In 2014, Johnson, then still Mayor of London, wrote a gushing paean to Winston entitled *The Churchill Factor* which hammered home the parallels between the war-time leader and himself, with all the subtlety of a pneumatic drill in a secluded rural hamlet on a peaceful Sunday morning.

According to Johnson, Churchill was Britain's greatest hero who "saved our civilisation" from the threat across the Channel for no other reason than that he had a great big personality and a winning way with words.

"He and he alone, made the difference," Johnson wrote.

Johnson's hagiography left many unconvinced. In a withering review in the *New Statesman,* eminent historian Richard J. Evans likened the work to being "cornered in the Drones Club and harangued for hours by Bertie Wooster". That is, perhaps, a little unfair on Wooster, the foppish comic foil to Jeeves in P.G. Wodehouse's classic comic novels. For while Bertie might be a bit of a fool, he is at least well-meaning and full of good intentions.

Johnson's book, by contrast, was on a mission. Or more accurately two missions. One to armour-plate Churchill's reputation, the other, to hop a ride on his legend.

The text is plagued with inconsistencies, factual errors and dubiously sourced events including the one about the cleaning lady, which Johnson claims he was told by Churchill's grandson, Nicholas Soames. The anecdote seems to have tickled the author because he reiterated it constantly while promoting his book and even at the 32nd Annual Churchill Conference in Oxfordshire in June 2015 where the audience seem to have soaked it all up unquestioningly.

Ending the tale, Johnson does at least confess that the story "has withstood all my efforts to verify it at the Churchill Archive or elsewhere."

Well I have, and in doing so, I have concluded that Mr Johnson can't have tried very hard.

The facts of the "Mrs Jones" story can be quickly and easily debunked by anyone with access to something called the internet.

Awards are archived in freely accessible public record databases and can be easily googled. The number of women who received DBEs in Winston's resignation honours lists in August 1945 amounts to a great fat zero. Of the 37 honours dished out on 14th August 1945, only four went to women and three of those were the Defence Medal (DM). All of those DMs went to Churchill's aristocratic Downing Street secretaries while his Assistant Private Secretary, Shelia Allison Minto, received an MBE.

Nobody got a DBE.

Dig deeper and you find that between 1941 and 1946, just 21 DBEs were awarded. None of them are gifted to cleaning ladies from the East End. All went to powerful, famous, well-connected and "eminent" women.

The story of the lady who got made a Dame for retrieving secrets from a puddle is no more real history than claiming that Mickey Mouse invented radar. It's a flat-out fabrication.

It might seem like a harmless fabrication. A "good story" and nothing more. But it matters.

The recent past shapes our recent present in more ways than we notice. Churchill's iconic life and deeds are increasingly used to shape our present. To define "who" we are. If we can't get Churchill right – we get nothing else that follows in our own history right either.

* * *

The historian Andrew Roberts, who has dedicated much of his life to the study and the cult of Winston, once claimed that "a thousand biographies" have been written about him – but if that is true, a good proportion of them will be filled with all the things Churchill never said and another with all the things he never did. Very few people in very recent history have been the subject of such mythologising.

Take the famous anecdotes and quips beloved of Churchill superfans – and known by all. There's the story where the PM, late at night, stumbles into the great Labour MP Bessie Braddock in the corridors of power: "You're drunk!" she says, to which Churchill replies, "and you're ugly, but in the morning I will be sober." Boris Johnson claims to have identified "the very spot" where the encounter took place. Which is fascinating, given that it is unlikely that it ever took place at all.

Churchill was a gentleman of the Victorian era, not a wise-cracking vaudeville act, and the gag is older, even, than him. It was first related by Augustus Hare in his diary about an encounter between two unnamed MPs in 1882, when Churchill was eight and Bessie Braddock had yet to be born. The joke was well-worn enough to have been used in a 1934 W.C. Fields film *It's a Gift*. So if Churchill ever said it, he was simply plagiarising a very old and corny joke.

The same goes for the tale where Nancy Astor, the first Conservative woman MP, tells Churchill that if she were married to him, she would put poison in his coffee, to which the PM replies that, if that were so, he'd drink it. A withering rebuff sure – but it wasn't Winston's.

That gag had been around since the days of Queen Victoria and had previously been attributed to everyone from David Lloyd-George, PM during the First World War, to the American author Mark Twain. Quote Investigator, the website dedicated to tracking down falsely attributed sayings, discovered that the line appeared in the 1935 movie *Bright Lights*, where the following exchange takes place:

Patricia Ellis: If you were my husband, I'd give you poison.
Joe E. Brown: Yes, and if I was your husband, I'd take it.

And that's just the start of it. Churchill never said that the Royal Navy was governed by "rum, sodomy and the lash". He never claimed that "if you're not a liberal by 25 you don't have a heart" and that "if you're not a Conservative by 35, you don't have a brain", and even if had he done so he'd have looked bloody stupid. For he himself was a Conservative MP at 25 and a Liberal one by the time he turned 35.

Winston never moved away from a Socialist MP at the Westminster urinals, fearing his manhood would be nationalised and he never wrote "this is the sort of English up with which I shall not put" in a letter to a publisher when criticised for ending a sentence with a preposition.

Despite a million internet memes with his picture on them claiming he wrote: "If you're going through hell, keep going", he never said it. That quote seems to have entered public consciousness via a religious article in an American Christian newspaper and has only been attributed to Churchill since the mid-1990s. He never declared that "courage is what it takes to sit down and listen" or that "an empty car pulled up at Downing Street and Attlee got out" or that the Labour leader, his wartime coalition partner, was a "sheep in sheep's clothing".

Attach a fairly anodyne quote to a picture of a famous person and you give it value. And Churchill like Freud, Einstein and Twain seems to be the gift that keeps on giving in that regard.

Churchill was a great coiner of phrase. Unlike many a modern politician he penned his own speeches and on the evidence of his books, or at least the ones he wrote by himself, he was undoubtedly capable of great wit.

But the magnified cartoonish Churchill of our popular imagination is no more the real man than Julie Andrews was the "real" Maria von Trapp. He has become as much a work of fiction as Sherlock Holmes or James Bond – and much of the groundwork of that characterisation was laid out by none other than Winston Churchill himself.

For as great a politician as he was – what he really excelled at was self-promotion.

Various sources claim Churchill stood up in the House of Commons in January 1948 and said that we should: "leave the past to history, especially as I propose to write that history myself."

Hansard, the record of all parliamentary exchanges, excludes it perhaps because it was an interjection, but here, at last, is a quote that fits the man.

The line anticipates one in the 1962 western, *The Man Who Shot Liberty Valance*, where a character sums up the folklore of the Wild West thus: "When the legend becomes fact, print the legend."

Churchill could not more perfectly be summed up.

He quite literally took control of the narrative in his six-volume *The Second World War*. Written collaboratively and published between 1948 and 1953, the books put their author centre stage. The highly subjective account, which was a global best-seller, reaped its author millions of pounds – but more importantly, forged his legend.

Churchill, alone among the wartime leaders, wrote an account of the events between 1939 and 1945 and his narrative placed himself firmly in the middle of things. By his account, his judgement is seemingly inviolable, with the great man deflecting blame for his own mistakes in Norway and Greece while taking full credit for things he got right – or didn't have much of a part in.

In reality, Churchill prevaricated over the planned invasion of Normandy in 1944 known as operation Overlord. He was wary of the plan, continually seeking to delay it or even postpone it indefinitely, but *The Second World War* bends the narrative to overstate his support for the assault and thus glory in its subsequent victory.

In the years since, his biographers and admirers have been all too happy to play along.

People love a great story. The one about the British Bulldog who spent years in a hermit-like wilderness only to emerge to lead a quasi-holy crusade against the unspeakable evil of Nazism is just such a tale. Over time, it has become ever more sacrosanct and the cult-like guardians of it ever more bellicose.

That reputation was only bolstered by the 2002 BBC2 TV poll, which determined that the wartime PM was our Greatest Briton. That curious national exercise placed him a mere two places ahead of his distant cousin Princess Diana in a list that included *Some Mothers Do 'Ave 'Em* actor Michael Crawford, Cliff Richard and – confusingly – at number 86, U2 frontman Bono, who is Irish.

Since that coronation by TV, Churchill has been our "national hero". And to question it is to risk being branded "unpatriotic" or worse.

"The history of the world is but the biography of great men," wrote Thomas Carlyle, the Scottish thinker, and for the likes of Boris Johnson, Andrew Roberts and many others in the UK and abroad, Winston Churchill is immutable. A still resonating political God.

But "great men" narratives and top 10 lists are a dangerous conceit where actual history is concerned.

* * *

Winston Churchill was first and foremost a product of wealth and nepotism.

Born into one of the most powerful and well-connected families in England on 30th November 1874, he was the scion of a veritable political dynasty. His father Randolph was spoken of as a future Prime Minister and was briefly Chancellor of the Exchequer before his early death. Winston was the grandson of the 7th Duke of Marlborough, who had been both the Lord Lieutenant of Ireland and a cabinet minister under two prime ministers. The Churchill and Spencer family trees peppered history with great leaders, politicians and generals all the way back to the 15th century.

Much has been made by biographers of Winston's dismal school years and how he overcame his academic deficiencies to get into the Royal Military College at Sandhurst on his third attempt. This forges a Cinderella-like narrative of an underdog, climbing above failure to make it to the top. None of it would have been possible if his family hadn't been so eminently well connected, though. Churchill was no pantomime Dick Whittington. He was a very posh chap from Oxfordshire, whose dad had been Chancellor and whose mum was obliged to keep telegramming round to find him a job because little Winnie had flunked out of his very expensive school.

Churchill was a privileged child who didn't have to do well at school, because whatever brickbats were thrown his way, he would inevitably fall back on his silk-stockinged feet. That doesn't make much of a story, though, so over time his origin tale has been edited to portray him "overcoming the odds" and "learning valuable lessons" on a path to destiny.

A lot of what really happened doesn't fit the bowdlerised narrative. For a start, the man who would later be celebrated as the saviour of liberty, spent much of his early life depriving people of that very thing.

His first taste of action, as a young army officer, came in 1895 when he was posted to Cuba as an observer during the island's war of independence against Spain. There, following his involvement in military skirmishes, he was awarded his first medal, the Cross of the Order of Military Merit, for helping the Spanish suppress the revolt. Which rather spoils the narrative of Churchill as the great defender of liberty fighting oppressive tyrants, as if he was fighting for the tyrants.

He travelled to India in 1896 and joined expeditions to the North-West Frontier to secure the borders of the British Raj and crush local uprisings. While serving in Sudan in 1898, Churchill took part in the Battle of Omdurman, in which the forces of the British Empire (together with Egyptian troops), equipped with machine guns, modern bolt-loading rifles and artillery took on poorly equipped Ansar followers of the local Mahdi and butchered them. Forty-eight British troops died in that engagement – and 12,000 Ansaris.

Churchill seems to have had twinges of doubt in the face of the slaughter and wrote that:

"These were as brave men as ever walked the earth. The conviction was borne in me that their claim beyond the grave in respect of a valiant death was not less good than that which any of our countrymen could make."

But even as he praised the heroism of "native people" pitted against the vast machinery of the British Empire, there was no doubt, for him, who the good guys were.

In a letter to his cousin, the Duke of Marlborough, dated 29th September 1898, he boasted about having taken part in what was to be the last great cavalry charge by the British Army against the Mahdi's men, contrasting the honourable close-knit fighting of his unit against the butchery elsewhere. But one doubts that this sympathy was much consolation to the families of the dead, or the people of Sudan, whose only consolation was that they were eventually to be ruled and exploited by British and Egyptians rather than the Mahdi or any of the other European powers with growing interests in Africa, such as the Belgians.

Churchill was a product of an Empire that believed itself culturally and morally superior to everyone else on Earth.

The young Winston was saturated with inherent self-regard that surpassed even that normally imbued as a product of the English aristocracy and the British public school system. This conceitedness was too much for some. One contemporary journalist, writing for the *Daily Chronicle*, dubbed him "Pushful the Younger".

No opportunity to promote himself went unmissed. When the Boer War broke out in 1899, the former army officer, now re-invented as a journalist, managed to secure the equivalent of £100,000 from London's *Morning Post*, to cover the campaign for just four months' work. His subsequent capture and escape from a prisoner of war camp were turned to his advantage and soon he was being feted as the living embodiment of the *Boy's Own** spirit.

Shortly after that, he entered politics – and part two of his legend began.

Until 1911, MPs weren't paid, meaning that politics was a rich man's hobby. Elected Conservative MP for Oldham, aged 25, in 1901, Churchill immediately embarked on an epic campaign of self-promotion, which culminated in him crossing the floor in 1904 to become a Liberal MP. His timing could not have been better. The Tory government collapsed shortly afterwards and the subsequent general election in 1906 saw his new party storm to power under Henry Campbell-Bannerman. Two years later, Churchill was appointed President of the Board of Trade and aged just 33 he became the youngest cabinet minister since 1866.

This was not a "path to destiny", though. Churchill was always first and foremost a politician, driven by aspiration,

---

* *Boy's Own Paper,* a magazine featuring dashing adventure tales for boys. Published in Britain between 1879 and 1967.

working to his own agenda to serve private ambition. Even as he moved from party to party, from post to post and hobby-horse to hobby-horse, the core mission was always, first and foremost, to promote Winston's interests, fuel Winston's ambitions, and one day to elevate Winston to the highest office in the land.

Over the course of his long political life, Churchill entertained many positions and veered from decidedly "Conservative" to strongly reformist tendencies.

His more enlightened instincts were there from the start but they were driven too by his indomitable wife Clementine, a life-long liberal, who in another time and place could well have made her way to the front bench on her own merits. And perhaps even to Downing Street herself.

For most of her husband's life, Clementine Churchill was his chief political advisor. Which is all the more remarkable when you consider that Clementine harboured a lifelong hatred of the Conservative party

When they first met, Clemmie was extremely hostile to what she viewed as the vile 'Tories' and seeking to impress her, Churchill described his own former party in a 1908 letter to his fiancée as:

"Filled with old doddering peers, cute financial magnates, clever wirepullers, big brewers with bulbous noses. All the enemies of progress are there – weaklings, sleek, slug, comfortable, self-important individuals."

Two years after writing that, as Home Secretary, he was pushing many decidedly progressive and liberal reforms, including the introduction of a distinction between political and criminal prisoners and the ending of imprisonment of children. He also commuted half the death sentences passed during his term.

In 1911, as President of the Board of Trade, he was responsible for the first attempts at creating a welfare state and, while it chimed with the mood of his party, undoubtedly Clemmie had a hand in it.

Over the next 50 years of his political career, his wife wrote hundreds of letters to him, often at key moments, that demonstrate a calm, guiding hand at the tiller – even as her husband rocked from one hobby horse to the next.

Clementine, like many wives and women in history, is the unsung hero of the Churchill legend. Operating behind the scenes and displaying formidable foresight and intuitiveness, her role has been dampened and downplayed by most Churchill biographers.

The predominantly male Churchill fan-base prefers the story as the tale of one man and his destiny, not one man and a highly intelligent woman working in partnership. But without Clemmie behind him, it is unlikely that the wayward Winston would have sustained his long career, let alone made it to that plinth in Parliament Square.

Left to his own instincts and devices, there were many times when Churchill's conflicting instincts left him playing an elaborate game of political Twister with a foot, simultaneously in every political camp.

Women's suffrage is a case in point. For most of the years that preceded women getting the vote, Churchill was implacably opposed to the notion of women voting, suggesting that it would be akin to a man demanding the right to have a baby. And yet, when the tide turned in favour, he began to thaw and professed that he was only willing to fully commit to it if the male electorate agreed in a proposed referendum on the issue.

Churchill was obsessed with popular opinion and what we nowadays call "optics". Image was everything and on his long path of self-promotion, no publicity stunt was to be missed. He often got it wrong.

When a violent Latvian gang was cornered by police at the Siege of Sidney Street* in January 1911, Churchill hot-footed it down to Stepney with his private secretary and a photographer in tow. There he made a show of "taking charge" of events including calling up the Royal Artillery, who shelled the quiet East End Street, setting fire to the terrace.

Churchill was roundly lambasted for interfering with the operation at the time and when footage, shot by Pathé News in one of their earliest film reports, was shown at cinemas it was apparently greeted with boos and four-letter words.

Two weeks after the siege ended an inquest was held and the former Conservative Prime Minister Arthur Balfour held the errant Home Secretary to account:

"I understand what the photographer was doing" he bellowed, "but what was the honourable gentleman doing?"

The man who would one day be dubbed the *Greatest Briton* of all time was also, frequently, to find himself out of his depth. When war broke out in 1914, for example, Churchill was First Lord of the Admiralty, a job he was singularly ill-suited to.

Many Conservative newspapers had attacked Churchill's appointment in 1911, deeming his temperament unfit for such a big role. *The Spectator*† declared: "he has not the loyalty, the

---

* A gunfight in a tenement building in the East End of London between police (and, later, armed forces), and members of a Latvian criminal gang, led to the deaths of three policemen, a fireman and the three gang members.
† Later famously edited by Boris Johnson himself

dignity, the steadfastness to make an efficient head of a great office." And they were on the money, because from the outbreak of war, his worst tendencies were on display.

Big on promises, he failed to support them with deeds.

In October 1914, Churchill visited the besieged Belgian city of Antwerp and promised to provide reinforcements to bolster the defence against the German army, but almost as soon as he was gone, the British army was withdrawn.

A greater disaster came the following year, when he personally backed a plan to relieve pressure on the Russians by attacking the Turkish army in the Dardanelles and opening a second front. That terrible miscalculation at Gallipoli ended in catastrophe, with 50,000 French, Australian and British Empire troops dead.

Following uproar and resignations in protest, Churchill was demoted to Chancellor of the Duchy of Lancaster before resigning in November 1915.

Ever eager to put out his own first draft of the Churchill legend, Winston later claimed that he was right and that the assault on Gallipoli would have worked if only he had been in overall control. Almost immediately he began to portray himself as a scapegoat who had been wronged; most historians strongly disagree.

"The attacks at the Dardanelles and Gallipoli convinced many of his contemporaries that Churchill was a man of blood, lacking sound judgment, and unfit for high office," wrote his official biographer Sir Martin Gilbert. Others, including the historian and author Christopher Bell, have suggested that Churchill got "swept up" in the misadventure – despite it being a patently bad idea. Disaster or not, 1915 is a pivotal year in Churchill mythology. Following the catastrophe at Gallipoli he donned a uniform and went out to France to fight on the Western Front.

This is the legend of the noble, repentant politician who accepts that his actions have cost lives and who therefore puts himself in the firing line in a powerful act of penance. The truth of Churchill's time in the trenches however is very different to the folklore.

Keen to be made a brigadier,* Winston actively canvassed for the rank but had to make do with being a mere colonel. Unfortunately, he proved so rusty, on account of not having been in uniform for 16 years, that when he gave parade ground orders to his infantrymen, he used anachronistic 19th-century cavalry commands, that left them all marching into one another in bewilderment.

In January 1916, he was sent to Ploegsteert (aka Plugstreet), a quiet part of the Western Front, eight miles south of Ypres. That was the closest he ever came to actual war.

He was undeniably a big hit with the men. Lax on discipline, he liked to strut about in a French army helmet and lead the troops in singsongs. As not much was happening war-wise, he spent a lot of his time painting watercolours and writing to Clemmie.

Boris Johnson's biography would have matters otherwise. In *The Churchill Factor*, he claims that Churchill ventured out into no man's land some "36 times". It seems highly unlikely, because Colonel Churchill was only at the front for six weeks and for most of that time in reserve.

Johnson suggests that Churchill was in the thick of things, but there were no major engagements in the area around Ploegsteert during his very brief stint at the front. The occasional rogue shell fell and the odd bullet may have whizzed past, but the idea that he was "constantly under fire" as Johnson and others would have it is demonstrably untrue. A complete fabrication.

---

* A senior rank above a colonel but below a major-general

The legend of Churchill at the front remains a beguiling and romantic notion, however, and one that suggests by inference that generally members of Parliament didn't do that sort of thing in the Great War. That by being there, Winston was embarking on something brave and unique, which set him apart from all those other MPs.

It's wholly untrue. Colonel Churchill was very far from being the only parliamentarian in uniform. By January 1915, 184 MPs from all parties were on active service in the armed forces and, unlike Churchill, many remained so for the duration of the war. Overall, 264 MPs served in some capacity during the conflict, or about 40% of all parliamentarians.

A good percentage gave their lives. Twenty Members of Parliament died on active duty.

One of those, Harold Cawley, Liberal MP for Heywood, was killed by a Turkish sniper at Gallipoli. A victim of his right honourable friend's woefully planned misadventure in pursuit of ambition.

By comparison with most of his serving colleagues, Churchill's stint in uniform was very short indeed. And anyway, within weeks of arriving at the front he was bored stiff and itching to return to Westminster.

By March 1916, he was back in London on leave and lobbying hard to get a cabinet job. Returning briefly to the front in April he sought again to resign his commission and had to be dissuaded by Clemmie, who told him in a stern letter, to be "patient" since it might play badly with "simple people".

"Your motive for going to France was easy to understand – Your motive for coming back, requires explanation," she wrote.

Churchill wrote to friends and colleagues asking for advice and clearly hoping that they would say what he wanted to hear. Most said he should stay in France.

And then he had a stroke of luck. In mid-spring his battalion was amalgamated with another, rendering him redundant. He returned to Westminster on 7th May 1916 and his brief and uneventful time at the front was over.

Like the Siege of Sidney Street or those quips he never uttered, the "he donned khaki and went to the front" story is critical to the Churchill myth. Repeated endlessly as proof of his integrity, upon examination, it falls apart like cigar ash in the wind.

It's disappointing to determine that stories we've grown up with aren't as thrilling or reassuring as we would like them to be. It's comforting to buy into the Churchill myth because as "our Greatest Briton", it shines well on us as well. He's our mascot. Our one great, towering modern hero. Why spoil it with inconvenient facts and examination?

None of this is to deny that Churchill was not a major presence in 20th-century British politics. He looms large in our collective consciousness precisely because he burned so brightly. There's much to like and much to admire.

He was undoubtedly a clever man, with a broad range of interests and an almost boyish interest in things. He wrote acres of books. He had a ferocious energy. He was knocked down countless times – both literally and metaphorically – but he always got back up and dusted himself down and started all over again.

That determination is admirable, but his irrepressibility was undoubtedly born of that innate sense of Spencer-Churchill privilege and entitlement.

As with his tenure as First Lord of the Admiralty, in his post-war career, he frequently failed to live up to the hype. His term as Chancellor of the Exchequer between 1924 and 1929 is a disastrous case in point. His decision to take the country back onto the Gold Standard in April 1925, though popular, caused the value of the pound to rise and exports to fall. That precipitated mass unemployment and deflation and, in turn the General Strike of 1926.

But very little is made of that or of Churchill's many other career failings, because "the big event" of his war leadership from May 1940 has come to eclipse everything else. Handed the office he had craved all of his life, Churchill finally and undeniably came into his own.

His greatest successes came out of mimicking the better decisions of the Great War, including the notion of creating a war-time coalition to steer the country through the crisis. He rallied the nation with commendable duty and purpose. He gave the impression of a capable commander at the centre of things and that's important in a crisis.

He was very good at playing the part. He set out a clear narrative and acted as a rallying figure for what was to follow. He defined the parameters of the war. Good against evil. Democracy against tyranny. Civilisation against despotism. He offered the promise of hope, of victory and eventual glory. He inspired his people to keep on keeping on.

Churchill clearly relished it all. He liked being at the blazing core of things. He was good at the big stuff. The bellicose language, the defiant speeches, the posturing with machine guns and the V for victory hand flicks. Undoubtedly a rallying figure is needed when a country is at war and Churchill made a very good one indeed. He was made for the job of wartime PM, because it suited his talents. And he was undeniably good at it, not least because he became a symbol and a beacon at the heart of government.

He was also undoubtedly popular with a broad swathe of the British public because, like Boris Johnson, he projected a personable X factor.

Time has turned the favourable hand into myth. Nations in need of heroes want their paragons to be bigger people than the rest – outsized and cartoonish. Imbued with super-powers. Churchill has been turned into fiction. His wit exaggerated, his intelligence amplified; his foresight, his integrity, his intuitiveness, his love of democracy, and his steely nerve in the face of the Nazi war machine all blown out of proportion to fashion a supernatural God.

The truth no more resembles the myth than the physical Churchill measured up to his three-metre-high statue in Parliament Square. But as we shall see throughout this book, very often people prefer to buy into the myth than the reality of what happened.

* * *

In the summer of 2020, as Black Lives Matter protests erupted in London, there were fears in some corners that activists might seek to topple Churchill's statue outside the Palace of Westminster.

Some of those fears were deliberately concocted.

Embattled by the Covid crisis engulfing the nation and recovering from his own brush with death*, Boris Johnson, now Prime Minister, seized the moment to appropriate Churchill once more and shore up his political base by defending the wartime leader.

Johnson took to his Twitter account.

The statue, he wrote, was a "permanent reminder of Churchill's achievement in saving this country – and the whole of Europe

---

* I was commissioned to write his obituary by a well-known publication that gave him a 50:50 chance.

– from a fascist and racist tyranny," adding, "we cannot try to edit or censor our past."

In the 55 years since his death, Churchill had become an inviolable, secular Tory God. Any attempt to question his perceived place in history was a blasphemy. How dare "truth seekers" bring up awkward "facts". To do so was to "rewrite" the past – or at least the "perceived past" in which Churchill had saved the world from tyranny. Boris Johnson the "ersatz Churchill" needed the real one to remain untouchable and unvarnished to serve his own narrative as his latter-day incarnation.

If Churchill fell, the man who had mimicked him, might fall as well. It was a fight worth having.

As the BLM protests intensified, someone wrote "was a racist" under Churchill's name on the plinth. Emma Soames, the late PM's grandaughter, began to wonder whether the effigy should be moved out of the square.

Writing in *The Daily Telegraph*, Johnson wrote that he would "fight with every breath in his body" to keep the statue up, and quite swiftly Twitter was erupting into one of its vicious Punch and Judy battles and commentators were demanding that soldiers be posted to defend the great man's memorial.

But by picking the fight, Johnson inadvertently set in motion the unpicking of the Churchill myth. Soon, academics and historians were emerging from dusty lockdown libraries, to point out the many paradoxes of Winston.

For all the cries from Tory supporters that Winston "wasn't a racist" or that he was "a defender of free speech and liberty" and a "defender of democracy", there was clear evidence to the contrary.

Take his record on Irish nationalism.

In May 1920, it was Churchill, who as Secretary of State for War, was responsible for the recruitment and deployment of the paramilitary Black and Tans into Ireland to crush the independence movement in what was then still part of the United Kingdom.

The Black and Tans were – as Roy Jenkins describes them in his biography of Churchill:

"A sort of Freikorps, for whom the war had not provided enough violence or the peace enough employment opportunity."

In November 1920, this violent, state-sanctioned unit murdered 14 civilians at a Gaelic football match in Dublin. In December they set fire to Cork and then proceeded to shoot at firemen who tried to put out the blaze.

The atrocities turned public opinion in England and galvanised the independence movement further on the island of Ireland. Churchill's officially approved thuggery arguably tipped the balance. He ignored pleas from his wife Clemmie to encourage Prime Minister David Lloyd George towards an equitable peace.

Celebrated as a "saviour of freedom" by British Conservatives still, the bit where Churchill sanctions paramilitary violence against ordinary Irish people is rather at odds with the point. Likewise, those seeking to claim that he was no racist face rather an uphill struggle.

Late in the 1930s, Churchill defended the suppression of Aborigines in Australia, arguing that: "I do not admit that a wrong has been done to these people by the fact that a stronger race, a higher-grade race, a more worldly-wise race to put it that way, has come in and taken their place."

The supposed great defender of freedom was violently opposed to Indian independence. He loathed Gandhi, who he called a "malignant and subversive fanatic" and said he wished he might be "trampled by an enormous elephant."

Churchill loved a hobby-horse, or a cause he could latch on to. And from 1931 to the early months of 1935, Churchill threw himself into the centre of the debate on India's future, despite knowing very little about it. He described Indians as "a beastly people with a beastly religion", despite only having been there once.

An appearance in front of the Joint Select Committee on India in 1933 "painfully exposed his lack of detailed knowledge of the subject" according to Robert Rhodes James, one of his biographers. And Churchill's subsequent lurch to the right, as he worked tirelessly to oppose Indian nationhood and other people's right to govern themselves, threw him into the company of some of the very nastiest elements of the Conservative right.

"Churchill idolatry" is now such that his implacable opposition to the self-determination of hundreds of millions of people is excused away as "typical of that time". In fact, by the 1930s, most sensible parliamentarians, on all sides of the House of Commons, accepted it as an inevitability. Churchill, almost alone among statesmen of the era, opposed it.

Uncomfortable as it might sound, his belief in democracy and freedom only really began and ended at the English Channel.

US civil rights leader Richard B. Moore, has argued that "the finest hour" was in truth but "a rare and fortunate coincidence" taking place at the moment "the vital interests of the British Empire [coincided] with those of the great overwhelming majority of mankind."

Certainly, the supposedly great defender of democracy was more than happy to throw in his wartime lot with Joseph Stalin, who as leader of the USSR was responsible for the enslavement, murder and imprisonment of millions of his own and other people.

Churchill was not a defender of democracy – he was a defender of the British Empire. And the two are not analogous.

On becoming President of the United States in 2009, one of Barack Obama's first acts was to remove a bust of Churchill from the Oval Office. At the time he claimed that he was simply returning it to its original place elsewhere in the White House. But it cannot have been coincidence that Obama's own grandfather was a survivor of what has been dubbed "Britain's gulag" in 1950s Kenya during Churchill's second term of office as Prime Minister.

In that painful episode, British Imperial forces set up "detainment camps" in East Africa, where hundreds of thousands of citizens were interned, brutalised and held against their will. There are numerous accounts of forced castrations and state-sanctioned torture. Prisoners were burned with cigarette ends and some were even electrocuted – many were summarily executed or beaten to death.

Some have sought to whitewash these horrors of late British colonial oppression in Kenya. Others have claimed that though they happened, as Churchill was now well into his dotage and clearly no longer at the peak of his powers, it was hardly his fault.

Hero-fashioning is all in the edit. Churchill the racist, Churchill the useless post-war leader and Churchill the suppressor of Irish, Kenyan and Indian freedom has to be left on the cutting room floor if the legend is to work.

* * *

Fake history blows both ways, and some of the accusations levelled against Churchill by his detractors over the years are untrue. The oft-repeated suggestion that he deployed troops to quell striking miners in the town of Tonypandy in the Welsh

Rhondda Valley after riots broke out in 1910 is a case in point. In fact, Churchill actually halted the deployment of cavalry and did not send the army in.

In Scotland, the so-called "Battle of George Street" has become a particularly persistent fake history tale, which lays blame on Churchill for something that literally didn't happen.

The myth claims that in January 1919 Churchill sent in troops to break up a trade union demonstration in Glasgow. On social media feeds, details are frequently accompanied with pictures of a tank rolling through the square. In fact, the images were taken a year earlier in a fundraising effort for the war. The story, which first appeared in a memoir by a Scots trade unionist called Emanuel Shinwell in 1973, has been exaggerated down the years to claim that "English" soldiers fired shots and even that people were killed but nobody died and no soldiers were present. There was a riot and the local Scottish police did engage with the demonstrators.

In all of it, Churchill played no part.

As we shall see throughout the book, the deemed big figures of history inevitably get appropriated by all sides. Lauded by some, denounced by others. Churchill is no exception.

Over the course of his long political life, he was prone to changing times and changing attitudes, and quite often he changed with them. His views on Europe, Jews, Ireland, Islam, appeasement and women's suffrage all altered – sometimes radically – over the 62 years that he sat in the House of Commons.

During the years following the EU referendum, Brexiters and Remainers both claimed him as their own. Both cherrypicked quotations to suit their needs. Both in a way were right. It was true that he had once called for a "United States of Europe" and also that he had seen Britain's place outside of it. Like any quasi-religious figure, his deeds and texts can be interpreted in any number of ways, depending on what you want to prove.

What is beyond doubt is that nobody actually knows what Winston Churchill's views would have been on Brexit, on account of his having died 51 years before it happened.

Lists of "greats", as encouraged by that 2002 BBC poll that put Winston at the top of the pile of Britons, are reductive. History is not the iTunes chart or some dance-off between the icons of the past.

The notion that one person can be claimed to be the "Greatest Briton' or the "Greatest prime minister" of all turns history into a beauty pageant.

Churchill undoubtedly matters as a figure of significant historical importance in a way that Jim Callaghan or Arthur Balfour do not. He was the man of the moment in 1940 and arguably the only parliamentarian who could unite the houses of parliament at a time of unprecedented crisis.

But the events that followed are far more complicated than the airbrushers would have it. Churchill was no flawless wartime leader. His personal and political faults were many and they frequently caused problems. He was over concerned with minutiae. His judgment was frequently wrong. He relied heavily on intuition and, as he had done with Gallipoli in the First World War, he instigated disastrous campaigns in Norway and Greece that led to heavy casualties and tied up valuable resources.

From 1943 onwards the US was pushing for an assault on France to hasten the war's end but Churchill and his commanders' preferred strategy of going up through Italy and protecting the British position in the Mediterranean delayed matters. By obsessing over air strength and strategic bombing over ground invasions, he undoubtedly played a part in prolonging the war.

Churchill did fall into line on D-Day and Overlord eventually, but only really because of the insistence of his more powerful partner, the US.

Much of our belief that things were otherwise is down to his success in shaping his legacy for posterity. In writing his best-selling six-volume history of the era, he did more than anyone to forge his own myth as the man who made all the difference.

In the words of the title of historian David Reynolds' book on the subject, Churchill's writing endeavours allowed him to take "command of history". He placed himself at the centre of things and expunged his contemporary doubts to create an image of himself as a wise and adept leader.

According to Reynolds, Churchill earned some £12 million, in modern money, from the six-volume work, written with a team of researchers, which set him up for the rest of his life. But the books also earned him his place as the key player of the war. Churchill the journalist was very good at writing himself up.

He even chose the spot where his statue would sit, marking the most prominent position on the edge of Parliament Square and thus ensuring that even after his death he was left looming as an eternal presence over British democracy.

Churchill's enduring significance rests on one brief – but of course, hugely pivotal – moment in time when Germany, in thrall to Hitler and Naziism, sought to overrun Europe and impose tyranny on millions of people.

Leadership and symbolism matter and Churchill and his long-honed act was central to unifying Britain and giving the people something and someone to rally behind.

He did not win the war alone. One of his great skills was delegation. He may have interfered too much in the details, but he was willing – when convinced – to go with decisions made by his military brass and core war cabinet of five.

In the final analysis, Churchill's reputation is ultimately damaged by those who seek to keep him "at number one". Politics is not a pop chart. Compiling lists and crowning people the greatest is all well and good for TV talent shows, but politics doesn't really work like that. Ranking prime ministers is a self-defeating task and who ranks highest is ultimately a matter of taste and private political prejudice.

Unlike Thatcher or Atlee, or Lloyd George and Tony Blair, Churchill did not make Britain itself "different" in any meaningful way. He didn't revolutionise the country. He guided it through a storm.

Having a sensible debate around his legacy has become impossible. As with other figures and other events we will encounter in this book, he has essentially become a religious figure. And you cannot bring logic or reason to bear on religious icons.

When President Biden removed a bust of him from the White House Oval office in January 2021, it was viewed by many British politicians as a deliberately provocative act. A threat to the so-called "special relationship". Obama removed it first. Trump put it back. Now Biden has removed it again. Churchill's effigy had become a political weather vane.

The same long ago happened in the UK. Churchill and his reputation have been weaponised in a way that no other British prime minister, or recent historical figure has. "Belief" in him and his deeds have come to determine what sort of Briton you are. You are obliged to be "For him" or "Against him". There is no middle ground.

In researching this chapter, it was striking to see that, without exception, British historians who have tackled the wartime PM have felt obliged to mitigate any criticism by assuring readers that he really was a great man who did great things. Viewing Churchill dispassionately, in the narrative of history, is akin to a sort of heresy. There is no neutral ground.

And that is as unfortunate as it is dangerous.

Many people want the history they read or watch and the individuals who populate it to confirm the existing biases they already hold.

But how we regard the so-called great men and women of our past is not necessarily how they were viewed in their time. Churchill is a case in point. He was not, for example, as popular as we like to think.

In the 1945 General Election, he failed to offer Britons the future they wanted and was given what he dubbed "the Order of the Boot" in a landslide Labour victory. Clinging on as Conservative leader, he failed to define a clear vision for the post-war era and was defeated again in the 1950 General Election. He fought again and this time won the 1951 election, which returned him to power. But what is often forgotten, is that he actually lost the popular vote. Labour received 200,000 more crosses in the box and Churchill only got back into Downing Street courtesy of the UK's antiquated first-past-the-post system.

The reason that his fame and reputation, not Attlee's, has resonated down the years, is in no small part thanks to his and his supporters' efforts in pushing his legacy boisterously to the front of history's queue.

What we think happened in the past and what we are encouraged to believe are not necessarily how things were. Events were not ordered or pre-ordained or clear cut. History, like the human beings who forged it, is complex and nuanced and all the more interesting for it.

But most people don't like "complex and nuanced". So ever more around the world populists, lobbyists, influencers and pundits have sought to strip events of intricacy, to reinforce false-hoods and cement myths that favour their agendas in the present.

In the process, history has been footballified – if I can use such a term. It's been turned into a game, with sides and jeering supporters. Detail has been traduced and the truth jeopardised, with events remoulded by populists to fit neat little narratives and to secure power for their own ends.

Johnson was wrong to suggest that Churchill's reputation should somehow be inviolable. On the contrary, we need to scrutinise him more. Nobody, not even Winston Churchill, should be above examination. For when invented anecdotes and half-remembered fairy tales get mistaken for actual history we are in serious trouble.

CHAPTER TWO

ANCIENT PEOPLE THOUGHT THE EARTH WAS FLAT

The story of Fake History

In the last week of August 1939, as Europe tumbled fatefully towards war, Otto Völzing, a German archaeologist working on an excavation in a valley beneath the Swabian Alps in southern Germany found some mammoth tusk fragments in the dried silt at the back of a cave and placed them carefully in an old cigar box.

The dig was led by 41-year-old Robert Wetzel, a palaeontologist, university professor and dedicated Nazi who had joined Hitler's NSDAP in 1933 and was now head of pre-history* at the University of Tübingen. Wetzel was a leading figure in the Ahnenerbe, a specialist SS† unit set up by Heinrich Himmler, that had been tasked with providing evidence for the Nazi party leadership's unhinged fantasies about the German people's racial origins.

The Nazi regime was not the first, or last, government to sponsor fake history for political ends. But the money and energy

---

* History before the written record
† Short for "Schutzstaffel" (meaning "Protection squadron"), Hitler's elite paramilitary organisation

they threw at the project and the willingness of otherwise respectable people, including Wetzel and Völzing, to go along with it is perhaps unparalleled in history.

Heinrich Himmler, the Reichsführer of the SS, had been nurtured on tales of Teutonic legends by his father and believed that the German people were responsible for nothing less than the creation of human civilisation. In the early 1930s, he fell under the spell of a wife-beating, alcoholic, Austrian occultist called Karl Maria Wiligut and a Dutch prehistorian called Herman Wirth, whose views further fed his fantastical illusions.

Wirth claimed the German race was two million years old and had created the lost civilisation of Atlantis. Wiligut believed that the events of the Old and New Testament had actually taken place in Germany and that Jesus Christ was an Aryan God called "Krist".

In the 1920s, Wiligut had been committed to an insane asylum and Wirth had been ridiculed by contemporary academics for using obvious forgeries as part of his "research". But by the mid-1930s they were two of the most influential men in Germany, receiving significant state funding.

Ahnenerbe agents were sent out to find archaeology to sustain the baseless nonsense these men had dreamt up. They conducted expeditions to Finland, Sweden and Tibet – and scoured the Fatherland for traces of the lost people of Atlantis. The Ahnenerbe were pseudoarchaeologists, completely unconcerned with empirical rigour, reason or methodology and wholly committed to the quest for confirmation bias. They misattributed artefacts and repurposed finds to fit the narrative they had been given.

The most important tool in the armoury of any archaeologist is a bullshit detector. The mental capacity to question evidence and to ask: "Is this what it seems to be? Does this support what I believe to be true, or do I simply want it to fit into my argument?"

When evidence is not critically evaluated, but instead used to shore up an existing theory or discarded because it disproves the original assumption or belief, confirmation bias has occurred. Or "lying", as we call it in the ordinary world.

You'll be shocked to learn that the Nazis weren't above cheating. When they couldn't find what they were looking for, they made archaeology up altogether. The SS had been created to evoke the spirit of medieval knightly orders and what they needed more than anything else was a nice grail. So, they commissioned the Chiemsee cauldron, an elaborate, 10 kg, 18-carat gold container that was ostentatiously decorated with Celtic imagery, and pretended it was an ancient artefact which proved that the modern "Aryans" were descended from an advanced civilisation.

That vessel was later dumped in a Bavarian lake by a retreating Waffen-SS* unit in 1945 – and when it was discovered during a dive in 2001 it caused considerable academic head-scratching and even sparked a protracted fraud trial.

Of course, there's no more such thing as an Aryan race than there is a tribe of purple pixies living under your floorboards. The whole myth of an ancient race of blue-eyed, blonde-haired Indo-Europeans was concocted by 19th-century racists and leapt on by 20th-century fascists to prop up their toxic and murderous ideology.

But, depressingly, some people still believe it.

The Chiemsee cauldron was but the gilding on that pseudo-archaeological Nazi farce.

---

* The military branch of the SS

In their determination to prove German cultural supremacy, the Ahnenerbe grew ever more wayward and ever more desperate. On little more evidence than the jottings of a 16th-century Lutheran theologian and some 12th-century carvings in the rock, Hitler's archaeologists determined that a natural sandstone formation in the Teutoburg Forest, known as the Externsteine, was actually a sacred pagan site. On Himmler's orders the Ahnenerbe was ordered to carry out an extensive survey of the area to prove that it was an Aryan observatory built to study the movement of the stars.

That dig was overseen by a deranged septuagenarian lay preacher called Wilhelm Teudt, whose works were broadly ridiculed right up until the point Adolf Hitler granted him a professorship on his 75th birthday.

If this all sounds like the script for an inferior Indiana Jones prequel, that's because Spielberg's films were partly inspired by these events. But the genuine inhuman excesses of Nazi atrocities are always bleaker than fiction. To facilitate his caprices, Himmler drove thousands of enslaved prisoners to their deaths. An entire concentration camp was established at Niederhagen, on the outskirts of Büren-Wewelsburg to provide labour to build a castle that would serve as "Himmler's Camelot", where the SS leader could indulge his Arthurian fetish.

At least a third of the inmates died.

In the pursuit of personal ambition, genuine archaeologists, academics and historians willingly conspired with this baloney – a nonsense, let us not forget, that was then used to justify the murder of millions of Jews, homosexuals, gypsies and other "undesirables".

And it was while seeking to empower that rotten mythos that Völzing stumbled upon the mammoth fragments in the caves beneath the Swabian Alps.

For decades it had been known that the Hohlenstein-Stadel caves in the Lonetal valley were rich in Ice Age archaeology. These and previous excavations had revealed a number of electrifying finds, including carved figurines of horses, bison and a rhino, but it seems that on that hurried last day of excavation, as war loomed just one week away, Völzing missed the significance of what he had found.

The cigar box, with splinters of ivory inside, was deposited at Wetzel's house and remained untouched for the next 30 years.

Wetzel and Völzing both survived the war, but their SS service haunted the rest of their professional lives. As the post-war decades passed and as both sought to eke out a living, they remained ignorant of the great treasure they had accidentally stumbled upon, which was still sitting in a cigar box collecting dust at the back of Wetzel's home.

When he died in 1962 his collection was gifted to the Ulm Museum and several years later a West German prehistorian by the name of Joachim Hahn began cataloguing it. One day in 1969 he opened the cigar box and immediately recognised what Völzing and Wetzel had missed.

It turned out that the fragments were parts of a figurine that was to become known as the Löwenmensch – or Lion Man. The object, made in the Upper Palaeolithic era of the late Stone Age and treasured by a forgotten tribe of early people for millennia afterwards, is the most ancient piece of symbolic art in existence.

It is head-swimmingly old.

The object was made by a group of early people known as the Aurignacians, approximately 40,000 years ago. To give that context, it was already 23,000 years old when the last mammoths died out.

But the value of the "Lion Man" is far more than the sum of its age. Carved from a single piece of tusk, it would have taken over 400 hours to complete. That constitutes an incredible investment of time for something that served no obvious practical purpose. Its surface has been worn smooth by thousands of hands over perhaps hundreds of generations, suggesting its value persisted long after its sculptor was gone.

We don't know precisely what it was for, but it clearly played a part in some sort of religious ceremony. And that tells us much about our ancestors 1,200 generations back. It liberates Stone Age people from the grunting, clubs and furs stereotype of cartoons and kitsch 1960s Raquel Welch movies. It renders them human beings, preoccupied with the same questions that consume us – their descendants today. "Who are we, where do we come from and what's it all about, man?"

Even as they struggled to subsist, even as they gathered berries and hunted and hid from predators lurking in the darkness beyond their camp fires, this tiny group of early humans was trying to make sense of the chaos of their world. They were trying to understand who they were.

These then were the first prophets, the first storytellers, the first scientists, the first historians and the first bull-shitters.

Our ancestors were born out of chaos and into chaos. Humans have a need for order and logic and reassurance amid the anarchy of the Universe and the terrifying randomness of it all. We see patterns of animals and ploughs in the night sky – where there are none. Many pray in times of need. So, like us, they sought to impose order on the things they could not understand and created gods and spirits.

Evolutionary instincts drove human beings to use superstition and storytelling to overcome the unbearable lightness of their being – and the darkness beyond it. They knocked on wood to wake up tree spirits to protect them as they walked through the forests – and we still "touch wood" for luck today.

The Lion Man was a product of that elaborate psychological defence mechanism, the first clear evidence of those twin human marvels, of human creativity and self-deceit. As civilisations grew and writing and language developed, dimly remembered events and the deeds of ancestors became inexorably interwoven with the prevailing beliefs and mythos of the times. And just like those tanks that never were in Glasgow's George Square – things got exaggerated.

Great camp-fire storytelling favours exaggeration and as we moved beyond the darkness of the plains and caves where our species dwelled for over 95% of our existence, that love of tall tales persisted.

The great narrative of the Bronze Age Trojan War, for example, likely evolved out of actual events, but once it was in the hands of storytellers, it was turned into a blockbuster event.

Ancient history was written by the spinners. The *Iliad* and *Odyssey*, both attributed to Homer, who may or may not have existed, were both products of oral history and ritual told and retold over and over by generations of poets. The stories were altered and reshaped and smoothed, much as the Lion Man was worn by generations of hands. Finally written down in the 7th century BCE, Homer's works hark back with a nostalgic yearning for a lost world where great gods and brave heroes do great deeds and where kids didn't waste their lives away staring moronically at wax tablets.

The *Iliad* and *Odyssey* were neither religious texts nor history. They served in part as entertainment but also to forge a common sense of values and shared principles of heroism and behaviour, based on the examples set by a lost golden age.

The works attributed to Homer are monumental in every way. They are the foundation of European literature and Western thinking – they are also the starting point of fake history. Although, to be fair, having created them, the Ancient Greeks did at least have the decency to try and address the problem.

Herodotus, born c.485 BCE, is frequently dubbed "the Father of History" and generally agreed to be the first person who tried to apply discipline and academic rigour to the study of the past.

By using "Histories", the Greek word for "inquiry", as the title of his work, Herodotus also invented the use of the term. The work itself, which was later split into nine books, explored the 150 years of events and conflict that culminated in the Greco-Persian war and the Persian defeat at the Battle of Plataea in 479 BCE, just a decade before he was born. His work is a masterpiece of early Athenian literature and scholarship, but as the narrative weaves back and forth across the Mediterranean and Middle East, it becomes much more than that. There's travelogue, yarn, gossip, sex, violence, food journalism and some cracking tales of revenge.

Some of his anecdotal titbits are illuminating. In Book 1 section 133, Herodotus claims, for example, that Persians made all of their big decisions twice:

"Moreover, it is their custom to deliberate about the gravest matters when they are drunk; and what they approve in their deliberations is proposed to them the next day, when they are sober, by the master of the house where they deliberate; and if, being sober, they still approve it, they act on it, but if not, they drop it."

The notion of drunk democracy sounds like America under Trump, but it's a methodology not that far removed from France's modern presidential elections. Two votes are held. In the first round there's essentially a drunk contest in which any Thomas, Richard or Henri can stand. In the second, the two remaining candidates go up against each other in a "sober" election and the French make their choice.

Whether Persian democracy really worked that way, however, is unknown because, unfortunately, some of Herodotus's other assertions can leave him sounding like a 1960s backpacker, high on Afghan Black, recounting stuff he's heard from a wasted hippy in a hillside yurt.

Herodotus talks a lot about snakes. There are snakes that fly, snakes that eat horses and snakes with horns. He claims that there are phoenixes in Egypt, gold-digging giant ants in Persia and sexy mermaids – the ancestors of the Scythian people – who drove themselves into a wacky psychedelic ecstasy whenever anyone died. He relates a cracking story about a singer called Arion who is rescued by a dolphin after getting kidnapped by some nasty pirates, and another one where a woman's urine is used to cure the eyesight of a blind king.

Please don't try that at home.

Elsewhere, Herodotus's narrative spills over into pulp fiction. One story tells the tale of Lydian King Candaules, who is so obsessed with the beauty of his queen that he convinces his favourite bodyguard Gyges to spy on her when she's naked. Gyges reluctantly agrees, but things backfire spectacularly when the Queen sees him gawping at her through the cracks of her boudoir and makes an indecent proposition to him. He can either be executed for being a horrid little peeping Tom or become her lover, murder the King and take the throne himself.

Being no idiot, Gyges chooses option two and, after committing regicide, rules over the Lydian Empire for 40 years. Four generations later the Gods, belatedly catching up on the box set of events unfurling below them, kill his descendant Croesus in revenge. Nasty.

These Homeric tendencies, twinned with an over-reliance on the sayings of oracles and deeds of gods attracted much contemporary ridicule. The great comic playwright Aristophanes trolled Herodotus mercilessly in early European theatre and, 400 years after his death, Plutarch was still laying into him in an essay entitled "The Malice of Herodotus". That polemic denigrated Herodotus for sloppy research, gullibility and an obvious bias in favour of the Persians. In the centuries since he has had as many detractors as defenders and Plutarch's rebranding of him as "The Father of Lies" has stuck – but it's not entirely fair.

Despite his moments, Herodotus was more than capable of expressing incredulity: "I am under no obligation to be persuaded... these are the things that I have been told," he wrote.

It seems too that even his wackier takes might have had some basis in fact, such as the one about gold-digging giant ants. In 1984 a French ethnologist, Michel Peissel, discovered that while "giant ants" weren't a thing, there were massive marmots* in the Dansar Plain, above the Upper Indus river in modern Pakistan, that do indeed dig up gold as they make burrows. Herodotus's translators may have mistakenly rendered the term for marmot into one for "giant mountain ants", because the two words apparently sound almost identical in Persian.

Similarly, the Scythians' "magic vapour" that got them all spaced out and wacky was undoubtedly good old-fashioned weed. There is sound archaeological evidence to support the account of

---

* A genus of large rodents

Scythians using hemp mounds to get stoned, probably as part of a funeral rite. Or at least that was their excuse.

Archaeology also vindicates his writings about Egypt. Herodotus expanded at some length about the unusual shape of boats on the Nile but for centuries his 23 lines describing them were written off by many scholars as little more than fantasy. However, in 2019 a dive off the lost port of Thonis-Heracleion discovered a miraculously preserved ship that exactly matched his description.

Even the "flying snakes" stuff might have been true; sure, no such creature exists in Africa or the Middle East today, but they do prevail in the forests of Southeast Asia and it's not beyond the bounds of credibility to suggest that he'd heard the story from some traveller and muddled things up.

Herodotus was the first "social historian", as interested in the habits, customs and gossip of ordinary people as he was in wars and big events. And as such, the Herodotean legacy has sometimes been dismissed even as that of his near-contemporary Athenian historian Thucydides has found great succour with academics.

Herodotus loved the lure of the tall tale; Thucydides was wedded doggedly and unremittingly to the pursuit of truth.

What we know of Thucydides' biography is sketchy and comes almost entirely from his own account of his life. Having survived the Plague of Athens – a pandemic that killed Pericles – he fought in the Peloponnesian war as a military general and was subsequently blamed, unfairly by his account, for the fall of the city of Amphipolis and sent into exile. Some historians, including the Greek scholar H.D Westlake, have wondered whether his version of events is but a self-justification for having lost the city to the Spartans. But perhaps no history of oneself can ever be wholly objective.

What is indisputable is that having been sent into exile, Thucydides sat down and wrote a history of the Peloponnesian war that almost single-handedly invented journalism, evidence-based history, political theory and critical thinking. He took a clinical, chronological, detached and unemotional approach to his work. Putting loyalties aside, he sought to write an unbiased account of recent events that examined the origins of the conflict and the motives of the various protagonists involved.

In the 21st-century age of invisible weapons of mass destruction, Brexit, China-US rivalry, and fake news, Thucydides has come firmly back into fashion. He is a popular reference point for journalists, historians and even politicians, hoping to evoke his spirit by name-dropping him. Steve Bannon, Trump's chief strategist* and the Executive Chairman of Breitbart,† which practically invented the fake news agenda, claimed to be a fan. As has Boris Johnson. Whether they have fundamentally misunderstood Thucydides, or were deliberately invoking his legacy to suggest that "their" history was "true history" is a moot point.

Thucydides is so hot in the 21st century, that he even gets name checked in a Wonder Woman movie where the villainous General Ludendorff whispers, "peace is but an armistice in an on-going war" to the eponymous hero, who immediately recognises it as the words of the great Athenian historian. It seems unlikely that the father of accuracy would be impressed, though, because this is actually a fake quote.

Neville Morley, Professor of Classics and Ancient History at Exeter University and a renowned Thucydidean, tasked himself

---

* From January–August 2017
† From 2012–January 2017 and August 2017–January 2018

with finding the origin of the saying in a 2015 article only to discover, rather embarrassingly, that its source appeared to spring from the walls of America's most prestigious military academy:

"The earliest definite attribution to Thucydides that I've found so far is actually in the 'History of Warfare' gallery in the West Point Museum, which includes quotations painted on the walls that were, so I am informed, supplied by members of the History Department in 1988 when the gallery was refurbished."

Thucydides' book is a hard read. Unapologetically elitist, it was never intended to shift copies or entertain readers whiling away their time on Mediterranean beaches. Thucydides' target audience were rulers, leaders and experts. His text is as unencumbered with gods and oracles as it is with the reassurances of notions of destiny. This was a man uninterested in the Herodotean fripperies of what people ate or the aqua-borne pursuits of lute-playing youths riding dolphins.

In many ways he was the forerunner of the sort of dusty, dismissive academics who lurk in one corner of Twitter, coruscating less-informed users with facts and bar charts and logic.

While Herodotus failed to unshackle history from mythology, Thucydides put truth to the fore. His work would elucidate the tiny band of rulers who would read it in his age and beyond. In his own words, this book would be "a possession for all time".

The work would become a cautionary tale of the impact of war and bad leadership on society. And it is one that is achingly relevant in the age of misinformation and the excesses of Trump and the hubris of Brexit.

The way Thucydides tells it, 5th-century BCE Mediterranean city states had seen the arrogance that informed Brexit exceptionalism 2,500 years before the UK left the EU.

As the Athenians embarked on an ill-advised invasion of Sicily in 413 BCE, they convinced themselves they were better and stronger than their enemy, who they believed would be quickly divided and driven into retreat. As with the Vote Leavers and Faragists* of 21st-century Britain, naysayers and critics of the misadventure were ignored or ridiculed. But everything swiftly turned to hell. Imbued with overarching self-confidence and conceitedness, the Athenians invaded, failed and ignominiously returned home, before the government was overthrown in 411 BCE.

Marx and ABBA both claimed in their key works that the history book on the shelf was always repeating itself. Thucydides errs slightly on the matter, suggesting instead there is a constant riffing in the present on the tunes of the past – not an exact repetition; history as jazz, not karaoke.

The characters might change but human nature and human folly do not.

* * *

The collapse of the Roman Empire and the rise of Christianity led to an extended neglect of the works of the great Greek scholars, largely because many people stopped being able to speak Greek. The works of many writers were lost altogether. In the popular imagination this is the era known as "The Dark Ages", which stretched from around 500–1000. It is popularly viewed as an intolerable time of anarchy and a sort of descent into collective stupidity, where nobody had nice things or did anything more than hoe turnips and stare at the empty landscape. But in truth, the Dark Ages weren't that dark.

---

* Followers of Nigel Farage – one time leader of UKIP and the Brexit Party

Yes, the collapse of the Roman Empire saw Europe plunge into a thousand years of Christian religious theocracy and yes, knowledge was "lost", but none of that was new. There had been multiple "dark ages" before.

Since the rise of the first Mesopotamian civilisations in what the West call the "Middle East", multiple empires and cultures had risen and fallen and knowledge had come and gone. In the 11th century BCE, the Mycenaeans, the first great European civilisation, had seen 500 years of sophisticated and advanced culture crumble to dust. But as always happens – something else rose in its place.

With the collapse of Roman omnipotence in Europe, everything didn't simply grind to a halt. In the 400 years that followed, for the vast majority of people these ages were no darker than any that had preceded them.

The term was coined long after the event, in the 14th century by Petrach, a man heavily biased in favour of Greek and Roman culture, who viewed this period in antiquity as the "golden age" of human civilisation. Because even in the 14th century, people were looking back to those lost "good old days".

In fact, despite its rather dismal mud and misery vibe, some very good things came out of the Dark Ages. In the north of Europe, technological advances in agriculture revolutionised the production of food. Beyond the boundaries of that continent, massive strides were being made in science and mathematics, by Islamic scholars and scientists – even as new ideas filtered in from China.

And the Monastic age – so unfortunately characterised as a period of shaven-headed men in sandals painting fancy letters while waiting for the Vikings to ransack them – was at its height.

These early monks were the first Western academics engrossed in a culture of study and academic enterprise. In well-stocked libraries across Europe they were busily engaged, not simply in the copying out of psalms and Bible verses, but also writing books of their own including the first truly great history of Britain: Bede's Ecclesiastical Histories.

The Venerable Bede was an English Benedictine polymath, living, working and writing in the 7th and 8th centuries, whose most famous work, which seeks to detail the origins of Christianity, is a masterpiece of the Early Middle Ages.

Bede drew on the extensive library at his monastery in Wearmouth-Jarrow and with astonishing clarity and accuracy told the story of "English" history and the emergence of Christianity in it up to that point. To read Bede is to be transported back in time. But what is most striking, given that he is a Christian monk, is that he takes a very Thucydidean approach. His work is remarkably accurate on dates, events and names, and filled with well-sourced material. His dedication to evidence and his remarkable ability to piece together fragments of information to make up a whole makes his greatest work one of the cornerstones of British and European history.

Unfortunately, for every Thucydidean scholar, history has an idiot propagandist waiting in the wings. In Britain the culprit is Geoffrey of Monmouth, whose batshit-mad medieval *Historia Regum Britanniae*, written much later than Bede's work, in the 12th century, created a series of pernicious myths of exceptionalism that fed fires which still need stamping out today. Some of those will be covered later in this book. Suffice to say it was Monmouth who made up the legend of King Vortigern inviting the fictional Anglo-Saxon mercenaries Hengist and Horsa to his

Kingdom. And it was Monmouth who invented the bonkers tales of King Arthur and his knights that so enchanted Himmler, and Monmouth who created the source material for *King Lear* and all the other fictional rulers of Britain.

Monmouth and Bede represent the eternal push and tug between actual history and fake history that began with Thucydides and Herodotus and which continues today.

Simply because Churchill's grandson tells the Old Etonian Mayor of London a story about Winston making a cleaning lady a dame, it doesn't make it true. But as in the case of dolphin-riding singers or Monmouth's "arrival of the Saxons", once it has been put in a book it can take on a truth of its own and the longer that persists, the harder it becomes to dispel. People prefer "good story" narratives to dull as ditch-water events that don't play to their prejudices. The knotweed of stupidism can sow deleterious ignorance of the past.

There is no better illustration than the Flat Earth fallacy. Ask your mates or Facebook friends to guess when they think people began to accept that the world was round.

I tried this out on 40 fairly well-informed friends and relatives and the majority guessed:

"Between the 15th and the 17th centuries."

Everyone knows after all, that Christopher Columbus sailed west to "prove that the Earth was round" in 1492 and therefore it must have been after that.

Many of us grew up with stories of Columbus's terrified sailors clinging onto the rigging for dear life, in the fear that their ships would fall off the edge of the world. It's a funny story and it gives us all a good laugh at the expense of Italian sailors, even though it's total hogwash.

Christopher Columbus did not sail west to prove the Earth was spherical. That wasn't even at the bottom of his "to do" list. Because everyone knew it already.

Stargazing is as old as eyesight. A handy Aurignacian-era mammoth tusk proves the point and suggests that humans were trying to chart Orion 38,000 years ago. The Bronze Age Nebra sky disc, a remarkable object discovered in 1999, and so perfect that it too was feared at one time to be a forgery, depicts celestial bodies 3,600 years ago. People in Ancient Saxony weren't lamenting the loss of Atlantis, but they were most definitely charting the stars.

It is unclear exactly who first worked out that the Earth was spherical. It may have been Phoenician sailors attempting to sail around Africa, or it could have been Pythagoras. Although as the Greeks had a habit of attributing everything to Pythagoras that should perhaps be taken with a pinch of salt*. Certainly, by the 3rd century BCE it was widely accepted, in the Hellenic world at least, that the Earth was a sphere and the knowledge was carried forward into the Roman era and beyond.

When not knocking off well-sourced history books, Bede dabbled in the phases of the Moon and the measurement of time, to which end he wrote in *The Reckoning of Time* that the Earth is:

"Not circular like a shield or spread out like a wheel, but resembles a ball being equally round in all directions."

So why do we think that they thought otherwise?

American writer Washington Irving is to blame. Best remembered for his novella *Sleepy Hollow*, the Rip Van Winkle stories and the term "the almighty dollar", Irving was America's first native-born "man of letters".

---

* There is considerable doubt in some quarters as to whether Pythagoras even existed. There are no primary sources.

During his long career, he tossed off many a book, including the one that would come to cement the origin myth of Columbus discovering America. The resulting work, written in 1828, was mawkish, whimsical, hagiographic and wrong, but to add insult to injury, Irving claimed that he was writing in the Thucydidean tradition and that:

"*I have avoided indulging in mere speculations...*" and endeavoured "*...to place every fact in such a point of view, that the reader might perceive its merits, and draw his own maxims and conclusions.*"

Irving's book was the salvo of American myth-making. The country was in need of an origin story and he provided it for the hungry young nation.

Christopher Columbus didn't "discover America". The Vikings had first sailed there 500 years earlier. Columbus never even set foot on the mainland, as he never travelled beyond the islands of the Caribbean. The suggestion that he "discovered America" is even more ridiculous when you remember that when he arrived in the region, 60 million people were already living there. And had been for 16,000 years.

Columbus also wasn't much of a hero, or a navigator.

In 200 BCE, Greek polymath Eratosthenes had calculated the size of the Earth to within a margin of 1%. When Columbus set off from Spain in 1492, he made the same calculation, but misjudged it by 25%, meaning that when he arrived in what became known as the West Indies, he thought he was in mainland China, or somewhere off the eastern coast of Japan. Columbus was like one of those annoying drivers who won't switch on the sat nav but who insist they know where they're going even as they drive around in circles.

The Italian never set foot on the northern or southern continents of America. Even as the Italian explorer Giovanni Caboto (aka John Cabot) made land fall on the coast of North America in 1497 on behalf of the English King Henry VII, Columbus was sailing about in circles, thinking he was somewhere near India and confusing the Amazon for the Ganges delta.

Columbus was not really an explorer. He wasn't even trying to do something useful, such as prove that the Earth was round. Why would he, when everyone knew this already? His motivation was wealth.

Many people have an image of Columbus the adventurer, or even Columbus the invader, but few are familiar with Columbus the violent thug, the brutal tyrant and the unhinged capitalist.

As Viceroy and Governor of the Indies, his leadership was marked by incompetence and barbarity. He ordered the mutilation and murder of people who mocked him for his lowly birth and ordered that their dismembered bodies be dragged through the streets.

In his defence, Columbus did create a bridge across the Atlantic and did kick-start the age of American trade and discovery. The notion that European exploration of South America upended some Edenesque paradise is deeply flawed and something we will be looking at later on in the book. But even by the standards of his time, Columbus was unhinged and excessively brutal in his treatment of the people he came into contact with.

He enslaved people on the island of Hispaniola – comprising modern-day Haiti and the Dominican Republic. He allowed his men to kidnap and rape Carib women.

Despite claiming high Christian virtue, he boasted about nine-year-old girls getting sold into sexual slavery. His maltreatment of the people in his charge was such that he was eventually removed from his position, arrested and sent back to Spain in chains.

By now many, including his patrons Queen Isabella and King Ferdinand, were distancing themselves from him. Columbus's religious zealotry had begun to boil over and he believed the end of the world was nigh and that he was a prophet of God, who was now speaking to him directly. He began signing letters "Christo Ferens" meaning "Christ Bearer" and his mental condition had clearly and deliriously deteriorated.

He died in 1506, aged 55, a neglected and marginalised figure who had become an embarrassment to all but his handful of devoted supporters.

And yet over time, the madness and the failure, the brutality and the folly were forgotten as he was turned into the Americas' founding father. There were other candidates for the role, including Giovanni Caboto and the Viking Leif Erikson, but Columbus fitted the bill better for an emerging United States. Unlike Cabot, he wasn't operating under the patronage of the hated English. And who wants to be founded by marauding barbarians in funny hats?

By the 19th century, Columbus had been repurposed in North America as a great hero who had "discovered" the continent, brought Christian light to the darkness and proved that the Earth wasn't flat. Inconvenient facts such as the one that he had never seen North America, or that everyone knew the Earth was round already, or that he had enslaved people and ordered summary executions before being sent back to Spain in chains – were trimmed out.

Irving's heavily fictionalised "Columbus", then, was a dangerous artifice. He was created, much like the Lion Man, to make sense of early US history for the faithful and to give the young country a founding myth. In that, Irving was little different from Monmouth and the Ahnenerbe. His work was no more genuine or well intentioned than the Nazi Chiemsee cauldron.

People buy into myths, whether it's the story of Camelot or the saintly Columbus, for no other reason than that they tend to be easier to grasp than the complex truth. Once they take root, they take on a truth of their own, as more and more people accept the deceit as established fact. For 200 years, Irving's Columbus was the only one on offer and naysayers and troublemaking historians who tried to persuade folks otherwise faced an uphill struggle. Challenging an established lie takes effort because the longer it is accepted, the more immutable it becomes.

Hundreds of millions of Americans invested in the fake history of Columbus and nobody likes to be told they are wrong. To question the false consensus is to risk attracting opprobrium and ire. Much easier to make hay out of protecting the falsehood. And many have.

In October 2020, with electoral defeat looming, Donald Trump sought to reclaim the ahistorical Columbus.

Speaking at the White House on the day named in the Italian adventurer's honour, the President declared:

"Sadly, in recent years, radical activists have sought to undermine Christopher Columbus's legacy. These extremists seek to replace discussion of his vast contributions with talk of failings, his discoveries with atrocities and his achievements with transgressions."

Trump was seeking to preserve the fiction because that false but established American history worked in his favour. Trump's supporters weren't interested in truth so much as "the truth" they had grown up with. The one where America, the greatest country on Earth, was founded by white Christian men, forged by white Christian cowboys, betrayed by liberals and Black Lives Matter activists and saved from the Antifa mob by an orange property tycoon.

The legends of "great men" can be forged out of greed, stupidity and barbarity. Shored up by liars and dissemblers, the myths can perpetuate and prosper, but not to the advantage of the vast majority of ordinary people – the pawns of history.

During the Trump years, expertise and truth were assailed by a hail of "alternative facts" and "alternative history". If his disastrous tenure and unsettling departure teach us anything then it is that truth matters.

CHAPTER THREE

BRITAIN COULD HAVE LOST THE WAR

*Why nationalism is irrational
and counterproductive*

In the late afternoon of 24th December 1954, in Chicago, Illinois, a middle-aged woman called Dorothy Martin led a small party of followers out into the street in front of her home and awaited the arrival of a flying saucer from the Planet Clarion.

This was the fourth time Dorothy and her sect, The Seekers, had prepared for the aliens but on each previous occasion their hopes had been dashed. Back in November, some confusion about the time difference between Clarion and suburban Illinois had meant a no show. Then, on the 17th December, the sect had received a message saying the spaceship had landed and that they needed to leave immediately, but by the time they got outside, the Clarions had scarpered. The aliens had been very specific about metal – insisting that it had to be stripped from clothes and luggage before they could meet – and someone had forgotten the metal in their bra.

A third prophecy changed the date to the 21st December, but the Clarions had been so busy chatting to God that they had lost track of the time. The aliens sent their apologies and promised that they'd pop down on the 24th. There was to be no more messing about – the 24th of December was it – and The Seekers were so convinced of it that they left jobs and marriages, sold possessions and homes, and even baked a flying saucer-shaped cake for the pre-departure meet and greet.

Earth was doomed and Dorothy's followers alone would be spared. The Seekers were going to live on Clarion and create new homes in a galaxy far, far away.

This disparate group of sci-fi fans and eccentrics were the chosen people, destined to sustain the human race and propagate the species on Clarion. And while they were enjoying the flight, Earth would be engulfed by floods and fires and earthquakes and all the other stuff that happens on your average Doomsday.

Being fundamentally decent people, The Seekers wanted to warn as many others as possible of the coming apocalypse. So, they tipped off the TV channels and local press.

As a result, by late afternoon on that December day, hundreds of increasingly impatient Chicagoans had gathered in the street in front of Dorothy's home. As 6 p.m. approached, rumours spread that someone had seen "a little green man" in the crowd. But when The Seekers went looking for him, he was gone.

The hour of first contact came and went. The Seekers checked their watches. They sang a hymn. More moments passed. They looked to the sky again and back to their watches, and after a brief conversation, went back inside to the warmth of Dorothy's home and ate the spaceship cake. Outside, disappointed Chicagoans, who had wasted Christmas Eve waiting for a spaceship that hadn't materialised, had to be dispersed by the Chicago City Police Department.

Leon Festinger, a social psychologist who had managed to infiltrate The Seekers, observed what happened next.

As on the previous occasions, instead of questioning the prophecy, The Seekers sought to explain why the aliens hadn't come. Or perhaps they had come. Perhaps the crowd had scared them away. Perhaps the mysterious "reporter" who had talked his way into the house was actually one of them. The Seekers communicated with the Clarions via a system of telepathic writing and, as they ate their cake, Dorothy was seized with the urge to put down an incoming message which she relayed to the group.

The Clarions had been talking to God, and it turns out that Dorothy and her friends' example "...had spread so much light [that] God had saved the world from destruction."

By baking a cake, taking off their bras and standing out in the cold, the Seekers had literally saved the world from destruction. Their sacrifice had not been in vain. And, having got over their disappointment about not being able to travel through space, the cult dusted off the cake crumbs and began to proselytise with renewed energy.

Festinger's research of this event, published in his book *When Prophecy Fails*, formed the basis for the psychological theory of cognitive dissonance. Human beings, from the carvers of the Lion Man onwards, have had an innate urge to believe, but dissonance can occur when those beliefs are challenged by evidence that refutes them. So, we offset the mental discomfort by altering our belief to restore balance.

"A man with a conviction is a hard man to change," wrote Festinger. "Tell him you disagree and he turns away. Show him facts or figures and he questions your sources. Appeal to logic and he fails to see your point."

Cognitive dissonance can affect anyone. A girl breaks your heart, so you convince yourself she wasn't good enough for you. Smoking will kill you but the cigarettes are needed to calm your jittery nerves. Christians are brought up to believe that Jesus was/ is a perfect being. And yet in the Gospel of John, Chapter 2, verse 15, Christ becomes so enraged by traders in the Temple that he smashes everything up.

Christ going mad with a whip doesn't fit with the Jesus brand and so most churches choose to ignore John and use the Gospel of Matthew instead, which doesn't mention it.

Studies into cults and cognitive dissonance have suggested that Festinger was wrong to conclude that a failed prophecy inevitably leads to cognitive dissonance or a need to offset it, because actually prophecies hardly ever fail in the eyes of the true hard-core believers and there's therefore no need to recalibrate. A committed cult rarely doubts itself and will instead incorporate events into its liturgy and make it part of their creed, or – in the case of the Nazi Ahnernebe – create things to fill the gaps.

It's easy to dismiss such delusional thinking. It's comforting to sneer at the mad excesses of The Seekers or the Nazi Ahnernebe. It's tempting to reassure ourselves that we would never be as gullible and self-deceiving as that. Delusion is the preserve of ancient peoples, or Nazi lunatics or Chicago housewives. We are modern, rational people. We would never fall prey to such nonsense. But even the most rational amongst us can be taken in by the lure of a cult.

* * *

When I was a *Star Wars*-obsessed boy of the late 1970s, failing my way through school, one teacher made all the difference. Mr

Higham didn't just teach history – he obliged you to fall in love with it.

When he spoke, that dusty Hertfordshire classroom transformed into the fields of Agincourt, or the gloomy back streets of plague-ridden London.

Mr Higham was particularly good on the Plantagenets, and in his hands the high tragedy of Henry II and Thomas à Becket became a struggle every bit as epic as that between Lord Vader and Luke. The story had it all. A charismatic English king wants to reform an injustice at the heart of his kingdom, namely that when they commit a crime, religious clerics – who in 12th-century England make up one-fifth of the population – are permitted to be tried by the local bishop in the bishop's court (governed by meddling, unelected Bishops in far-off Rome), rather than the secular courts. A bishop's court would often move for acquittal and would certainly not enforce the death penalty, so, clerics could quite literally get away with murder. When a priest committed a secular crime, he was punished with prayers; if an ordinary subject committed the same offence, he had a foot chopped off.

Seeking to level things up, Henry appoints his hedonistic friend, Thomas, the Archbishop of Canterbury, believing free-spirited Becket will bend to his whims. But Thomas goes all happy-clappy and refuses to come over to the dark side. Seven years of tit for tat, exile and rage culminate in high drama.

On a drunken Christmas night in 1170 at his castle in Bures, Normandy, Henry yells: "Who will rid me of this turbulent priest?" Four knights cross the Channel, ride to Canterbury and slay Thomas in cold blood as he prays at the altar of the great cathedral.

Soon miracles are being reported and sainthood follows. Each year on the anniversary, Henry is whipped in public by monks to cleanse him of the curse of this episcopicide.*

Mr Higham captivated his audience of 10-year-olds with this tale. But even as he spoke, there was something that stirred the inquisitive mind of that otherwise indolent child – something that didn't make sense.

If Henry II was King of England, then why was he in France all the time? Weren't there castles to be built and *Domesday Book* sequels to be written? And not just Henry – they were all at it. Why did Richard I die at the hands of a crossbowman, clutching a frying pan, on the outskirts of Limoges? What was wrong with Bishop's Stortford?

And what was so good about France anyway? I'd been there and it smelt funny. The milk was weird. The water, according to no less a source than my mother, could poison you if you brushed your teeth with it. They lived off raw steaks and a peculiar green fruit called an "avocado". Cutlery, seemingly, had yet to be invented, for when they ate breakfast, they dunked their pastries in hot chocolate.

They didn't know which side of the road you were meant to drive on. The TV didn't speak English. And worst of all, they were peculiarly unacquainted with Britain's central role in creating the modern world.

Too timid to raise my arm and seek elucidation, the question of those endless French breaks bugged me for years and it was only much later that I connected the dots and realised that selective historical engineering had been at play. Mr Higham hadn't

---

* episcopicide – the murder of a bishop

exactly been lying to us but he had been extremely economical with the vérité.

Like many children born in the late 1960s and 1970s, I spent my childhood believing that Britain was best. And school history lessons reinforced the point.

The way we were told it, William the Conqueror had invaded in 1066, much as one might seek an upgrade from Economy Class to First. No longer the mere Duke of a bit of western France he was now ruler of the greatest country on Earth and, subsequent to his arrival, we had all lived happily ever after.

Mr Higham had edited out the not-insignificant fact that, from 1066, England had become little more than a colony of Normandy, ruled by Norman nobles, who spoke Norman French and whose leaders lived in France. Also, the people who had been conquered, who we now call the "Anglo-Saxons" (but more on that later) spoke a language that was easily intelligible to the "volks" on the other side of the North Sea.

And, in a further humiliating blow, the language of the Angles was one that the Norman kings didn't bother to learn for centuries. It was only when Henry IV came along in 1399 that a British monarch even bothered to speak it.

The Britain which I grew up in, of the late 70s and early 80s' was haunted by the ghost of its lost Empire and struggling to find its groove. The then so-called 'sick man of Europe' was flailing about in a tide of economic failure and political impotence. Like an ageing rock star, desperate for relevance, the country and curriculum were falling back on its greatest hits, to make up for the lacklustre new material, like the "three-day week" and the "winter of discontent".

Fake history was providing the heavy sedation to offset the cognitive dissonance.

Mr Higham, like my parents, had been raised in an era when being British meant something.

For half my dad's life, the map had been painted pink and London had sat at the heart of the greatest Empire the world had ever seen. Britishness was a byword for excellence and he and my mother – and most people – still bought, unquestioningly, into the conceit of our inimitability.

Dad was a rational man, but when it came to domestic engineering and British superiority all reason was lost. Despite bad experience after bad experience, he insisted on buying British cars. At some point, in the 1980s, he purchased a metallic blue Austin Montego that seemed to sum up the cognitive dissonance of British exceptionalism. It was ugly, but he insisted it was beautiful. Bits kept falling off, but he swore it wasn't the car's fault. On one occasion, the driver's seat snapped in half when he was putting his seatbelt on and he blamed himself for leaning back too hard. It rarely started, but that wasn't the Montego's fault. It was the fault of everything, anything apart from the machine itself and sacred British engineering.

Brainwashed into a dogma that preached a potent, self-reinforcing mantra of our own island's brilliance, my father, unwittingly, was a paid-up member of the cult of "British exceptionalism". The creed was fairly straightforward and it went like this:

The British were a chosen people. Greatest on Earth. And to be British, was to have won the lottery of life.

"Britain is not just another country; it has never been just another country!" Margaret Thatcher declared in a 1987 BBC interview, tapping into a widely held sentiment. And I suppose, back in childhood and undoubtedly as a result of the environment in which I was raised, I believed it too.

* * *

For most of human history, nation states didn't exist and most people didn't notice or care.

Our peasant ancestors were too busy working the land, struggling to pay tithes to their feudal overlords and seeking to provide enough food and shelter for their families to worry about what country they came from. People defined themselves by the villages they lived in and the lords they pledged their fealty to.

It was only from the 1400s onwards that anyone in Europe began to define notions of nationality or care about them much – and those people were the rulers with time on their hands.

The idea of nation states suited monarchs. People with one identity are easier to control and easier to mobilise. But to create a collective identity and set up your "nation" stall, you first need people to buy in.

The Anglo-Irish political scientist Benedict Anderson defined nations (and empires) as "imagined communities" – social constructs that are essentially imagined into being by leaders and people who consider themselves to be a part of the group.

Imagined communities, by their nature, forge something else – an exceptionalism that we shall call *"the conceit of we"*. *The conceit of we* insists that the citizens of nations act homogeneously. That they think and act as one. That the people have "habits" and a shared collective heritage and a common identity.

"We" drink tea. "We" invented democracy. "We" have a better sense of humour than you. "We" have stiff upper lips. "We" won the war. "We" are a Christian country. "We" have never done this. "We" have always done that. "We" have more history. "We" – let's face it – are better than "you".

Politicians like nothing more than talking up a bit of "we" in a crisis. "We survived" the bubonic plague and the Blitz and the Napoleonic wars so "we" will survive Brexit and coronavirus.

"We" thinking is cult thinking and, depressingly, it's one that millions of people ascribe to. In its broadest form, it is probably better known as "nationalism".

In his essay "Notes of Nationalism", George Orwell sums up the "indifference to reality" that lies at the heart of the condition.

"All nationalists have the power of not seeing resemblances between similar sets of facts. A British Tory will defend self-determination in Europe and oppose it in India with no feeling of inconsistency."

Einstein called it an "infantile disease, the measles of mankind" and its most obvious symptom is the abrogation of reason. The idea that people born in a geographical region have some common spirit and a common destiny is nonsense, but it's compelling nonsense.

In 1996, 30 years after England's one World Cup win against West Germany, England hosted the European Championship. With Britpop and Cool Britannia at their height, there was a sense that the stars of destiny had aligned, that it was England's sacred right to overturn 30 years of hurt. The comedians David Baddiel and Frank Skinner and musician Ian Broudie put out a single entitled "Three Lions" that tapped into the oracular mood, and soon the notion that "football was coming home" became a kind of prophecy.

When England came up against a newly reunited Germany in the semi-finals, 50 years of jingoism boiled over and unhinged xenophobia took hold.

The *Daily Mirror,* under editor Piers Morgan, declared "football war" on Germany and having initially planned to drop leaflets over Berlin, instead put out a front-page featuring England players in military fatigues with the tag line "Achtung! Surrender". Inside the paper, further depths were scraped:

"There is a strange smell in Berlin and it's not just their funny sausages, it's the smell of fear" the comments page gushed, adding, confusingly: "zey don't like it up zem" in reference to the catchphrase of Corporal Jones, an English character in the long running BBC sitcom *Dad's Army* about the British Home Guard – of which there will be more in a moment.

Not to be outdone *The Sun* screamed "Let's Blitz Fritz", leading to a complaint by the German Embassy. The German Captain Jürgen Klinsmann expressed fears that the inflammatory language might end in violence, and Labour and Conservative MPs tabled an Early Day Motion* in the House of Commons condemning:

"The frenzy of jingoistic, notably anti-German nonsense in the tabloid press."

But England was too wrapped up in the coming prophecy to notice.

In the end it was Klinsmann – not Piers Morgan – who was proved right. England lost – and things turned very ugly indeed. If England couldn't win on the pitch, they would win off it – and to offset the dissonance, violence erupted. There were riots in Trafalgar Square. Tourists were assaulted. In Brighton, a Russian student was stabbed by a mob who mistook him for a German.

Failed prophecy and punctured self-belief had descended into an orgy of drunken violence.

Nobody chooses the place of their birth. Nationality is happenstance. But condition millions of people into believing that their tribe is better than everyone else's and you create a vicious and dangerous climate of extremism.

---

* Motions which aren't generally debated but are used to put on record the views of MPs, which often attract public interest and media coverage.

If England had been drawn against Spain or Italy in the 1996 European Championship semi-final it is unlikely that anyone would have been stabbed. The events of that night were predicated on our opponent – Germany – because Britain in 1996 and Britain in the 21st century remains dangerously obsessed with the country and wedded to the myths surrounding both world wars. If nationalism is our illness, then Germanophobia is the symptom.

The Second World War ended in 1945, but many in Britain have never come to terms with the win. Britain has a seemingly incurable case of war delusion and for much of the month of October and early November the cult indulges in "war Christmas" – an orgy of flag waving, poppy-wearing and misty-eyed remembrance for a conflict that 98% of us cannot remember.

Challenge the sacred texts of either that or the Great War of 1914–18 that my both my grandfathers had fought in, or worse, suggest that we should move on from all of this indulgence, and you risk inviting significant ire.

Several years ago, I wrote an article for *The Independent* newspaper questioning how long we should continue with remembrance now everyone who had been involved was dead. Subsequently, I was invited onto BBC Three Counties Radio to discuss the piece and soon an elderly chap from Bedfordshire was ringing in to suggest that I be put against a wall and shot.

I wasn't proposing dismantling of the Cenotaph. I was simply suggesting that it was getting unhealthy, and worse, that contemporary politicians were appropriating those events and the lives of those lost men and boys for modern political aims. I was suggesting that we were at risk of turning the war dead into victims and saints.

I suggested that what was needed was more balance and context and truth, that it was unhealthy to keep looking back and to constantly be in thrall to the mythos of war.

But it was too much for him – or any of the later callers.

The awkward truth is that remembrance in Britain no longer has much to do with the wars. It has become a nationalistic tribal indulgence. The poppy has become a badge of fealty to faith in the cult. Its absence from the lapels of television presenters is called out and condemned. Fail to wear one and you're accused of "hating this country".

No symbol has been more sentimentalised or weaponised or so tragically dragged through the mud.

Britons no longer go to church, because there's no need. The de facto state religion is the two world wars. Their symbols are our iconography, their events our scripture.

Today's reading is taken from the Gospel of Dunkirk.

In the beginning, Britain went reluctantly to war. By late May 1940, everything had turned to shit and the Wehrmacht had punched a hole into France and cut the Allied forces in half. Fearing death or capture, thousands of British Tommies fell back to the small French town of Dunkirk and awaited their fate. The overcrowded seafront was easy pickings for the Luftwaffe. As the Royal Navy tried to work out how to evacuate over 300,000 men from the shallow water German pilots sprayed the beaches with bullets and spattered the sand with English blood.

Then, a miracle happened.

Hundreds of tiny boats, made up of a rag-tag armada of small craft and pleasure cruisers came to the rescue. British indomitability and the resolute courage of ordinary people had turned disaster to triumph. They had brought salvation to the French coast.

The "little ships" story is the defining Dunkirk legend. It ranks alongside 1066 and Guy Fawkes in the national consciousness.

But an awful lot of what we believe and assume we know about the event is nothing more than myth.

It is true that, to their surprise, the German army advanced rapidly into France in May 1940 and routed the Allies. In a period of just six weeks the Wehrmacht had overwhelmed the opposition and cut the Allied forces in two, causing hundreds of thousands of servicemen to retreat to the port of Dunkirk to await rescue. But "the Miracle at Dunkirk" that followed was no miracle.

In 1965, 25 years after the retreat from France, a flotilla of the original boats recreated the voyage to Dunkirk of those original "little ships". Hundreds of sailors and fishermen took a day trip to France and the moment was captured by a Pathé newsreel that tellingly describes the participants as "pilgrims".

If you go to the Imperial War Museum (IWM) in south London, one of the boats that was filmed on that day is on display.

The *Tamzine* is a tiny fishing vessel less than 15 feet long that could at most hold perhaps eight people. After being featured in the newsreel, it became iconic and was bequeathed to the IWM in 1981 by its owner Mr Ralph Bennett to make up part of their permanent display.

Looking at this exhibit, it's hard to imagine how a fleet made up of such tiny craft saved hundreds of thousands of people and brought them safely home. And that's because they didn't.

The purpose of the "little ships" was to ferry soldiers from the shore to the awaiting transport ships and destroyers – not to cross the Channel. And despite what you might have gleaned from war movies, this wasn't done by "ordinary people". The *Tamzine* like the rest of the flotilla was not skippered by its owner but by Royal

Navy personnel and Coast Guard officers who had requisitioned it without the owner's knowledge or permission.

The Dunkirk Association of Little Ships admit that:

"Very few owners took their own vessels, apart from fishermen and one or two others."

The "one or two" others included Charles Lightoller, who had been second officer on the *Titanic* and was a decorated former Royal Navy Commander. Lightoller was a proper hero. Having heard that the navy was appealing for private vessels to help with the evacuation, he took it upon himself to sail his private motor yacht to France and, with the help of a sea cadet and his son, rescued an estimated 127 people under fire.

Lightoller's adventures inspired the character of "Mr Dawson", played by the actor Mark Rylance, in the 2017 film *Dunkirk*, but in that movie, as with the 1958 film, the experienced Lightoller becomes an ordinary English Joe – one among many – heeding the call.

Lightoller was the exception, not the rule.

This was a dark chapter in British history and as we debunk fake history, it is important not to underplay that. Between 10th May and 25th June 1940, 68,000 British soldiers were wounded, lost or captured in the Battle of France along with vast quantities of vital equipment. This was a catastrophe in every way. But the cult of British exceptionalism cannot abide the notion of "British failure" any more than my father could accept the disaster that was his car.

The story was deliberately spun and turned into a victory of plucky Brits outwitting the Nazi war machine. "We" won through, despite the odds. Just like "we" always do. "We" snatched victory from the jaws of defeat.

So as soon as the evacuation was over, the spinning began. Managing expectations on the 4th June, Prime Minister Churchill told the House of Commons that he had expected that only "20,000– 30,000 men might be re-embarked", but that thanks to the redoubtable efforts of the navy and air force, hundreds of thousands more had been delivered.

"Wars are not won by evacuations," Churchill cautioned, but less famously added, "there was a victory inside this deliverance, which should be noted."

Quite swiftly, the national and local newspapers were leaping on the event and celebrating how marvellous "we" had been.

"Heroic British defenders refused to surrender Calais," trilled the *Western Morning News* on 5th June, while the Bex*hill-on-Sea Observer* marvelled at the bravery of a local lad, who had crawled wounded for a mile through an open ditch to salvation.

Meanwhile in the US, sympathetic journalists and writers leapt on the story of the "little ships", and turned it into a tale of stalwart, decent Englishmen standing alone against Nazi aggressors. The 1942 Hollywood film *Mrs. Miniver* has the eponymous hero's husband sailing to France to rescue troops in his pleasure boat along with others. It didn't happen – but people came to think it had.

By the 25th anniversary, the flotilla's mission had become a sacred event. The *Tamzine* was no longer a fishing boat, but a holy relic.

The more I read and researched about the story of the *Tamzine*, the more sceptical I became. Parts of the story didn't seem to add up. There's only the late Mr Bennett's word to say that it was ever at Dunkirk – and as we will see in the next chapter, families do have a tendency towards "tall tale history". The vast majority of smaller vessels and rowing boats were abandoned on the French coast in 1940, but remarkably, at least according to the official version, this tiny craft was brought back to Margate, by a Belgian trawler, where it was reunited with its owner. And during what was unquestionably one of the most chaotic and desperate periods of the war.

Is it really believable that during a desperate retreat in the midst of war, a Belgian boat manned by Belgian crew would take the time and effort to reunite a rowing boat with its owner in Margate?

Much is made in the legend of the *Tamzine* that the boat was spattered with the "bloodstains of soldiers" – but nobody ever proved that it was human blood. Retreating soldiers would not all have been wounded and those that had would have been dressed.

More likely, those bloodstains, not unusual in a fishing vessel, were the result of decades of catch being gutted before being taken to the shore. But there's more poetry in the blood of retreating men.

Is it possible that the *Tamzine* never went to Dunkirk? And that perhaps, caught up in the excitement of the 1965 commemorations, the owner had simply claimed that it had?

When I raised this suspicion with Ian Kikuchi of the Imperial War Museum, he and his colleague Sean Rehling responded that such a deceit:

"Would [have required] the owner to have been consistently making up a story about Tamzine's participation, from the late 1940s until 1965 and thereafter up until his death."

It's a very good point, and anyway, perhaps, it doesn't really matter.

Like the murder of Becket, or the legend of Churchill, Dunkirk has transcended reality and become a sacred event. In that faith the *Tamzine* is both a miracle and a relic.

That religionisation of events has grown unabated since 1940. Come the 80th anniversary in 2020 you could even buy an amulet – the 80th anniversary "quarter sovereign" that had been "sandblasted using sand from the beaches of Dunkirk" for £99. I wrote to the purveyors of the amulet and asked them to explain what it all meant. But sadly, I received no reply.

Like all the best cults, the Dunkirk faith ignores the stuff that doesn't fit the narrative. The role of 40,000 French soldiers who fought the rear-guard that enabled the evacuation is barely referenced in films or documentaries. Most Dunkirk narratives fail to acknowledge the 140,000 French, Polish, Dutch and Belgians who were also present on the beaches and who were also evacuated. They also ignore the Belgian, Dutch, French and Norwegian fishermen who played a critical role, while the presence of Indians, Poles, Canadians and North Africans in Dunkirk in May 1940 is disregarded altogether.

The role played by Adolf Hitler in inadvertently helping the Allies tends also to be overlooked. His "Halt Order" issued on 24th May 1940 stopped advancing panzer divisions just 12 miles from Dunkirk. Why Hitler did this has been a matter of furious conjecture ever since – but most likely it was a strategic decision made by Field Marshal Gerd von Rundstedt to save his tanks.

Whatever the motive, the halt order provided three crucial days.

The triumphs of war and retreat are as much predicated upon the mistakes of the enemy as they are by the decisive actions of the victors. The chosen people at the heart of *the conceit of we* prefer to believe in divine deliverance instead. "Dunkirk Spirit" and British inimitability are uplifting notions. It's more comforting to indulge in them than to waste hours troubling ourselves with the actual chain of events and whether a small vessel really did cross the Channel in the late spring of 1940.

* * *

Dunkirk is but one strand in the celebrated narrative that claims that "we" could have lost the war.

In 1968, the BBC began broadcasting *Dad's Army*, a comedy television series about a fictional platoon in the war-time defence force known as the Home Guard, a real-life unit made up of men with reserved occupations and others too old or too young to fight.

By the early 1970s the sitcom was a staple of Wednesday and, later, Friday-night viewing, and thanks to endless repeats over the next 45 years, it acquired "national treasure" status.

Dad's Army revolves around a bank manager called Mainwaring, living in a fictional English coastal town, called Walmington-on-Sea, who takes it upon himself to marshal up a local defence force to fend off the coming German invasion. Appointing himself Captain, he enlists the support of his clerk "Sergeant Wilson" and junior, Private Pike, along with a local butcher, Lance Corporal Jones; an undertaker; a retired gentleman's outfitter; and a black-market spiv. Soon, the platoon is capturing felled Luftwaffe pilots and submarine crews and fighting the even greater threat that comes in the shape of the local air raid warden, Hodges.

After initial teething problems, the real-life Home Guard was not as hapless and comical as *Dad's Army* portrayed it. Many units played a useful and active role in manning anti-aircraft guns; they were given key strategic defensive roles and 1,206 men lost their lives in action – mostly protecting the public from fallen bombs. Nor were its ranks filled entirely with languorous old men falling asleep on chairs. Over a million coal miners, dock workers and school teachers were deemed to be in "reserved occupations" and thus unable to join the regular army, so half of the Home Guard was made up of individuals aged 18–27.

Some were selected to join the Auxiliary Unit, an elite band of men, trained in the dark arts of sabotage and guerrilla warfare, who had orders to set up resistance networks if the Germans ever invaded. More SAS than SAGA.

Dad's Army itself was not meant to be an exercise in jingoism. It is beautifully written and in between the pathos and the ribald comedy, it does a fairly good job of accurately depicting what life was like for some in wartime Britain: the role of the black market, the small mindedness, the class envy – and the fear – at least in the late summer of 1940 – that the Germans were on their way.

Unfortunately, and unintentionally, the programme cemented in the mindset of millions one of the most enduring myths of war. The one that suggests "we" were nearly invaded.

Each *Dad's Army* episode begins with an animated sequence showing three huge animated arrows, adorned with swastikas, pushing a shrinking Union Jack back across the Channel. Those 57 seconds, repeated unremittingly on British TV over 50 years, hammered home the notion that in 1945, isolated and imperilled wartime Britain stood "alone". Captain Mainwaring and his platoon were the last line of defence – small town Britain was naked before the aggressor and only the defiance and fortitude of ordinary people overcame the odds.

The impression all of this gives was that Britain was the David to the Nazi Goliath. The Nazis rode about in staff cars, while our officers fitted bicycle clips to their trousers and cycled off to war. It's a potent storyline, but it's not true.

At the start of the war, Britain was not held together by plastic tape and pieces of string. It was one of the world's three great superpowers.

The UK was a manufacturing giant, sufficient in coal and steel, and headed a vast Empire capable of pulling on extraordinary resources. By July 1940, the British army was 1.65 million strong.

French, Polish and Belgian servicemen who had escaped from Dunkirk joined Indian, Canadian and New Zealand soldiers who were already stationed in Britain. Across the world, the country could count on thousands of "Empire" troops. By the war's peak, the King's African Rifles numbered 300,000 and the Indian Army comprised 2.5 million troops, making it the largest volunteer force in history. That wasn't because all Indian Army personnel were excessively loyal to Britain, but rather that army pay was relatively good and the life of a soldier attractive for many from poorer rural areas. But the editing out of those many millions of men's part – in both world wars – is an egregious slight on their significant contribution to victory, which has yet to be rectified.

On the 16th July 1940, Hitler issued "Führer Directive 16" that spawned "Operation Sea Lion" – the plans for the invasion of Britain.

Hitler hoped Churchill would strike a deal. He calculated that there was nothing to be gained for Britain entering a protracted war and reasoned that the pragmatic Winston Churchill had more interest in the Empire than in fighting with Germany. Churchill's great achievement and lasting legacy – is that he didn't – largely because he had made the same calculation as the German High Command.

For Hitler and his chiefs of staff knew any invasion would fail.

The Royal Navy was more than double the size of the German Kriegsmarine and undisputed ruler of the waves. The German navy had recently suffered heavy losses during the two Battles of Norvik and ensuing offensives between 10th April and early June 1940, in northern Norway, weakening it further. Crossing a narrow channel of water, while the most powerful navy on Earth, or rather oceans, blasted what was left to smithereens, wasn't an appealing prospect.

German General Alfred Jodl suggested an invasion would be like "sending troops into a mincing machine".

Hitler knew that before it could even be contemplated, air superiority would have to be established. So as soon as Dunkirk was over, the Luftwaffe began attacking British air bases, hoping to knock out the RAF – or at the very least push Churchill to sue for peace.

Warfare is not neat, but history loves a simple narrative, and so the story of that conflict became encapsulated under one pithy label. In May 1941, the Air Ministry published a pamphlet that bestowed the collective name "Battle of Britain" on what was actually a series of largely unrelated events. This 32-page document became a bestseller and the term was immortalised. The fairly arbitrary dates used in that pamphlet claimed the "battle" began on 8th August 1940 and ended on 31st October.

This was "our" Darkest Hour; the moment when so many came to owe so much, to so few; but at the risk of ruining every war film you've ever seen about it – the tale of "The Few" is more myth than reality.

The RAF and Luftwaffe were fairly equally matched and British planes actually slightly outnumbered German. Churchill's biographer Roy Jenkins suggests the British had 1,032 airworthy fighters in 1940 while the Germans had 1,011.

But contemporary propaganda, which created a "David and Goliath" myth and perpetuated it since, has led most British people to assume that the RAF were vastly outnumbered and imperilled.

Again – untrue. By late July 1940, the UK was out-producing German aircraft at a rate of 2:1 and the British had more fighter pilots than the enemy.

The Luftwaffe's problems didn't end there. Every match was an away game; if German planes were downed, the pilots were lost. If RAF fighters crashed, the pilots took a bus back to base. In the course of the three months and three weeks of the Battle of Britain in the summer and autumn of 1940, the Luftwaffe lost 4,245 pilots and bomber crew to death, capture or injury while the RAF suffered fewer than 2,000 casualties.

Countless post-war movies have hammered home the notion that the British planes, prior to the arrival of the sacred Spitfire, were inferior to their German counterparts. That again is untrue.

The notorious Stukas might have had a fearsome reputation but they were no match for the RAF planes they met in the skies over England. Designed to be a dive-bombing terror weapon, the Stuka was effective when used against convoys and in the Battle for France, but as the Battle of Britain proceeded it swiftly became clear that it was the wrong tool for the job. The plane was slower and less agile than the RAF fighters and was easily picked off. The Messerschmitt 109 fighters, that made up the bulk of the Luftwaffe fighting force had limited range and could only last 10 minutes in the skies above England before being obliged to turn back.

By contrast British Hurricanes, which made up the vast majority (75%) of RAF fighter aircraft in the summer of 1940, were nimble, reliable, fast, and once converted to high-octane fuel were every bit the match for the Messerschmitt.

Britain's integrated radar system – the first of its kind in the world – allowed 29 monitoring stations to track enemy planes within 100 miles of the coast, meaning that fighters could be scrambled long before the Luftwaffe arrived.

The British also had significantly better cryptography.

In January 1940, British code-breakers at Bletchley Park, in collaboration with a French and Polish team in Gretz-Armainvilliers, 25km east of Paris, had broken the German Enigma code and begun deciphering messages sent by the German army, navy and air force. The Germans had total confidence in their system, believing their codes unbreakable. They were wrong though. From early August 1940 onwards, Enigma decrypts at Bletchley were able to reveal the strength, structure and formations of the incoming Luftwaffe attacks.

None of this was known when *Dad's Army* first aired.

The secrets of Bletchley and the breaking of Enigma only seeped out into the public realm in the mid-1970s. For years the truth that lay behind Britain's success in fending off the Luftwaffe and the game-changing contribution of code breakers went unsung. Instead victory was explained away with the pluck of "The Few" and that unique "British Spirit".

The British were not the underdogs. Far from it. They held most of the cards. And could quite literally read the Germans' cards too.

The RAF also had better leadership. Goering was a chaotic commander who kept switching his targets. RAF wing command took a clinical, professional approach that efficiently saw off the marauders again and again.

After an RAF bombing raid on Berlin on 25th August 1940, Hitler and Goering made the fateful decision to switch from attacks on RAF bases to a campaign of terror against London and the docks. That event, which began on 7th September and which was to become known as the Blitz, spelled fear and devastation for London and other cities including Liverpool, Birmingham and Glasgow, but the change in tactics meant that the Battle of Britain was effectively over. The Luftwaffe was no longer seeking to achieve air superiority and as such the threat of invasion, for what it was worth, was over.

It may never have been more than a bluff in the first place.

Field Marshal von Rundstedt later claimed that Hitler was never serious about the plan to invade. The attacks on all British targets were psychological not strategic. Hitler's hope was that sustained bombing would bash Britain's leaders into submission.

Churchill certainly didn't believe they would try. He told his cabinet that any invasion would be "suicidal". His calls to fight on the beaches and never surrender were a rallying cry – as much aimed at the politicians in Washington as they were the citizens of Britain and her Empire.

Even if the Germans had defied the Royal Navy, the Wehrmacht would not have got much further than the beaches of Kent.

A war game conducted at the Royal Military Academy Sandhurst in 1974 by military historians ended with all six umpires (all former senior military officers, three of whom were English and three German) concluding that the Germans would have been soundly defeated. Without air supremacy and unable to defeat the Royal Navy, their supplies would have been cut off. The German 9th army would have been annihilated.

Hitler switched his attention to the East and, in 1941, launched Operation Barbarossa against the USSR. That decision sealed the fate of the Axis powers. From the arrival of the Americans and Russians into the war, it was not a case of "if" Germany and her allies would lose but when.

The fear of invasion in Britain in 1940 was real but it was also encouraged by the government. The fear corralled the British against the common enemy and the notion of "imminent threat" played a significant part in dampening criticism and creating a sense of a united front. The idea of defiant Britain standing alone against Nazi terror also generated sympathetic press in the USA. Churchill knew that American entry into the war would be a game changer and stoking fears of invasion played to that agenda. If Britain was conquered – then what was to stop America being next?

None of which is to underplay the misery and terror caused by the bombing. The devastation and loss of life was only too real. Over 40,000 ordinary Britons died in the Blitz. Two million homes were destroyed. Families were torn apart. Children grew up nervously looking to the skies and cowering in tin shelters.

To walk around the streets of south and east London today is to see the extent of it. Barely a road went untouched and the Victorian terraces are dotted with later additions – testament to the misery of war, the lives lost, the innocence destroyed.

But next to the suffering of other European nations, Britain got off lightly. Compared to the more than 300,000 French civilian deaths or the millions of Polish and Russian lives lost, not to mention the Holocaust, it was slight. Indeed, more Hungarian and French civilians died in the Second World War than all British civilian and military losses.

* * *

WWII remains a dangerous and unhealthy fixation in the UK.

The false notions it bred informed Brexit and the resurgence of far-right post-millennial sentiment. Like a cloying poison, it still crawls across the British political landscape. Decades after its end, it ever more influences the country's global outlook. "We" stood up to be counted and "we" are owed a debt of gratitude as a result. Britons born long after the event have appropriated its perceived glory. Yes, we might lose the football but remember, "we" won the war.

That attitude stands in contrast to the people who were actually there.

Most Britons who survived the events of 1939 to 1945 did not revel in the victory. They spent six years separated from loved ones, living in fear and subsisting off paltry rations. Life was colourless and empty. Childhoods were swallowed. Young lives wasted in fighting a horrible and protracted war.

As such, VE Day celebrations were brief and largely muted. Most people wanted to move on and build a happier and safer future. The British of 1945 had their eyes firmly on what was to come and not what had been. That's why they voted Churchill out, opting for a vision of a better world instead, which Attlee offered.

And yet in the years since, the Blitz and Dunkirk "spirit" have become sacred to many. A secret weapon to be summoned up in times of need. During the Covid-19 pandemic, this banal nonsense was resurrected and people were told to "keep calm and carry on" (more on that later) as if endurance was particular to the British and these qualities were imbued in their DNA.

An old soldier, Captain Tom Moore, who gamely decided to raise money for NHS charities, was turned into a national hero. Knighted, celebrated and elevated to the top of the music charts, when Sir Tom died in February 2021 there was national mourning and even talk of erecting a statue to him. Tom Moore was a wonderful old man who wanted to make a difference but his fame became amplified out of all proportion. Much of that lay in his value as a veteran of the dark days of WWII. Had he been a former coal miner – or a woman – it's unlikely that he would have become so revered and become such a national treasure.

Britain, almost alone among European nations, has not been conquered or defeated in a major war in the last 200 years. It has never had to stare into its soul and question what it is. Instead, it has fallen back on those imagined and propagandised moments of glory.

While defeated countries put their propaganda away and sought to come to terms with what had happened, the United Kingdom's efforts became post-war Saturday matinee television; the propaganda became the perceived reality. And in the years that followed, "war" films and fictionalised versions of events became a staple entertainment, blurring the margins of reality.

In many a mind, the 1963 epic *The Great Escape* is a faithful account of the escape by Allied airmen from Stalag Luft III prisoner of war camp. In fact, characters were made up and situations embellished for blockbuster entertainment. The barbed wire-leaping Cooler King played by Steve McQueen was an amalgam of people and fantasy.

The phrases of war too persisted. In recent years the phrase 'Keep calm and carry on' has come to adorn a million cups and posters in offices across the land. In fact, the phrase was not used during the war and only entered the public consciousness in 2000. But its association with the events of 1939–45 was enough to cause a merchandise avalanche which persists to this day alongside all the other religiosity of war.

As organised religion has faded, the Second World War and the British people's role in it has become something to unite us and take its place. Akin, almost, to faith. But the British people who lived through WWII didn't have some special spirit that got them through. They didn't have a choice. War faith has indoctrinated many to believe it was otherwise, though.

Britain is not alone in its exceptionalism. Many, perhaps all, countries believe themselves apart. Every nation puts itself at the centre of the world map and their place at the nucleus of history.

China, troublingly, persists in the propagation of the myth of the country's "5,000 years of unbroken history" – a wholly artificial conceit but one that the nation's 1.4 billion people seem for the most part to buy into. Many Americans have no doubt that they live in the greatest democracy on Earth, despite the huge gulfs in wealth between rich and poor, the lack of basic universal healthcare and the gaping flaws in their electoral system.

Coronavirus exposed a global pandemic of exceptionalist thinking. President Lukashenko of Belarus told his people they could overcome the disease by "drinking vodka" and "driving tractors", while in Indonesia, President Joko Widodo suggested that Indonesians were protected by "God and the climate".

And our near neighbours are little different to the British.

Christophe Prochasson, a French historian, once put it to *Le Monde* that France remains wedded to the notion of itself as "a great power promised with an exceptional destiny". Many French remain rooted to a belief in the primacy of their culture. French academics and politicians have long maintained, perhaps with some justification, that France was the birthplace of 19th-century revolutionary enlightenment and thus the modern world, that French culture and language are supreme, that their cuisine is *the* cuisine and their wine the only one that should be taken seriously.

The paradox of exceptionalism is that the conceit is not unique to any one country. All nations are susceptible to the condition. But all exceptionalism is "cultism" whether we like it or not. It creates pigeonholes and notions of groupthink. It encourages division and walls. At its worst, it leads to football violence, to acts of monstrous self-sabotage and even war.

Some believe in horoscopes and others in fairies, while some folks believe in the "little ships" myth of Dunkirk spirit. But cling to that nonsense and you might as well believe in aliens from the Planet Clarion.

CHAPTER FOUR

THE ROYAL FAMILY IS GERMAN

How unreliable family history blinds us to reason

All families have myths of their own.

Mine has a first-rate one about great-grandad Harry, who was sent as a missionary to Papua in the 1880s to replace a colleague who'd been eaten by cannibals.

Harry was a Congregationalist, the hard-core, apocalyptic wing of the judgmental Puritan tradition; the same joy-sucking miserabilist tendency that had banned Christmas in the 17th century. Harry was a convert who like so many converts before and since took to his faith with the zeal of an extremist. A distant cousin once told me that having tried and failed to convert his brother, a trainee doctor, to the cause Harry instead stole the skeleton he kept in his bedroom – and buried it by moonlight while his mother – who he had perhaps managed to recruit to the faith – held a lamp.

By 1883, aged 28, Harry was ready to take his piety out into the world and, having completed training as a missionary, he headed to Southeast Asia with his wife Mary at his side.

Their destination was Mer – known then as Murray Island – an atoll that sits in a scattered archipelago of 452 islands in the shimmering blue waters of the Torres Strait. When Harry and Mary arrived, the place was populated by the Meriam people, descendants of a Stone Age Neolithic tribe who had pitched up on its shores 3,000 years previously.

Harry's assignment was to take over the running of the mission school that taught local islanders to be good Christian pastors. The couple also ran an elementary school – and clothed the naked scholars, partly, in paper.

"The girls wear loose print garments of fancy patterns and at Sunday services hats made out of old newspapers and trimmed with any finery my wife can spare," he wrote in the London *Mission Gazette* of April 1886, adding: *"The boys and men wear... shirts and loin cloths. Trousers denote a scholar."*

Harry's mission to bring his Congregationalist God to Mer faced one not insignificant problem. They had one already.

The Meriams believed in "Bomai", a shape-shifting sea spirit, who had come to them as an octopus and united the eight island tribes under his watchful eyes. At some point, in fulfilment of a prophecy, Bomai had sent Malo, his nephew, to Mer as well and subsequently the two gods had become one: Bomai-Malo.

Bomai's name was considered so potent that it was blasphemous to say it out loud. The twin gods gave the Meriams' religious leaders an origin story. It also gave them dominion over the seas and guardianship of the land.

These were a chosen people – another chosen people.

Sixty years after Harry's sojourn, Australian historian Clem Lack described the Meriams as:

"A proud, and independent people who regard other Island-ers, as well as the mainland aborigines, with contempt; arrogantly conscious of their racial superiority and of a warrior ancestry that reaches back into the dim past."

English-born Harry must have felt right at home.

The similarities between Mer culture and English Congrega-tionalism didn't end there. After all, both cultures also believed in eating flesh.

"This is my body, which is given for you; do this is remem-brance of me."

The United Reformed Church, which sprang from Congrega-tionalism, believes that Communion summons up the "pneumatic" presence of Christ – a sort of Christian voodoo. And that likely struck a chord for the Meriams, whose faith held that the spirit of Bomai-Malo could be awoken through ceremony and dance. Their tradition of exo-cannibalism, the eating of enemies – was done in remembrance of him.

Despite their fierce reputation, the islanders welcomed the missionary couple and even demonstrated a willingness to incor-porate some Christian teachings into their belief in Bomai-Malo.

Harry, meanwhile, threw himself at the task of translating St Mark's gospels into Mer; although as the language was hitherto unwritten and the people of the island largely illiterate, it's unclear who read it.

The missionary couple had a daughter while there and came to see the islanders less as anthropological clay and more as fellow – if perhaps inferior – human beings.

A string of letters beginning "Dear Everybody", written by Harry to his family and friends, sent news of the mission back home. Much of it is touching even if it is faintly ridiculous. In one memorable episode in the sweltering heat of early November 1886, he instructs the native children in the story of the Gunpowder Plot, before concocting an elaborate celebration of the event using palm torches.

And yet, even as the 5th November bonfire raged outside in the sweltering tropical heat, something else was burning away inside Harry. While the Meriams were happy to join him in celebrations of Christmas and Christian feast days, they refused absolutely to disavow the old faith. As he strove to rid them of their old gods and replace them with his own, while fighting off the ravages of recurring bouts of malaria, my great-grandfather seems to have descended into psychological torment.

According to my father's cousin Michael, two years into the mission, in a fit of rage, Harry marched into the hills, uprooted a statue to Bomai-Malo and tossed it in the sea.

Soon afterwards, the couple left the island. The official reason was illness but again, according to Michael, that may have been a euphemism for the "mental breakdown" from which it is clear from wider family stories and mission sources, Harry never quite recovered.

In the century that followed, the eight clans of Mer conspired to forget Harry. But as they did, the bowdlerised events became scripture to my own people. As the 20th century proceeded, the cargo cult of Harry-Mary and their time on Mer became my family's very own Bomai-Malo and the founding saint of our narrative.

The legend of my missionary great-grandfather loomed over the family like a sort of faith. It was also a source of considerable pride. In the grand tradition of adventurous Victorians, he and Mary had set out into the South Seas and faced down danger.

While some folks are descended from chartered surveyors, carpenters and crooks – we had head-hunting defying Victorian adventurers in the blood. These were good, honest and brave people whose courage and fortitude shone well on them, and by dint of that, on us.

My family was large and clannish and convivial. My uncle, aunt and cousins lived across the road from us and there were other cousins galore who would descend at Christmases and Easters and gather to gossip, feast, drink and laugh. Inevitably – at some point – the tales of Harry and Mary would pop up.

But much like branches of a faith or versions of gospel, everyone had a slightly different chronicle of events. Some people knew stories others didn't. Others remembered things differently.

My father's left-leaning academic cousin Stephen, whose mother had been born on Mer, took a Thucydidean approach to events. The Norfolk branch of the family, which included cousin Michael, were heretics who deemed it all a lot of old nonsense and the perpetual fascination with it baffling.

Meanwhile the larger Essex chapter, from which I sprang, were enthralled by the story. In our Herodotean version, the narrative became ever more exaggerated. Harry had been hand-picked to replace a previous missionary who was eaten by cannibals and spent his years on Mer constantly escaping a giant cooking pot, while hungry warriors chased him about. All attempts by Stephen to correct the false narratives were brushed away. Like Columbus and the flat Earth – we liked our story and we stuck to it.

In all of it, nobody in my immediate family actually troubled themselves to read Harry's letters and avail themselves of the truth. To do so, is to get a story very different to the one that I was brought up believing.

For a start, he didn't replace a recently devoured colleague. Cannibalism – by Harry's own account – had not been practised on the island for 20 years, and he and Mary were far from the only white European people on the island. The Mission was fairly long-established. There were regular visits from colonial officers, and their stint on the island was relatively short, lasting just two years.

These details were ignored by his descendants. At Christmas lunches and family events, the Meriams were forged into little more than comic extras in my grandparents' central tale. A homogenous lump of predatory savages, devoid of names, emotions and culture, who served as little more than foils to our origin narrative.

The notion of savage black people boiling well-intentioned white men in a giant pot served as part of the justification for the grotesque injustice of colonialism. Those who still seek to defend the actions of British Imperialists argue that "the Empire was a good thing" because it ended the barbarity of cannibalism.

But this myth of cannibalism, like a lot associated with the Empire, is a deceit. The practice was nowhere near as wide-spread as imagined and many accounts were undoubtedly made up to facilitate the excesses of their imperial greed. The British used their "mission of civilisation" as an excuse for invasion and conquest.

Despite what my family wanted to believe, Harry and Mary were the religious wing of a vast machinery of oppression that robbed the Meriams and their neighbours of their lands, culture, way of life and dignity. But that narrative didn't suit my immediate family and their love of Harry "defying the cannibals" and so we chose to ignore it, if we ever took it on board in the first place.

* * *

All families lie about themselves. All of them are, to some extent or other, engaged in a perpetual information war of edit and spin.

A miniature version of the "we" narrative of nationalism on a familial scale.

Many forge Fake Family Sagas (FFS) which bend our ancestral narratives to give us a unifying story and make us feel good about who "we" are. And this was what mine had done with: "Harry and the Cannibals".

The FFS starts in the cradle. Your big nose is the fault of a Norman ancestor, your red hair signs of your Celtic blood. Your A in GCSE maths comes thanks to the great aunt who broke the Enigma code, and your love of Guinness and that passionate heart heralds from the ancestor who came from Dublin.

In re-editing the past, the FFS alters it fundamentally.

The violent drunk becomes an "old rogue". The sex pest becomes a "ladies' man". The family soldiers are uniformly trans-formed into "heroes" of whom everyone must be proud. Gener-ations that follow are groomed by the sanitised narrative and the fake history it engenders. The complex stuff, the awkward stuff and the stuff that is probably more interesting than the rest is "best forgotten" or, rather, edited out.

Genealogy traditionally focuses on male lines, thus propa-gating the bizarre and sexist trope whereby family trees follow one name back into the past. Almost everything contributed by women gets disregarded.

Most of us can name our four grandparents, but few know the surnames on the matriarchal lines that extend beyond them. Those people, who are every bit as much our ancestors as those whose names we bear, are excised from the tale. I know nothing of the woman, my direct ancestor, who held Harry's lamp while he dug that skeleton's grave. I don't know her name, or where she came from. I know less about her than the life of Columbus or the people who inhabited those Paleolithic caves beneath the Swabian Alps, where the Lion Man was found by Nazi archaeologists.

Fake family sagas aren't drawn to complexity or truth. They put people in the wrong place, at the wrong time. They invent missionaries who were eaten by cannibals. They promote distant relatives to direct forebears and turn urban myths into truths.

Some myth making is benign. It doesn't hugely matter in the grand scheme of things that Aunty Irma didn't see The Beatles at the Cavern Club in 1961, even if she – like millions of others – claims that she did. She might have mixed them up with someone else – but so what? Irma likes the story of rejecting John Lennon's advances and you might even enjoy her telling it to you for the billionth time.

The problem with the FFS lies not in the genial gossip of aunts and uncles, but in the way it cultivates a far wider duplicity. Family stories sit in the headwaters that feed the tributaries of the great toxic river of fake history. The past we know best, the one that is told about our families, by our families – the one that is subjected to generations of tinkering and reshaping – is at best unreliable – at worst downright untrue. It is these stories that leave us looking at the people of Mer like idiots and the members of our own families as players in the great tales of our nation's extraordinary altruism.

It is the stories that are forgotten that matter most of all.

In 2013, it was revealed that Nigel Farage, England's best-known populist right wing anti-immigration tub-thumper, was actually the great-great-grandson of penniless German refugees who had arrived in Britain – without papers – in the 1860s. Mr Farage has never made any comment on the issue of his German ancestry, but it is quite likely he never knew about it. Artful forgetting had expunged his family's immigrant past.

This same tendency to deliberately disremember chunks of family history is the reason you never meet an aristocrat who crows that the family pile was built on the profits of slavery.

We don't simply forget the bad things. Often, family members are deliberately forgotten, for the simple reason that they were "different". Gay and non-binary relatives are erased or rewritten, giving the false impression that they weren't there or simply never "met the right person". Since most amateur genealogists follow their own bloodlines back, unmarried "confirmed bachelor" uncles or "spinster" aunts are frequently papered over, lending weight to the lie that the LGBTQ+ community is a recent phenomenon, or that "that sort of thing" didn't happen in "our family". It did, and undoubtedly so because homosexuality is as old as heterosexuality and, well, humanity itself.

LGBTQ+ ancestors are not the only people who vanish. The dishonour of poverty and the embarrassment of the poorhouse means that most of us know nothing of the ancestors who ended up either there or in debtor's prison. The "shame" of disability and mental health has long been covered up or artfully forgotten.

It was only in the late 1980s that it was revealed that two of the Queen's cousins, Katherine and Nerissa Bowes-Lyon, whose deaths were recorded in 1940 and 1961, to avoid "scandal", were found to be alive. Nerissa and Katherine were living in a 'mental hospital' – and had seemingly been deliberately hidden away and written out of the Windsor family narrative.

Many of us will have Nerissas and Katherines in our family trees. Most of us, apart from the most determined researchers, will never have heard of them.

Most are familiar with the workhouses and lunatic asylums that dotted Britain in the 19th and well into the 20th century, but few appreciate that they were frequently repositories where the disabled could be dumped. Many thousands more ended up on the streets begging – but who ever brags that their ancestor was a beggar?

Childless men, straight or gay, can defy the odds and be remembered into the next generation, but only if they have the good sense to die "heroically" in a pointless war. The Facebook friend sharing those Remembrance Sunday pictures of "Uncle Billy who was killed in WWI" is keeping his memory alive, but it also serves as a badge of honour that reflects well upon the poster.

Given the nation's cultish devotion to the wars, having a relative who fought, or died, is one step away from sainthood.

Nobody now living can recall the First World War or anyone who lived through it. Most of the people who lost their lives between 1914 and 1918 did so at the murderous end of a machine gun or shell. Great Uncle Billy was as likely conscripted – as volunteered.* He likely didn't want to be there and he certainly didn't want to die.

Billy may have been one of the 306 men shot for desertion or cowardice or been one of the 228,000 British victims of the 1918 flu pandemic. But his regimental grave won't give those details, or any other of the possible causes of death – including accidents or suicide.

People want their ancestors to be interesting and charismatic. They don't want them whimpering fearfully in a trench or getting run over by a truck. Uncle Billy best serves the FFS lying in his silent grave; his fate forever defined by that brief moment in his fleeting life when he was sent across the seas to provide filler on Facebook.

* * *

---

* Of British troops in WWI, 2.4 million volunteered and 2.5 million were conscripted

The challenges with family history do not end with dodgily sourced Facebook posts and the stories your own tribe spun. "Ancestry" can be weaponised by others.

Throughout his two terms of presidency, Barack Obama was dogged by accusations, led by none other than Donald J. Trump, that he wasn't a "true American" and couldn't be because he hadn't been born in the USA. This was, in a way, the warmup act for what was to follow in Trump's assault on truth and his dangerous dalliance with QAnon. The followers of that conspiracy theory came to believe that Trump was a secret agent, working to overthrow a global paedophile ring led by the Clintons and Rothschilds.

This earlier conspiracy sought to prove that Obama was not American. According to the US constitution, only "natural-born citizens" can become president, or vice president of the country. So, if it could be proved that Obama was not American-born, he could be disbarred from the presidency.

The "birther" narrative was obviously and repugnantly racist. A deliberately vile inquisition by Twitter trolls and conspiracy theorists, it hinged on Obama's skin colour and the fact that his father, Barack Sr, had been born in Kenya. Barack was American. He had demonstrably been born in America. It was easy to prove. But proof was not enough.

No evidence could convince Trump and his conspiracy theorists. Birth certificates were produced, hospital records were dug up. A contemporary announcement of Obama's birth in Hawaii was unearthed in a local newspaper, but all to no avail.

The "birther movement" ignored Barack Jr's white mother, Ann Dunham, born in Kansas, who could trace her family back to the 17th century Pilgrim Fathers. Clearly, women didn't matter in the equation.

Nor did proof. Trump and his co-conspirators didn't care about proof. Facts weren't the point. *They* had decided Obama wasn't American – and, like any good cult, the belief was enough. No evidence could be unearthed that would undo it.

It was inconceivable to them that the son of a Kenyan could ever be the true President of the United States, whoever his mother was and whatever his birth certificate might say, for the simple reason – and let's not pretend it was anything else – that he was black.

Trump too is the son of an immigrant. His mother was Scottish and his immigrant grandparents were German. But no "birther" insinuations were ever made against him. He deliberately and dishonestly weaponised Obama's family history and used it against him because it was all he had. The "birther" accusation demonstrated aptly that Trump detested Barack Obama because he feared him. Obama was smarter, more erudite, more widely admired and better looking than the frat boy who inherited a property fortune and who harboured his own ambitions to be president. Obama posed a threat to the shell of Trump's puffed-up empty privilege, and so Trump focused on one of the only means he had of taking him down: Obama's race and heritage.

In fending off accusations about heritage, Obama has common ground with Queen Elizabeth II.

For years there has been an enduring belief that "The Royal Family are German", which stems back to 1714 when George – Elector* of Hanover – became King of England. Oh, and that Queen Victoria married Prince Albert of Saxe-Coburg-Gotha in February 1840. According to this logic, everyone who followed is "German" despite Germany not existing in 1840,† let alone 1714.

---

* Prince of the Holy Roman Empire
† The Unification of Germany took place in January 1871

The trouble begins with Queen Anne, who, having lost all of her children in childbirth and infancy, came to the throne of England in 1702 without an heir. Anne was to reign for 12 years in a peaceful era that sat in sharp contrast to the 100 years that had come before it. Parliament didn't want those Jacobites, who supported the claim of the Roman Catholic House of Stuart, getting any funny ideas.

So, in 1701, following the passage of the Act of Settlement, which ensured that only a Protestant could sit on the throne, Sophia, Electress of Hanover, became Anne's heir. As she was not English-born, she had to be naturalised, and so, in 1705, the Sophia Naturalization Act was passed. It declared that, henceforth, any issue of Princess Sophia's body would automatically become a British citizen.

The act was only repealed in 1948, meaning that if you were born before that and can prove that Sophia was your ancestor, you still have every right to a British passport – if you want one.

According to the "royals are German" subscribers, Sophia was a bratwurst-munching Hanoverian, though actually it's a bit more complex than that. Born in the Dutch Republic to a Scottish mother, Elizabeth Stuart, the only daughter of James I and his wife, Anne of Denmark, spoke faultless English. Yes, technically Sophia was a bit German, a bit Danish, a bit Scottish, English and probably everything else, but then so too is Nigel Farage.

We're all human mosaics. There is no such thing as purity in DNA. The "race chromosome" does not exist.

Sophia never made it to the throne, though. Anne outlived her by two months – much to her apparent satisfaction – and Sophia's son Georg Ludwig, known to us as George I, became king instead. George was 54 and had grown up in Hanover. German was his first and main language, so yes, if you want to be picky, it's fair to claim that he was "German" – as was for his son George II.

But George III was as solidly British as anyone else in the realm. He thoroughly embraced the place of his birth and in his accession speech to Parliament in 1760, aged just 22, declared:

"Born and educated in this country, I glory in the name of Britain."

All of this occurred before the Unification of Germany and even before the American Revolution and the formation of the United States. Suggesting that Queen Elizabeth II is German because one or two of her ancestors down one particular line were renders the admittedly curious logic of nationality completely void. Indeed, nobody in the US would be able to claim they were American. And at the risk of invoking him three times in one chapter, it would make Mr Farage German as well.

Likewise, if logic determines that one of the Queen's seven-times grandfathers being born in Germany makes her German and not properly British, then there's barely a person alive in the UK who can claim they are a proper citizen of the country. Go that far back and somewhere you'll find a relative who wasn't born in the country that you now reside in. George I and II are the direct ancestors of David Cameron and Boris Johnson, but nobody has ever suggested they were German.

As far as the Queen's German ancestry goes, the lingering suspicion might stem from a name change in 1917 when it was decided that being called "Saxe-Coburg-Gotha" wasn't exactly a great look for the King of the United Kingdom and the British dominions in the midst of a war with Germany.

But that family name is unsurprising given that the royal families of Europe had intermarried for centuries. Indeed, in 1914

King George V was first cousins with both Tsar Nicholas II of Russia and Kaiser Wilhelm II of Germany.

Kaiser Wilhelm was even said to have been Queen Victoria's favourite grandson by no lesser source than Kaiser Wilhelm II. And who are we to doubt him. But nobody ever claimed that Wilhelm II was British – despite being the son of an English woman.

Some families argue about the truth of their missionary ancestors; others go to war over the Balkans. From 1914, anti-German feeling in Britain meant that anyone with a link to that country was viewed with suspicion.

Unfortunately, in addition to having a German surname, George V's wife, Mary, known as "May", had the very non home-counties surname of Teck. Mary was a princess of Teck, in the Kingdom of Württemberg but, confusingly, her father had been born and raised in Austria and was himself the son of a Russian-born duke. Some claim that Kensington-born Mary spoke with a heavy German accent, but audio of her delivering a message to "the boys and girls of the Empire" in 1923 suggests she spoke in that curious, affected drawl used by the older members of the British Royal family even today.

So why does the myth of the "German Royal Family" persist? Perhaps – as with Obama, it's to de-legitimise them.

The British public and press's fantastically odd and dysfunctional relationship with their royalty is matched only by their odd and dysfunctional relationship with Germany.

Perpetuating the notion that the "Royal Family are German" knocks them down a peg and keeps them in their place. It's the ultimate Fake Family Saga. It hints that the Queen and her family are "second rate" products by dint of their ancestry. Not "proper Brits".

None have propagated the story of the royal Teutonic myth more than the enduring cuckoo cult that is Britain's self-styled "upper class", a tiny, wealthy, self-obsessed elite within an elite whose members eek out their brief time on Earth engaging in affectation. Britain's "upper classes" are particularly obsessed with the wholly artificial notion of pedigree. Many will claim, with little or no prodding, that they are descended from William the Conqueror and invest in grand family trees to prove it. Lineage transformed into a game of eternal one-upmanship.

Those who buy into this nonsense view family heritage as a bespoke motorway between two destinations. There may be slip roads and perhaps once or twice someone makes a brief diversion; but just as the M6 runs between Catthorpe and Gretna, so the lines of Britain's oldest families stretch from the muddy hill at Battle to the muddy green wellies on their feet.

And from this well of tripe springs all manner of endemic stupidity.

The notions of class and of social rank remain curiously embedded in Britain. Since *The Daily Telegraph* began printing "forthcoming marriages" in the paper in 1911, it has done so according to a mysterious system of social ranking. Those who seek to make announcements on the pages of the paper await publication with fingers crossed as the paper's Court and Circular editors decide who is posher than whom and then grade them accordingly.

Struggling to believe that such a thing still went on, I contacted the paper's Social Editor, who kindly confirmed to me that the process still happens.

The British people curiously remain susceptible to the drawl of an upper-class accent and seem not only willing but eager to elect men who are the products of Eton classrooms, believing perhaps that they are somehow a "Rolls-Royce" product, put on Earth to govern us.

Cap doffing still runs deep. Many Britons like nothing more than to spend their weekends trapsing around unimaginatively built stately homes that they might thrill at the portraits of the grand families that built them and perhaps catch a glimpse of one of their descendants.

This grooming of the national mindset explains the retention of 92 "hereditary peers" in the House of Lords: individuals who are gifted a right to sit in the nation's upper chamber and facilitate laws for no other reason than that their ancestor was the illegitimate child of some prince, or willing to spaff a few quid on a title when David Lloyd George was selling off gongs for bribes.

As of September 2020, in addition to the life peers who you might hope had been appointed according to some degree of merit, there were four dukes, 24 earls and a host of other viscounts and barons in the House of Lords. The misogynistic nature of hereditary peerages precludes women so, with one exception – the Countess of Mar,* who served in the House of Lords from 2014–2020 – they are all men. The unforgivable blight on modern democracy that is the House of Lords is blighted further by this archaic hangover which goes unnoticed by many while it is tacitly tolerated by others.

"Aristocracy" no more exists than "Blitz Spirit" does. Like claiming the "Royal Family are German", it is nothing more than the embedded narrative of fake history. Self-styled upper-class people are no "better" than anyone else. You can't swab for

---

* The Scottish upper classes are evolved enough to at least pass their titles down the female line to the oldest daughter – but only when needs be.

pedigree. There is no such thing as blue blood. The idea that some families are "older" than others is patently ridiculous.

The Queen's "royal line" didn't spring magically to life in 1066 any more than my family began with Harry sailing to Mer. Elizabeth Windsor's ancestors are the same people as yours and mine. Paleolithic cave dwellers, priests and paupers – rich men, wise women, thugs, whores, beggars and thieves. Early royals, like the religious leaders on Mer – claimed that they had been put there by divine provenance and everyone bought into it. Apparently exceptional people need "exceptional" leaders, and who better to fit that bill than one put there by the Octopus God Bomai-Malo or Yahweh?

There is no "royal DNA". The House of Windsor is a conceit. Nobility a myth. Not that this has stopped people trying to prove otherwise.

Burke's Peerage, established in the 1820s, is a niche genealogical publishing firm based on a business model that might be best described as "vanity readership". Each year it used to produce a flagship directory listing the "peerage, baronetage and knightedge (sic) of the landed gentry of the United Kingdom" and beyond; the "FFS" as class confirmation bias with names added or cruelly edited out as the publisher deemed fit.

The book was ridiculed as far back as its publication began. In *A Woman of No Importance,* Oscar Wilde has one character advise another to study peerage because: "It is the best thing in fiction the English have ever done."

But thousands more, flattered by their names being included, bought willingly into the deceit.

By the 1980s, a new meritocracy had taken hold and even posh people were distancing themselves from their aristocratic pasts. As such, Burke's was in financial trouble and, having sold off its flagship publication, set about producing books about general aristocratic genealogy instead. American-born journalist and financier, Harold Brooks-Baker, was hired to get things back in shape and, to that end, began issuing attention-grabbing press releases about the royal family. This included the claim that Queen Elizabeth II was a descendant of the Prophet Muhammad via Princess Zaida of Seville.*

Brooks-Baker also dreamt up the bonkers "most royal candidate theory", a "study" – and I use that word cautiously – which claimed that the winner of US presidential elections would always be the candidate with "most royal blood". In 1984, Brooks-Baker seemed to hit the jackpot when he correctly predicted, early in the race, that incumbent President Ronald Reagan would beat his rival Walter Mondale in the election that year. This snake-oil research was based on the findings of Burke's chief genealogist, Hugh Peskett, who claimed to have spent three years working out that Reagan was descended from "eight" royal households of Europe including Brian Boru, King of Ireland in the 11th century.

Poor old Walter Mondale, with his family tree pathetically lacking royal stock, never stood a chance.

Brooks-Baker sat very much at the back of the class of the Geoffrey of Monmouth school of historical research, using dodgy history and questionable sources to make money out of the gullible and credulous – as well as those who liked a "good story". His "most royal candidate theory" provided fodder for tabloid newspapers and conspiracy theorists, including lizard-botherer David

---

* Zaida was an 11th-century Muslim princess who converted to Christianity and became the mistress of King Alfonso VI of Castile.

Icke,* but it came a cropper in 2004 when John Kerry, the supposedly most royal candidate – lost to George W. Bush.

In 2012, a teenage girl in Salinas, California took up where he left off and made headlines after working out that every single US president bar one had been a direct descendant of King John of England. BridgeAnne D'Avignon (and yes, it's a real name) told radio station WFMY that the reason for this apparent coincidence was that: "They all have the trait of wanting power", suggesting that over the course of 1,000 years the descendants of John had carried some sacred genome.

Martin Van Buren, the one non-descendant of King John who made it to the White House, must have done so as a fluke.

When Biden won the 2020 US election, much was made of his Irish roots, and there was considerable debate about how it might affect foreign policy and that British obsession "the special relationship". But dig into those Biden ancestors and you discover, surprisingly, that he's no more Irish, than Nigel Farage† is German. Just two of Biden's sixteen great-great grandparents were Irish-born. He has far more recent English ancestry, but claiming that you "come from Sussex" doesn't play as well with all those self-identifying Irish voters in the US.

Life is too short to dig into your own family tree, let alone other people's and, anyway, the idea that all but one of the US presidents have royal ancestry, rather belies one inconvenient fact: everyone, of European heritage is descended from royalty. And a high percentage of people living in the United States are descended

---

* David Icke – former footballer and broadcaster, who has claimed that the royal family are in fact giant, bloodsucking, shape-shifting alien lizards and who has made a career out of conspiracy theories.
† That's four references, dammit!

from King John. Wherever you come from and whoever you are, one of your ancestors was royal. And if you're British or of British Isles descent there's a good chance that some of them are fairly famous and fairly recent.

In 2016, the British actor Danny Dyer appeared on the BBC TV programme *Who Do You think You Are?* and was astounded to discover that he was a direct descendant of King Edward III. It was a great bit of telly, but if you are reading this and have some fairly recent "British" ancestors, then there's an extremely high probability that you are descended from King Edward III too. Some estimate it as being as high as 99%. You are very likely descended from Charlemagne as well – because most European people are.

It seems incredible – indeed, hard to fathom – that our families could somehow forget this, but they do. In 1999, Joseph Chang, a statistician at Yale, deducted that everyone living in the late 20th century had a common ancestor in the 11th century.

Those of European descent – which means anyone with just one European ancestor – have a shared ancestor 600 years back. As British geneticist Adam Rutherford is prone to pointing out, family trees are not really made of branches. They are really more like enormous webs. It's what Rutherford calls "a numbers game". If you go back through your two grandparents, four great-grandparents and so on, you theoretically have to keep multiplying, meaning that you would sit at the bottom of a giant inverted pyramid with literally millions of ancestors above you. Of course, there are more people alive today than at any point in history, so in fact those tracts of web fold back in on themselves, meaning, in Rutherford's words: "...you can be and in fact are descended from the same person many times over."

While we might not be lucky enough to all claim that we are German, we can at least comfort ourselves that we are all royal.

The late Harold Brooks-Baker was ridiculed for claiming that the Queen was a descendant of Mohammad, but – for once – he may not have been far off the mark. According to Chang's modelling, it's quite likely that the vast majority of Europeans are. Even the most rampant Islamophobe, insisting upon their intrinsic nationalist identity and European heritage, will have a Muslim ancestor.

Likewise, all of those self-styled aristocrats who claim descent from William the Conqueror are right. They are indeed descended from him. But they're also descended from whoever cleaned his toilets.

If you think your family history is dull, boring or limited, this is only because generations of your family have edited it to make you think it so. You sit at the edge of a vast unexplored familial cosmos that stretches in all directions and across all continents.

Forget the FFS – and console yourself instead that your great-great-great etc grandfather signed the Magna Carta. No family is older than another and no one people more ancient. We are hindered in how we look at ourselves by defining our own limitations of who we are and who we want to be.

* * *

Nowadays, you can spit into a tube and send away a sample and get back a reading that will break down the tiny bits of thread that harbour faint traces of where our ancestors lived. This might tell you that "you" are 4% Asian or 19% Northern European or 52% African – but it doesn't tell you much else.

Sometimes, however – the results are illuminating and eye-opening.

In 2006, Leicester University appealed for volunteers who had traced their ancestry to donate DNA samples for a study into the movement of world populations.

One volunteer was John Revis, a 75-year-old retired surveyor and genealogy hobbyist who had traced his family back to the 1700s.

"One line went to the States and became very successful while my immediate line stayed in the North of England and were mostly bakers," John told *The Mail on Sunday* when they tracked him down in January the following year.

What John didn't know, at least until Leicester University informed him of it, was that he was also the descendant of a West African ancestor. For he carried an extremely rare Y chromosome marker, M31, that had only previously been identified in a small number of men from West Africa.

When Mr. Revis, who had been blonde-haired, blue-eyed and "Nordic looking" in his youth, informed his wife she struggled to make sense of it:

"John has always seemed very English to me," she said, adding "he likes his roast beef and Yorkshire pudding on a Sunday. He has never asked me to cook anything unusual."

An appeal to find people with the same relatively rare surname discovered that 7 of the 18 men who had it carried the same chromosome.

There were two possible explanations. It is known that in around 200 CE, Rome brought a garrison of North African men to the north of England to build Hadrian's Wall. Perhaps John and his distant cousins were descended from one of the members of that unit who had stayed behind and had children locally. More likely they were the descendants of a far more recent arrival, courtesy of the brutal 18th-century slave trade. By the time of the abolition of slavery at least 10,000 black people were living in England, but their story has all but been erased not only by the official account but also by the narrative of exceptionalism that casts Britain as the hero that rid the world of the very slave trade it had created.

"This study shows what it means to be British is complicated and always has been," said Leicester University's Professor Jobling, adding: "Human migration history is clearly very complex, particularly for an island nation such as ours, and this study further debunks the idea that there are simple and distinct populations or 'races'."

You can't swab for Englishness any more than you can for Thai or Indonesian, Danish or Indian – but as more people try and as the science improves, we might all have a chance to unwrap stories as fascinating as John's. Stories that tell us who our ancestors really were, and not simply who we want them to be.

Of course, having an ancestor who came from West Africa 300 years ago does not make you "African" – but it does dispel the lies of the FFS and perhaps makes the notion of what we came from more interesting and thought provoking. Our history is human history. There's no Union Jack, St Andrew's flag, Stars and Stripes or tricolore printed on your DNA.

But this hasn't stopped people trying to claim otherwise, and DNA tests, processed in anonymous commercial labs, are increasingly used to lend scientific authority to heritage bias.

Quite how reliable they are was laid bare in Canada in 2018 when a man called Louis Côté, who was suspicious of his own recent DNA test results, sent samples of his girlfriend's pet Chihuahua, Snoopy, for analysis.

When the test had been done and the results delivered, Snoopy was declared to be 20% Native American and a descendant of an indigenous tribe. The dog was not available for comment, but his tale serves a useful commentary on the dangers of commercial enterprise serving the confirmation biases of ancestry that so many increasingly seek.

In Snoopy's story, we see bad science and dodgy business practices, conspiring with bad history, to disseminate a "good story" narrative.

History and culture are more than the faint traces of genetic markers from the past.

CHAPTER FIVE

CURRY COMES FROM INDIA

The great deceit of language and food

A little over 30 years ago and well into the long, dark culinary void stretching beyond it, British cuisine resembled nothing less than a horrific crime scene.

In the post-war era, good food, like showers and cologne, was something continental people did. British cooking was defiant in its inedibility. The culinary wing of the same dreadful exceptionalism that imposed the Austin Montego on my father and our family.

The collective amnesia in the decades that followed mean that it's hard to fathom quite how bad things were. Basic stuff found on supermarket shelves today simply didn't exist. Nobody had heard of hummus, crème fraîche or pesto. Garlic was something the French wore round their necks to ward off Englishmen. Coffee was instant and the texture of paint. Bread was just about the only thing that came in varieties and you had a choice of four: white, brown, sliced or unsliced. Olive oil was kept in the medical cabinet from where it was fetched every now and then to unblock the wax in ears. The only avocado anyone ever saw was the colour option on a bathroom suite in the seventies.

Most people ate shit: frozen fish, curiously white sausages of questionable provenance, beans, oven chips and powdered mash – which was considered a wonder food. You might have a roast on a Sunday but the vegetables would be prepared in much the same way that Vesuvius "prepared" the people of Pompeii in 79 CE.

Most British people stewed the living taste out of everything.

Eating out was no better. Most ordinary people had to make do with Britain's insipid chain restaurants, which offered up over-priced cardboard with milky cups of tea. Pubs served the same crap you ate at home but with a sprig of parsley on the side. Drinking wine that required the pronunciation of foreign words was viewed suspiciously, while vegetarianism was liable to get you reported to the security services.

It is easy – and tempting – to lapse into imprudent nostalgia for the days when we had all our teeth and hair. But you would have to be utterly deranged to long for British food of the sixties, seventies and even a little way beyond. As late as the 1990s, Tesco was having to put out ads featuring the comedian Dudley Moore, almost as a public service, to explain what Prosecco and tiramisu were.

Quite why the British put up with this prolonged self-harm is unclear. Perhaps because of wartime rationing, which lasted until 1954, people simply became grateful for what they got. Not so much "keep calm and carry on" but more "shut up and eat it". No alternative was available. British food was endured, much like the weather, because nobody knew any better. But all the while – and just beneath the radar – a quiet revolution was going on.

For from the 1960s onwards, migrants from India, Pakistan and Bangladesh were bringing gastronomic relief via affordable restaurants and a novel style of cooking that – radically – actually tasted of something.

Curry was not new to Britain. The first "Indian restaurant", the Hindoostane Coffee House in London, was opened in 1809 or 1810 (accounts differ) by Sake Dean Mahomed, an enigmatic, Bengali-born adventurer, businessman and travel writer who moved to Ireland with his friend Captain Godfrey Barker in 1784, settled in Cork and then promptly eloped with a local girl called Jane Daly with whom he had seven children. Ten years later the family moved to London to pursue business opportunities.

Mahomed was one of those extraordinary entrepreneurs who don't let failure get in the way of their ambition. The Hindoostane was a case in point. The businessman hoped to cash in on the taste that repatriated members of the East India company had acquired for authentic Indian cuisine, and to that end he set up shop near Portman Square, where many of them lived. It was a lavish establishment with a hookah room and oriental decor, and in theory his timing could not have been more perfect.

In the early 1800s Britain had yet to affect its suffocating all-consuming grip on India, or indulge fully in its unwarranted, perverted faith in European racial superiority over the people who lived there. Many of the first British migrants – for that is what they were – adopted local ways. James Kirkpatrick was a case in point. The British Resident (aka ambassador) at Hyderabad from 1795 arrived in Asia every inch the British Imperialist hoping to suck a fortune out of the credulous South Asian people, but he quickly went native. He adopted local dress, learned the language, converted to Islam, and married a (disturbingly young) local girl with whom he later had two children.

This was not uncommon. Research by the English historian William Dalrymple, for his 2002 book *The White Mugals*, showed that in the 1780s, more than a third of British men working for the East India Company took local wives and had children – although their descendants, at least those who returned to Britain, mostly deliberately forgot this. Dalrymple himself discovered, to his amazement, that he had Indian ancestry but this had been edited out over time as his family had artfully buried it.

Perhaps as many as a million people around the world and at least 100,000 white "British" people in the UK have Anglo-Indian ancestors from a relationship during this era – but most won't know it.

The love affair with India ran deep and stretched all the way back home.

In the early 1800s no less a figure than the Prince of Wales, later George IV, began work on converting parts of what was then known as the "Marine Pavilion" in Brighton into the classic Indo-Saracenic manner that would make it famous. New styles of Indian cloth and design dominated contemporary fashion. The interior designs of respectable homes took on a distinctly Asian aesthetic.

And the taste for Eastern spices fed into culinary landscape.

Long before the Hindoostane opened, Indian flavours were infusing British cooking – with the classic British Christmas pudding being a case in point. Hannah Glasse's best-selling book *The Art of Cookery Made Plain and Easy*, first published in 1747, contained no less than three ways of preparing pilau curries.

And yet, despite his seemingly impeccable timing, Mahomed's venture failed. By 1812, he was bankrupt and although the restaurant did continue under new management for the next 20 years, its moment – like Britain's early respect for India – passed. Dean and his family moved to Brighton where he introduced something called champooi or "shampooing" to the British public – but who knows what became of that.

While the Hindoostane might have been and gone, the passion for Indian flavoured food, albeit with a very English twist, hadn't. British takes on Indian curries featured in cookbooks throughout the Victorian era.

Mrs Rundell, the Nigella Lawson of her day, included several recipes in her iconic *New System of Domestic Cookery*, which was first published in 1806. By the 64th edition, printed in 1840, the editor Emma Roberts had added 16 further "curries" to the book.

Mrs Beeton's legendary *Book of Household Management*, first published in 1861, included a fairly uninspired recipe for "poulet a l'Indienne". This dish demanded "one tablespoon of curry powder" and sliced apple, which seems to have been a thing.

But the undoubted "curry-head" of the age was Queen Victoria. Crowned Empress of a place she never visited, she was fascinated with the jewel in her crown and, under the tutelage of her close friend Abdul Karim, became surprisingly proficient in Urdu. It was Abdul, who in 1887, first cooked the Queen an elaborate Indian meal, and she was reportedly as taken with it as she was by him – to the horror of her courtiers.

The taste for Indian food was seized upon by British manufacturers and, throughout the Raj era, domestic rip-offs of Indian food became familiar staples of the British diet across all classes. Branston Pickle, first manufactured in 1922, was basically a bland "chutney" by another name. Kedgeree, a derivation of the South Asian Khichdi, became, along with mulligatawny soup, a standard of the age... if you were wealthy enough.

Away from the posh homes and middle-class kitchens, in the busy backstreets of London's East End and other ports about the country, another world of Indian food thrived.

Most of us think of Raj-era migration as a one-way street, but this wasn't the case. Asian migration to Western Europe was happening long before the 1960s and even prior to Sake Dean Mahomed first pitching up in Cork in the 1780s.

From the mid-1600s onwards the Royal Navy (RN), the merchant fleet and the East India Company began to hire thousands of "lascars" – sailors, soldiers and militiamen – from South Asia to serve on British ships. The number of willing recruits was so great that the RN and Merchant Fleet began to look more Indian than European, and in the end the Navigation Act 1660 declared that henceforth "three fourths of the Mariners [on English ships] were to be English."

The "lascars" later sailed on Captain Cook's HMS *Resolution*, making up a fifth of the crew. They were present at the Battle of Trafalgar in 1805 and at almost every major sea engagement and maritime adventure that followed right up to the beaches of Dunkirk, from which propaganda, history and popular culture subsequently sought to expunge them.

Indeed, one of the first "British" prisoners of war to escape German custody in the Second World War was the Indian Army soldier Jemadar Jehan Dad, who, having been captured in France in June 1940, disguised himself as a demobbed French North African soldier and made his way to Gibraltar. Dad would have had a better time of it than his lascar forebears.

Paid as little as 5% of the wage of their white counterparts and often handed the very worst jobs, the 19th-century lascars suffered appalling poverty and discrimination only to be deliberately forgotten by the very Empire they helped to create and sustain.

Many lascars settled in Britain's ports and, like their white counterparts who had gone East, married local women. Some of these same people set up local cafes and sold food. So, in the century that followed the closing of the Hindoostane, "curry" was no more absent from Britain than "Indian people" were from the streets.

By the 1950s, approximately 8,000 south Asians were living permanently in the UK with their numbers supplemented by many thousands more students, soldiers and sailors.

They were joined in the 1960s by South Asian migrants, with British passports, who were mostly expelled from Africa's newly independent states (of which more later). Further phases of migration from India, Pakistan and Bangladesh followed. Many, particularly in the later waves, came as manual workers but were soon setting up businesses.

British cities witnessed a dramatic population decline in the war years and things didn't change for decades. Between 1939 and 1991, London shed almost two million people, one quarter of its pre-war population and, as a result, property was cheap. Some of those early South Asian pioneers bought empty business premises and turned them into restaurants. They then sought to exploit a gap in the market.

"Native" pubs closed at 11 p.m. so by extending their licensing hours, Indian restaurants cashed in on the trade. "Curry houses" provided beer-satiating, affordable food that prospered on the principles of fusion and flattery. Dishes were tailored to suit the tastes of the locals, even as they subtly altered them. And with breath-taking speed, the bland, unimaginative standard fodder of the British diet was edged out in favour of the twin marvels of "Balti curry" and chicken tikka masala (CTM, for brevity, for the rest of this chapter).

Like all great institutions, both have their origin myths.

The CTM one, which is perhaps a little better known, goes like this.

On a freezing cold night in 1971, a bus driver recently off his shift, walks into a restaurant called Shish Mahal, on Gibson Street in Glasgow and demands a chicken dinner. Shish Mahal doesn't do "chicken dinners" so the waiter recommends "tikka" instead and a few minutes later and with some trepidation, sets a plate of food before the surly Glaswegian, who stubs out his cigarette and prods it suspiciously:

"What's this?" he asks.

"Your food," the waiter replies.

"Where's the gravy?" barks the bus driver.

With the exception of toast and Rice Krispies, almost all British food in 1971 comes with gravy (this part is true). It is practically a law and the plate set before the Glaswegian bus driver – is unequivocally gravy-less.

"Can't eat that!" he says and pushes it away.

So, the flustered waiter returns to the hassled chef, Mr Ali, who also happens to be the owner of Shish Mahal, and says:

"The big guy wants gravy!"

At which point and perhaps a bit pissed off, Mr. Ali takes out a can of tomato soup, pours it in a pan, adds some yoghurt and shoves the hapless waiter back out saying:

"Tell him it's called chicken tikka masala."

The meal is set before the bus driver, who eats the lot. Mr Ali has inadvertently invented a classic dish and soon people are queuing round the block to sample Shish Mahal's authentic Indian chicken tikka masala.

It's a lovely story and one Mr Ali's family and others have told repeatedly ever since. In 2009, Mohammad Sarwar, then Labour MP for Glasgow Central, even tried to get the dish granted EU Protected Designation of Origin status, but his attempt fell at the first hurdle for the simple reason that it's impossible to know who first "invented" CTM.

Indeed, like all fake history, the "great story" of how CTM was invented falls apart the moment you start to examine it. Shish Mahal was, if not an upmarket joint in 1970s Glasgow, then certainly popular with a certain type of esoteric and student clientele. The notion that a circumspect bus driver, familiar with the city, might just randomly walk in thinking he could order a "chicken dinner" doesn't really ring true. Because it isn't.

The late food historian Peter Grove and his friend the restaurateur Iqbal Wahhab made the story up.

Iqbal, owner of The Cinnamon Club, one of London's best known "Indian" restaurants and founder of *Tandoor Magazine*, confirmed this to me in a brief but entertaining email exchange.

In the early 1990s – having just launched his magazine – Wahhab inadvertently became an information hub for lazy journalists who wanted to write about curry. Tiring of endless calls about the origin of tikka masala he and Grove concocted the "Campbell's Soup" story over a bottle of wine. Grove, editor of *The Real Curry Restaurant Guide*, backed the "legend" up in his book and from there everything got out of hand.

Ali Ahmed Aslam aka "Mr Ali" was a gifted PR man and, ever with an eye on the next column inch, latched on to the story and claimed it as his own.

Nowadays, Iqbal is reconciled to his inadvertent creation of a folklore. "About 15 years ago I saw that Heston Blumenthal was staying in the same hotel as me in Delhi," he writes. "We got chatting and it turned out he'd come to research a documentary about what they had heard about the origins of chicken tikka masala. He wasn't too pleased to hear I'd made the whole thing up."

Iqbal suggests that really CTM is a bland UK version of murgh makhani, an Old Delhi dish which was probably on offer in the UK as far back as the 1950s.

The provenance of balti is every bit as mired in myth. As with the CTM, the European Commission rejected an attempt to grant protected food name status to the "Birmingham Balti'. The application specified that the sauce must include "a base mix of onions, garlic, ginger, tumeric, salt and garam masala…" and it should be cooked in a traditional metal bowl called a "balti".

Ah, the famous "balti" bowl.

Well, I'm sorry to break it to you, but there's no such thing in South Asian cooking. A balti is actually the Bengali and Hindustani term for a bucket of the type used across Asia to wash, to flush the toilet and perhaps clean your backside.

The metal bowl used in Birmingham to serve up curry is a "karahi" – a small wok used in Pakistan, Northern India, Afghanistan and Nepal.

In 2008, journalist Ziauddin Sardar wrote a provocatively entertaining book called *Balti Britain*, in which he journeyed through British Asian culture present and past. As part of his travels, he visited restaurants that claimed to have invented the balti and, having heard several unconvincing origin tales, he landed at Imran's Restaurant and Sweet House, in Sparkbrook, Birmingham. There the owner, Afzal Butt, confessed that he and his brothers had started calling the curry "balti" as a piss-take.

"We tried to civilise the natives by introducing different kinds of cuisine," he told Sardar. "In particular, we introduced the tandoor and karahi dishes. We soon discovered that the 'white people' had problems pronouncing the word karahi, so as a joke we said 'why not call it a balti. It will make life easier for them.'"

"It's a joke. Hundred per cent joke," Butt added. "It was an invention for the goras [white folk]."

In the early 1970s, Britain's South Asian communities faced an incessant tide of bigotry as part of everyday life. Overt racism was endemic.

Kids told racist jokes in playgrounds. The "P" word was hurled freely at people going about their business. Persistent urban myths about dog meat being used in Indian and Chinese restaurants sought to steer white people away from them.

The newspapers drove the fear. And then, as Ugandan dictator Idi Amin sought to expel South Asians from the country in 1971, the tabloids went into a frenzy:

"There are 200,000 Asians in East Africa," the paper declared in a lead article on 12th February, "all possessing British passports, who may come here soon."

Soon all of the papers were whipping up fears of "a stampede" of migrants and the National Front and far right were capitalising on them. There were few dissenting voices. Prime-time entertainment delighted in playing up the comical stereotypes and television – then the all-powerful force of popular entertainment – conspired to fuel the discrimination.

In 1975 Britain's best loved comedian Spike Milligan wrote a sketch called "Pakistani Daleks", which is painful to watch for anyone who, like myself, loves Spike. The BBC sitcom *Till Death Us Do Part* and its bigoted central character, Alf Garnett, was written with the intention of "satirising racists", but contemporary research by the BBC showed that his racist diatribes were popular with viewers, many of whom agreed with them.

In 1973, the Corporation polled viewers only to find that a clear majority liked Garnett and that they considered him to be a "common sense" character.

The subsequent report concluded "that the series may have reinforced existing illiberal and anti-trade union attitudes". Director-General Sir Charles Curran concluded that the report demonstrated that it was impossible to make "anti-prejudicial" comedy.

But the show was a big ratings hit and so the research was quietly shelved.

The hugely popular sitcom *It Ain't Half Hot Mum*, which aired from 1974 and was created by the same team behind *Dad's Army*, makes for painful viewing nowadays, too. The comedy about a wartime entertainment troupe was set in Burma but featured just three non-white characters. The best known was *Bearer Rangi Ram* – a manipulative and untrustworthy two-dimensional stereotype of an Asian man, played by a white actor, Michael Bates, who browned-up for the role.

Racism was by no measure limited to portrayals of Asians on British TV in this era. Even as viewers ate Smash and sausages they could tune into *Love thy Neighbour* whose entire "comic" premise was based on a white couple having a black couple living next door. LWT's *Mind Your Language*, first broadcast in 1977, was built entirely upon the conceit of "funny foreigners" who couldn't make themselves understood in a language school. The appalling *The Black and White Minstrel Show*, which ran, unforgivably, until 1978, featured white men in black make-up singing musical numbers and slave ballads as Saturday night primetime entertainment.

Britain's best-known comedians, including the then popular Jim Davidson, got laughs from telling racist jokes at the expense of Britain's black community, including his notorious "Chalky White" persona and his appalling exaggerated West Indian accent.

Anyone who challenged this endemic landscape of bigotry was told that it was "just harmless fun". When the BBC received complaints from the Campaign Against Racial Discrimination about *The Black and White Minstrel Show* in 1967, the BBC Board of Management effectively turned a blind eye.

Minutes from the time demonstrate that the then head of the BBC's publicity department sought to justify it by turning to the letters page of the *Daily Mail* and reading out laudatory missives from white readers, who didn't want the show taken off air.

In the years since their heyday, figures like Davidson have tried to claim that it was white liberals who were offended and that black people loved Chalky.

In a 2018 interview, Davidson told Piers Morgan: "When I did that Chalky stuff it was about an accent. The only reason he was black was because I could do the accent."

Watching footage of the act, in which "Chalky" is reduced to the worst stereotypes of white racist thinking about West Indian men, it is very clear that it was more than that. By legitimising intolerance, Davidson and the broad swathe of light entertainment of the era fed the flames of persecution and intimidation against families whose only "crime" was to be different.

Even as the UK boasted that it was the country that had saved the world from Nazi racism – its primetime comedians mocked other human beings for the colour of their skin.

It's satisfying to imagine that Afzal Butt and his brothers named a dish after a washroom receptacle used for washing your arse. It's a small act of defiance, far funnier than the crass, domestic, racist humour on television at the time, and one that had a life that stretched beyond the stultifying 1970s. For in time, balti became an enduring British cultural entity all of its own – even as Jim Davidson and his fellow bullies lapsed into obscurity.

Summing up his quiet act of "balti" revenge in that 2008 interview with Sardar, Afzal Butt ends by saying:

"A Balti is like curry. It exists and doesn't exist. Do you know what a curry is? I have never had a curry in my life!"

What fresh madness is this? you might be thinking as the cognitive dissonance runs rampant in your head. Why, it would be almost like saying that curry doesn't come from India.

Which, it doesn't.

The word "curry" derives from the Tamil word "kari" meaning "sauce" or "gravy", which is made from leaves from the curry tree (*Murraya koenigii*), although in Asia, where it heralds from and is pervasive, it is known by several names. Confusingly there's also a curry plant (*Helichrysum italicum*), but if you feel tempted to rustle up a nice "balti" bucket from the one in your garden, then resist, as it is inedible and will probably make you vomit.

Neither is to be confused with curry powder, which is to Indian cooking as instant Smash is to mashed potatoes. South Asians don't use curry powder any more than they "eat curry". That catch-all term was coined by British people to describe any spicy food they came across – first in India and then elsewhere, which is why you also have Malay, Thai, Balinese, Singaporean and even Japanese "curry".

"Curry" is equivalent to branding all European food "potato" and then opening restaurants called "potato houses" where you eat Swedish meatballs, pizza, moussaka, a caviar side and plenty of French baguette – all washed down with traditional pints of Guinness.

But if you're setting up restaurants, in a climate of racial hostility, you can't spend hours lecturing everyone about the complex and nuanced history of food before you dish out menus. It was simpler for migrant communities to play along with British assumptions, to tone down the heat and create a mashup of existing recipes, which in the process spawned a new genre called curry.

For many Britons in the 21st century, having an "Indian" is as much a part of the way of life as going to the pub. Although, in truth, most Indian restaurants aren't technically "Indian". The overwhelming majority of South Asian restaurants in the UK are run by people of Bangladeshi origin. Some – including the BBC and *Daily Mail* – have put the figure as high as 90%.

Trying to ascribe order to chaos and complexity is what humans do. The people sitting round the camp fires 40,000 years ago, passing their Lion Man from one to another, were trying to make sense of the Universe, and the Europeans have done the same thing with "Asian" food.

Quite simply, people are drawn to clear narratives and plain certainty. They want to believe in Churchill the great hero and that pizza comes from Italy and vindaloo from India, when in fact pizza originates in the Middle East and vindaloo is a twisted take on the Portuguese dish *carne de vinha d'alhos* (meaning "meat in a garlic marinade") .

How do you stick a provenance on food? How do you designate, as the EU tries to do, where something comes from and whether it is "authentic" enough? How do you decide who owns what and how it should be produced?

My late father-in-law Alan would always insist that he "only ate English food" and his favourite meal was fish and chips. While other family members tucked into our Saturday night – very British – Indian takeaway, he would comfort himself with his indigenous meal of cod and chips, unaware, that he was enjoying something gloriously exotic.

But what exactly is "English food"?

Battered cod was introduced to Britain by Sephardic Jews in the 17th century – via Holland – but the cooking style originated in Andalucia in the south of Spain where *pescado frito* (meaning "fried fish") is still eaten today.

Potatoes arrived in Europe from South American in the 1600s, but the deep-fried potato strip only appeared in the UK in the late 19th century when it was introduced by Flemish migrants.

Mushy peas owe their modern incarnation to a Dutchman, R.J. Mansholt, who began breeding marrowfat in the Netherlands in 1901 before exporting them to the UK. Vinegar was introduced to Britain by the Romans. Tartare sauce is French.

As Alan ate his fish and chips and mushy peas, he was enjoying something cosmopolitan and global – in every way.

The curse of nations has turned the human race into claim-stakers.

The process used to make champagne – the méthode champenoise – is French because everyone knows Dom Pérignon invented champagne (in 1697) – right? Well, no – wrong, because it was in fact created in England at least 30 years earlier. It was

Christopher Merrett, an English scientist and physician, who, in 1662, first set out the method of putting fizz in white wine in a paper to the then newly formed Royal Society. Champagne is French but the *methode* is English.

The English too have their closely guarded culinary chattels and believe, for example, that their blessed land is home to the sacred scone. If encouraged (but please don't), some English people will even prattle on about the order in which jam and cream should be applied as if their English god ordained that it should be so. But even the sacred scone is not straightforward in its provenance.

The word "scone" is of Scottish origin and is itself derived from the Dutch "*schoonbrood*". Scones themselves are closely related to Scots bannocks, which in turn can be found in indigenous Inuit cuisine that predates first contact with Europeans by, well, forever. Scones may be Scottish, or Dutch, English, or Inuit – or even much older – nobody really knows.

To misquote Spinal Tap – you can't really dust for food.

But that doesn't stop people trying.

Sometimes the debate over who created what becomes an extension of regional antipathy writ in culinary form. Take the vicious "who invented hummus" debate. An on-going saga in which the Greeks, Turks, Israelis, Lebanese, Egyptians and Syrians all try to claim the dish.

The chickpea dip is a matter of particular national pride in Lebanon and when their neighbour, Israel, began exporting their own brand to Europe in the early 2000s, the Lebanese viewed it as nothing short of an assault on their culture. A failed attempt to get the EU to recognise hummus as uniquely Lebanese escalated matters and soon the spat had turned into an extended, ridiculous metaphor for all the tension and animosity that continues to blight the lives of ordinary people in the Middle East.

By 2008, Israel and Lebanon were facing each other down in the "Hummus War".

Israeli hummus backers came armed with scripture claiming that the first reference to it appeared in the Old Testament Book of Ruth, written 3,000 years ago:

"And at meal-time Boaz said unto her, 'Come hither, and eat of the bread, and dip thy morsel in my 'hometz'." (Ruth 2:14)

This surely was game, set and match. Clearly, if it was in a holy book, it belonged to Israel – it was the word of God and anyone who doubted that hummus was Israeli was a blasphemer. But not to be outdone, Lebanese academics countered that "hometz" was actually the Hebrew word for "vinegar" not "hummus" and that Ruth was thus dipping her bread in something else entirely. While everyone started reaching for religious texts, Lebanese Minister of Tourism, Fadi Abboud, opened a second front by ordering up the "largest tub of hummus" in history, so that the nation could secure a Guinness World Record in 2009.

When the batch was finished, the event made news across the region and the Lebanese relished (sorry) in what was to be but a brief victory. For, across the border, an Arab-Israeli restaurant owner, Jawdat Ibrahim, was blending up a counteroffensive. That attempt saw 4,000 kg of chickpeas, oil and lemon juice emptied into a vast satellite dish and Israel declared home of the biggest tub of dip for the 2010 Guinness annual.

The Lebanese weren't having that and mounted a monumental hummus counterattack, whipping up 10,500 kg of dip, which they might well still be eating now.

A sort of "cold dip war" has rumbled on ever since and, as with all great farce, it is garnished with an equal degree of tragedy. There could be no better demonstration of the shared heritage and culture of the Middle East than hummus, whose history predates every nation state on Earth. But instead of celebrating that commonality, politicians and nationalists have preferred to use it to sow division.

Since people first gathered together to eat, food has been the great unifier of our species. Its history has defied the limitations of artificially imposed borders. If you sit down to break bread, you are tapping into a strand of shared experience that runs all the way back to the Swabian caves. Food is beautiful. It is the great validation of the sharing instinct deep within our species. And yet there will always be some who seek to ring-fence it – claim it – and use it to set lines in the sand.

* * *

Our attitudes to language are much the same as those of the players in the great hummus war.

It is impossible to pin down precisely when people first started speaking but it probably occurred before the era of "behavioural modernity" – that vast stretch of time between 40,000 and 100,000 years ago when homo sapiens started getting ideas about themselves and began behaving differently to other primates.

Some speculate that the first stabs at language were onomatopoeic attempts to turn sounds into meaning. And it's seductive to believe that words like *woof, cuckoo* or *bang* have their origin in the grunt-and-club stereotype of early cave men and women. Unfortunately, there's no archaeology and therefore no obvious trace.

Some words are common to many languages and one word is common to all.

In 2013 researchers at the Max Planck Institute for Psycholinguistics at Nijmegen, in the Netherlands, published the results of a cross-linguistic study which revealed that most languages of the world shared one universal word and it was – drum roll – "huh".

Some critics suggested that this was a bit silly, because "huh" is not a "real word" but those critics are wrong. Babies don't say "huh". "Huh" is complex. Mastery of it doesn't come until around the age of five – long after kids have perfected words like "want, "iPhone", "no", "mine", "chocolate" and "Brexit". "Huh" has a meaning – in fact, depending how you use it, it has many.

It can mean: "Sorry I didn't catch that", "What?", "Are you talking to me?", "So what", "That's funny" and multiple other permutations. The Dutch researchers concluded that the word had derived out of "cultural evolution" over time but it also could be one of those very old first words – a tantalising echo-fragment of the much-postulated theory of an original "mother tongue".

The concept of a "mother tongue", unlike chicken tikka masala, did actually start life in India.

On 2nd February 1786, Sir William Jones, a 39-year-old judge at Fort William in Bengal, gave a celebrated address to the Asiatic Society in Kolkota (then called Calcutta). Jones was a classical scholar, fascinated with India and, as a passionate philologist, particularly taken with its many languages. Having set out to learn Sanskrit, he was stunned to discover that it bore a striking resemblance to the classical Greek and Latin he had studied at Harrow and Oxford.

Sanskrit was not just similar to the classics – it was similar in a way that "could not have been produced by accident; so strong, indeed, that no philologer could examine all three, without believing them to have sprung from some common source," according to *The Story of English* by Robert McCrum, William Cram and Robert MacNeil.

Jones suggested that a now extinct common Proto-Indo-European (PIE) language had once been spoken by the ancestors of up to a third of the people on Earth and that it was the mothership of almost everything now spoken in Europe and South Asia.

The case was compelling. Language groups as apparently diverse as Gaelic, Gothic, Sanskrit and Farsi (Persian) seemed to share distinct characteristics. The mood-board of grammar – the nouns, tenses and use of masculine, feminine and neuter clauses, were conspicuously alike. Some words were pretty much identical. The Sanskrit "*bhratar*" was close to the Latin "*frater*" and the Greek "*phrater*" and closer still to the English word "brother". The Sanskrit word for cow was "*gau*", mother was "*matr*" and even relatively obscure words like "*nara*" meaning "nerve" hinted that all of this was more than coincidental.

Jones rather spoiled his copy book by elsewhere propagating some wilder theories. He suggested, wrongly, that ancient Egyptian and Chinese derived from PIE and was also responsible for cultivating the false racist notion of Aryanism. His belief in an original civilisation and racial divide later fed into the Nazi pseudo-scholarship that informed the Ahnenerbe's digs and all that other garbage.

The idea that Hitler, Goebbels and Göring were descendants of a master-race of blonde, blue-eyed super-beings was and is patently absurd. But the notion that they might have grown up using words related to those used by people in India – not so.

Linguistic archaeology of the pre-written era is a bit like looking for evidence of dark matter with the naked eye. You know it's there but it's impossible to trace it. And yet the extraordinary parallels Jones first spotted and subsequent work suggest that the languages spoken by many of us, like the food we eat, did indeed branch out from a very limited common source – or sources. As early people began to travel out beyond those first tribes, they took their legends, myths, food and even their "huh" with them.

It's far easier to work out where the languages we speak today came from, although most people give it no more thought than they do the provenance of their lunch.

Learning our mother tongue is like beautiful magic. Transmitted to us by parents and family and later on by teachers and school friends, we learn the complex rhythms, poetry, syntax and grammar, almost without thinking. And yet this glorious music of communicable sounds becomes intrinsic to who we are.

English is like a soup. Just as you can blend chickpeas and oil to make hummus, or tomato and tikka to make masala, so English is the product of a recipe that includes Old German, Norse, Norman French and Latin – with a pinch of everything else.

When the Romans left Britain in the 5th century CE, most people spoke one of the many shades of "Common Brittonic" and some British Vulgar Latin – a distinct local strand of the language of our former Imperial overlords. Over time the two languages intermingled, as languages in close proximity tend to do, and waited for "Anglo-Saxon" and Jutish to pitch up.

Bede has the legendary Saxon mercenaries Hengist and Horsa turn up from Denmark in the late 400s and eventually wrestle power from King Vortigern and kick off the Anglo-Saxon age and all the language replacement it entailed. Vortigern actually means "Great Ruler" and while some have cast doubt as to whether he actually existed, the numerous references to him in early source material suggest he probably did. Hengist and Horsa, however, are likely fictional – and the idea that two mercenaries led an invasion by stealth is to oversimplify matters considerably. More likely the "Anglo-Saxons" came in waves of migration and raids over a very long period of time.

Despite that, most modern Britons still believe that Anglo-Saxons, Jutes and Frisians "invaded" Britain in this era and drove the "native" people to the west or even to extinction – but that theory too is now widely discredited.

It is true that following the withdrawal of the Romans, groups of Frisians, Saxons and others came here. Unfortunately, most of the sources for what happened rely on "Anglo-Saxon" oral poetry and folk tales, which are highly unreliable. The only historian on the ground at the time was Gildas, a monk – whose work *On the Ruin of Britain* was bitter and polemical propaganda which argued that the "Ancient Britons" had deservedly lost their territory because of their wicked depravity.

It's likely that much like later Viking raiding parties, the "Anglo-Saxons" first came to loot and pillage, but later on to settle and rule and that, in time, settlements grew up and a language shift from Brittonic and Latin, spoken by our "natives" of the time, to "Old English" took place. The change would have come about as a small warrior class embedded itself in the local population.

In many post-colonial societies, the former imperial language has embedded itself and then infused with the pre-existing culture. In India, a distinct linguistic alloy has occurred between English and Urdu, Hindi and other languages to create what some have dubbed "Hinglish". In Tunisia, French and Arabic have moved ever closer together and, from the pidgin languages of the Torres

Straits to Haitian creole, "new" languages have forever sprung from the mergers, acquisitions, trade, love and war that our species carries about.

Like "curry", all languages are ultimately fusions and English arguably more so than many.

If you accuse your colleague of *kow-towing* to the boss, you're using Chinese. Tell him he's a *tosser* and you're using Norwegian. Subsequently get the *sack*, and it's happened in Greek. Go to the *sauna* to *get it off your mind* and you're deploying Finnish and Middle English. Though, in truth, by using *get* in any of its multiple meanings you're really speaking Norse. Get *drunk* on *alcohol* and you're speaking Dutch and Arabic. Take an *Uber* home and you've now switched to German. Suffer a *mammoth* headache and you're lapsing into Russian. Send a sad-looking *emoji* the next morning and you're deploying Japanese. If you get the *gist* of my argument then that's because you understand one of hundreds of modern French loan words in English.

Language, like food, goes deep to the core of who we are. We feel it to be a part of us and just as some lay claim to hummus, others feel driven to lay claim to words and language.

From the 17th century onwards, those newly emerged nation states began to view "their language" as something intrinsic to "their identity" and tried to impose order on the chaos.

It was by no means straightforward, because most nation states had many languages. There were at least 40 distinct tongues spoken in Italy at the time of unification, but subsequent Italianisation has sought to weed them out. France too had dozens of distinct local languages, with many still surviving, but as far back as 1635, Cardinal Richelieu was setting up the Académie Française to create a standard.

That frankly bonkers institution persists to this day, with many laws and regulations in place in the country as a last line of defence against perceived "Anglification" of French – which, when you consider that a good third of the English language is already French, is a bit laughable.

In 17th-century England, nobody gave a fig (*Provençal*) about regional variations of English let alone spelling or where words came from. Six surviving examples of Shakespeare's signature exist and he magnificently spells himself six different ways. As long as the reader understood, nobody cared and this was manna to printers – who could typographically justify lines in texts by adding extra letters, embedding mad spelling rules in the process.

Samuel Johnson's *Dictionary*, first published in 1755, committed many to a permanence from which they are unlikely ever to escape.

If you think English spelling has logic – and many cling to that ill-fated belief – consider how "ough" is pronounced before proceeding to say the words: bough, cough, hiccough, Slough and ought. Mad, huh?

As the 18th century went on, the English language came to become a building block of fake history and our notions of exceptionalism.

So, the British began setting down "rules of grammar" and codes of spelling and insisting that everything was logical and ancient and perfect – when it wasn't.

And from this sprang the fallacious belief that the English of England was somehow "original" and that its rules and spellings and the pronunciation of a small elite who spoke Received Pronunciation (BBC English) was correct and that anyone who veered from it was wrong.

By contrast, Americans (it was said) spelled everything wrong and used funny Americanisms that still excite rage in conservative British pedants, largely in the pages of *The Daily Telegraph,* to this day.

In 2011, the BBC magazine asked readers to nominate their most hated Americanisms and were inundated with contributions from angry correspondents. Nominations included "I'm good" for "I'm well", along with "touch base", "fanny pack", "deplane" and "gotten".

"What kind of word is 'gotten'?" wrote Julie from Warrington, adding "it makes me shudder."

Well actually it's a very old English word, derived from "getten" and taken west at some time around the departure of the *Mayflower.* It's used repeatedly in the King James Bible of 1611 but it's much older than that.

The word is there in Chaucer and has probably existed in Britain since it first stepped off a Viking longship in the late 8th century.

As with many perceived Americanisms, including "fall" and "diaper", it originated in the British Isles and was commonly used in the England of the 16th and 17th centuries, but fell out of use here as language shifted and fashions changed. Autumn is a fairly new French import. The word "nappy", which comes from "napkin" has only been used since 1927.

Claiming that "English English" is original and that "American English" is "wrong" is itself wrong. English English is no newer or older than any other form of the language. There is no such thing as a pure language. Arabic speakers might claim that the "best Arabic" is heard in Saudi Arabia, Germans may argue "the best German" spoken in northern Germany – but only because both were homes to the ruling classes who spoke that way.

In the 1950s, Nancy Mitford, scion of one of England's self-appointed "upper class" families, wrote an essay entitled: "The English Aristocracy" in which she created an extended glossary of terms that aristocratic people used and compared them unfavourably with those used by the "Non-U[pper]" classes. The essay sent social-climbing idiots into a frenzy of self-evaluation – and some of it persists to this day, but Mitford, for all of her snobbery and artificial airs and graces, knew nothing about language formation.

There is no inherent rule that the English of Liverpool or Preston is "inferior" to that of Oxford or Windsor, or that "toilet" is wrong and "lavatory" right. It is nothing more than preposterous bollocks, propagated by the equally preposterous Nancy Mitford.

Received Pronunciation is the product of a historical quirk. If Durham had become the preeminent university in Britain in the 19th century, then the teachers who sprang from it would likely have taken that brogue into the classrooms of the nation's elite private schools. Instead, they were mostly educated at Oxford and Cambridge, cementing the southern dialect of those academic seats of power as the "Standard English" still used today.

Unfortunately, English is now a global language – meaning that British people no longer feel obliged to learn others. Although there are some who say they never did so in the first place. Either way, that stroke of luck has only added to the nation's sense of entitlement and exceptionalism and isolationism, embedding that sense that we have inherited the world and that "our" language is *the* language.

In fact, modern English no more belongs to England than curry comes from India.

The many English variants spoken in the British Isles, Ireland, Australia, Canada, New Zealand, Jamaica, India and the United

States are but branches off the tree of the regional pidgins that sprung up here in the (not so dark) Dark Ages. They have as much right to declare themselves "proper English" as Mr.Angry of Tunbridge Wells. Noone owns English. And none have the right to exclaim their English "original" any more than one country can lay claim to hummus, or any restaurant the invention of chicken tikka masala.

But, like all fake history, facts rarely stop people trying to claim that the "truth" is otherwise. It's how cults work.

CHAPTER SIX

THE AZTECS WERE SLAUGHTERED BY THE CONQUISTADORS

How political apologies are weaponised

Friday, 1st March 2019 and Andrés Manuel López Obrador, the newly inaugurated President of Mexico, holds a press conference, to announce that he has written letters to Pope Francis and King Felipe VI of Spain, demanding an immediate and unequivocal apology for the invasion of his country 500 years earlier.

Obrador, the first left-wing President of Mexico in 70 years, has come to office on a populist tide, promising to deliver radical reform for ordinary Mexicans. He pledges to end corruption, improve healthcare, tackle the cartels and be a champion of the poor and the dispossessed. But there's more. This self-confessed history nut seeks not only to right his country's present – but also, to rectify the wrongs of its past.

The two letters are the first salvo in a counter-attack on historical injustice.

Having stirred the diplomatic waters, Obrador retreats to the ruins of the Mayan city of Comalcalco in the state of Tabasco and delivers an impromptu history lesson to his Twitter followers on the transgressions of the Spanish conquistadors:

"There were massacres," he begins helpfully, "the so-called conquest was done with the sword and the cross. They raised churches on top of temples." Spain and the Holy See, he declares have a duty to seek "forgiveness of indigenous peoples for violations that are now known as human rights" and it is up to them to make the first move in reconciliation.

The Vatican maintains a dignified silence, but Madrid is *totally* triggered. Soon the Spanish government bites back: "The arrival, 500 years ago, of Spaniards to present Mexican territory cannot be judged in the light of contemporary considerations," they say, in an official statement, adding pointedly that "our two brother nations have always known how to read our shared past without anger and with a constructive perspective."

Or in other words: "Jog on, troll."

Later that day, Spanish Foreign Minister Josep Borrell tells reporters that it is a bit "weird to receive this request for an apology now, for events that happened 500 years ago", while practically circling a finger by the side of his temple.

In Mexico, things haven't quite gone to plan for the President and he is widely ridiculed. The former Interior Secretary Miguel Ángel Osorio Chong goes as far as to suggest to *Mexico News Daily* that the President: "should be subjected to constant medical evaluation."

Multicultural Mexico has been independent for 200 years. What possible responsibility does Obrador think 21st-century, democratic and left-leaning Spain have for the actions of an adventurer who died in 1547?

Many doubt the Mexican President's true motives in dragging up Cortés. Senators accuse the populist Obrador of deploying a "dead cat" strategy.* The stunt looks very much like an elaborate distraction tactic. An attempt to divert attention from the mountain of promises Obrador has vowed and yet failed to deliver.

At a literary festival in Argentina, the Nobel Prize-winning Peruvian essayist Mario Vargas Llosa sums up the mood: "The Mexican leader mistook his recipient. He should've sent that letter to himself, and given us an answer as to why Mexico still has so many millions of Indians marginalised, poor, ignorant [and] exploited."

It's easy, in opposition, to pledge Heaven to the people of the Earth. Much harder to deliver. Obrador's promises of a brave new world have so far come to nought because you can't deliver social justice overnight. It takes dollars, pain, effort – and crucially – time.

By rekindling an ancient "us against them" narrative, Obrador tapped into Mexico's very own brand of exceptionalism, otherwise known as "Indigenismo".

Modern Mexico was forged from a protracted sequence of uprisings that took place between 1910 and 1920 and which are known collectively as the Mexican Revolution. From them sprung a cultural revolution and the contrivance of an origin myth that placed "native" people at its heart. Indigenismo is a political and cultural sentiment that strives to create a collective national identity based on pre-colonial Mexican culture, while advocating for the rights of indigenous people.

---

* A "dead cat" strategy is a political tool whereby politicians distract the public by throwing a metaphorical "dead cat" onto the table. People are too busy talking about the cat to worry about the situation unfolding about them.

Notable revolutionaries, politicians, writers and artists including celebrated painters Frida Kahlo and Diego Rivera propagated the notion throughout the 20th century, and Mexican politicians have long evoked that nativist mood at times of need, in much the same way that the British dust off the Blitz spirit whenever it suits them.

Indigenismo may have created some great art and design and given politicians and academics much to talk about, but it has done little for the people it was first intended to celebrate. Notions of spirit are all well and good, but they can't alleviate acute poverty, and Mexico's indigenous groups remain very poor indeed. According to the country's Census Bureau, nearly 80% of the indigenous population live beneath the poverty line, with just over 40% classified as in "extreme poverty". Encouraged by community leaders, these dispossessed voted in their droves for Obrador in 2018, helping secure his win on the back of his promises of land reform and improved social equality.

Now, struggling to deliver on any meaningful change, Obrador had deployed his dead cat.

The notion that 16th-century native people were living idyllic lives before the arrival of those dastardly Europeans is a long-established trope in some corners of Central and Latin America. But it defies actual logic and historicity, not least because most 16th-century Europeans, like most of those living in the 16th-century so-called Aztec Empire, were poor, bonded and suppressed. On both sides of the Atlantic, the vast majority of people led short, and often pitiful lives at the expense of rulers who exploited them.

If you were a slave, it makes very little difference who is holding the whip. And 16th-century Mexico was no Eden. On the contrary, the Aztec Empire was one of the most brutal and egregious tyrannies of that – or any era.

Montezuma II, ruler at the time of the Spanish invasion, was no credulous Disney king heading up a benign kingdom in a halcyon jungle setting. He was a ruthless, barbaric despot, overseeing a vicious culture that had cowed, beaten and slaughtered its path to regional supremacy.

Known to its people as *Ēxcān Tlahtōlōyān* (or "Triple Alliance"), the Aztec Empire, was, as the name suggests, a confederation between three city states: Mexico-Tenochtitlan, Texcoco, and Tlacopan. They didn't call themselves the Aztecs,* nor were they just one people – things were complicated – but as we have seen, popular history abhors complexity and so, over time, things got simplified and homogenised.

Though founded on the bones of older civilisations, *Ēxcān Tlahtōlōyān* had really only existed for less than 100 years before the arrival of Cortés, the Spanish invader. In historical terms, they had barely unpacked their xiquipillis† when the conquistadors turned up.

Life in the Empire was dominated by belief in a sadistic, end of days, death cult. While Dorothy Martin and her Chicagoan Seekers (back in Chapter 3) baked cakes and removed bra wire to feed their cognitive dissonance, the Mexica offset theirs by killing people and eating their innards. Most Armageddon cults resemble one another, but the "Aztecs" were at least unique in one regard. They believed that the Apocalypse had already happened – four times in fact – and that the cycle of creation and destruction had eventually worn the Universe out. The Sun was now weak and needed "human sacrifice" to keep it going. Blood was the fuel and if people weren't killed on a daily basis, the local star would peter out and die and subsequently the Earth with it.

---

* They referred to themselves as "Mexica"
† The bags carried by Aztec rulers

In feeding this mass delusion, hundreds of thousands of people – perhaps millions – were slain. *Ēxcān Tlahtōlōyān* sustained itself on butchery, pillage and tribute, and the addiction to human sacrifice sometimes spilled over into cannibalism.

"Aztec Christmas" was the Festival of Toxcatl. Witnessed and later described by the appalled Spanish conquistadors, the celebrations around it give an insight into life under Montezuma II and the Aztec's homicidal belief system.

Held in May at the height of the dry season, Toxcatl, meaning "drought" or "great thirst" was dedicated to the veneration of the god Tezcatlipoca – the supreme Mexica deity who was responsible for light and shadow and thus needed to be placated because of the whole "sun" thing.

I've called it "Aztec Christmas", but Bing Crosby crooning by a festively decorated tree, while chestnuts roast on an open fire, it was not.

In the year-long build-up to the big day, a youth would be appointed, or rather obliged, to play the role of Tezcatlipoca. The young man, usually a prisoner of war, would be dressed in fine robes and ankle bells, taught courtly manners, provided with four virginal wives and then, on the big day, be made to ascend to an altar – where he would have his heart ripped out in front of a live studio audience to much joy and celebration from all.

Having done that, the priests would chop off his head and throw his body roughly down the stairs – at which point his flesh would be flayed open and eaten by the attendant faithful.

Mince-pie anyone?

The people of Mer Island ate their enemies too of course, but it did at least have a sort of poetic logic to it. The Meriams believed, wrongly, that cannibalism imbued them with the strength and courage of their enemies – and they were dead anyway. The bestial theatre of Aztec human sacrifice was something else. It was depraved, nightmarish, and in its lust to feed the Sun – unremitting.

For centuries, it was assumed that the only victims of the killing were young men and that the Spanish had exaggerated matters for the purposes of "atrocity propaganda", of which more later. However, the principal 16th-century source on Aztec history comes courtesy of Diego Durán, a Dominican friar who was no nascent Goebbels. Durán developed a strong affinity for the "native people" he sought to convert and, in his writing, he frequently criticised the conquistadors. Unfortunately, he was also prone to inflating figures, claiming for example that 84,000 prisoners had been killed in four days during the inauguration of the Templo Mayor (Great Temple) in 1487. That number has been bandied about for 500 years and is still cited in defence of the conquistadors, most recently in a 2011 article for *History Today* magazine by British historian Tim Stanley. Quite how Durán arrived at the figure is unclear, but there is little evidence to prove it.

The more general academic consensus, supported by the archaeology is that hundreds – possibly thousands – of men, women and children were killed in multiple acts of murder during the reconsecration of the Mexicas' most sacred building.

Durán and others also recorded that in front of the Great Temple stood the *Tzompantli*, a gigantic pyramid-shaped rack containing thousands of skulls, that was eventually pulled down by the conquistadors. For centuries, it was assumed that once again this was deliberate exaggeration or even myth – Spanish misinformation used to discredit the Aztecs and justify their conquest. But following a huge excavation, which began in 2015, archaeologists unearthed thousands of decapitated skulls and the remains of the frame, which proved that this truly horrible pyramid of the dead really had once stood.

Human sacrifice was not reserved for annual religious events. It was everywhere and incessant. It's thought that even voluntary self-sacrifice was practised, suggesting that the entire population were in thrall to a sort of psychotic frenzy, brought on by their faith.

Ēxcān Tlahtōlōyān society was a terrifying place and likely already collapsing in on itself, under the weight of paranoia and competing interests, when the conquistadors turned up. Given the carnage and the fear it imbued, it's unsurprising that having arrived in Mexico, Cortés found willing allies among the Aztecs' many enemies, who were only eager to help in hastening things to their end. Prominent among them were the Tlaxcala, a loose tribe of Mayans who were engaged in perpetual war with their more powerful neighbour.

The Tlaxcala were critical to the success of the Spanish conquest – and without them the Aztecs could never have been defeated. Cortés was, first and foremost, a skilled diplomat and the alliance he forged demonstrates how adept he was at wooing allies and outsmarting his enemies. With just 500 men of his own he knew that without the help of locals he stood no chance of toppling the Mexica elite, so the Tlaxcala were rewarded for their loyalty and game-changing contribution to the victory over the Aztecs.

That does not fit the narrative of "European invaders" upending the "noble savages", though, and as such they are often marginalised in the tale – or edited out altogether.

By 1521, Cortés and his allies had overrun the great city of Teno-chtitlan, which lay at the heart of the Empire. But they were helped in no small measure by a smallpox outbreak which devastated the

Mexica population, allowing Cortés to seize control of the Triple Alliance and its territory.

The Spanish had not so much slaughtered the "Aztecs" as taken advantage of the circumstances that presented themselves and played off the existing rival factions for gain. It was a victory built on locally forged allegiances, bad leadership on the part of Montezuma and the intervention of an epidemic that hastened things to their end.

Cortés was certainly no liberator. Despite his and Spain's purported "Christian Mission", his chief motive was greed. But that made him little different to the Aztec rulers, who had carved out their Empire through conquest and avarice.

Had they been less addicted to their unhinged cult of death and more concerned with the business of governing, the existing elite may perhaps have seen off the tiny Spanish expedition. Instead, the Empire was largely brought down by itself.

And while the Spanish subjugation that followed was hardly an improvement for the ordinary people of the region, the orgy of violence did at least come to an end. Trade was later to flourish and a new and better world – our world – was born out of it.

Obrador has yet to ask the descendants of the Aztec people to apologise to the descendants of those they disembowelled and beheaded to feed the Sun. Nor has he suggested that they seek forgiveness from the distant grandchildren of the neighbouring regions who their antecedents ethnically cleansed. To do so would be to invite ridicule and anyway, where would the political capital be in that?

Much easier to simplify history, point the finger at the old colonial power and throw some dead cats around in the process.

* * *

Like spandex, leg warmers and the inexplicable rise of the mullet, the fashion for political apologies has its roots in the 1980s.

As the Cold War ebbed to its end, it was another Pope, John Paul II, who set the trend. In August 1985, on a trip to Cameroon, he expressed sorrow for Christianity's role in the slave trade – the first of more than 100 expressions of papal regret that he was to make before his death in 2005.

The speech was a big deal at the time and made front-page news across the world, in the days when front-page news still mattered. In truth, it wasn't much of an apology.

Having flown to Douala, the major port in Cameroon, the rock-star Pope was – according to a contemporary *New York Times* account – in an "exuberant mood". He joshed with the crowd of young people who had turned out to see him and then launched into his sermon. He covered African theology, the need to respect local traditions and then, having name-checked the Good Samaritan – suggested that back in the day, some Christians had not always behaved in a particularly Christian manner.

"In the course of history, men belonging to Christian nations did not always do this, and we ask pardon from our African brothers who suffered so much because of the trade in blacks."

John Paul did not mention Catholicism. Instead, the blame was spread more thinly to encompass all "men belonging to Christian nations". This was less an apology, more a cry of "It wasn't only us!" A diplomatic duck and dive that ignored the facts of the case.

For over the course of its history, the Catholic Church had demonstrated a complex and at times inconsistent approach to the malfeasance of slavery. During the crusades, the Vatican mirrored Islamic clerics in banning the practice – but from the late

Middle Ages onwards as powerful Catholic European nations, most notably, Portugal and Spain, began to extend their reach into Africa, Pope Nicholas V issued a series of Papal Bulls that gave Catholics the right to engage in human kidnap and trafficking for profit. By 1488, Pope Innocent VIII was accepting slaves as gifts and from the very late 15th century onwards – as long as the victims were not Christians, anything went.

That foul culpability went unaddressed by John Paul II. Not so much glossed over as blanketly ignored.

And this was not without calculation. As with Obrador, there was an agenda at work. The Pope's apology came in the midst of his mission to launch a "Second Wave of Evangelism" on Africa. With congregations declining in Europe, the Church needed new faithful and Africa was deemed to be fertile ground for converts. The visit was a mission. The apology itself, ultimately motivated by other self-serving rationale. It might as well have been written in sand, beneath the breaking waves of a Cameroonian beach.

Such faux-apologies came to define JPII's papal term. And none more so than his lacklustre address to Jews in 1998.

From 1945 onwards, the Catholic Church had been widely condemned for wartime inaction over the Holocaust. And for most of those 53 years, the Church tried to dodge the issue, by ignoring it altogether.

When it was announced that the Pope would finally seek to make restitution in the late 1990s, there was considerable anticipation that Pope Pius XII's dereliction of Christian duty during the war would finally be held to account. But the resulting letter was a fudge. The Pope accepted that "Christian countries" had been responsible, writing:

"The fact that the Shoah* took place in Europe, that is, in countries of long-standing Christian civilisation, raises the question of the relation between the Nazi persecution and the attitudes down the centuries of Christians toward the Jews."

But once again, he was careful not to implicate the Catholic Church. No liability was accepted. No redress made for failing to step up to the mark.

Jewish groups were unimpressed.

"We are very sad, very disappointed," Rabbi Leon Klenicki, director of the Department of Interfaith Affairs of the Anti-Defamation League, told the BBC.

"Those of us engaged in the dialogue have not yet succeeded," the World Jewish Congress added.

The Vatican was seeking to have its holy wafer and eat it, but nothing could dismiss the truth that the Church was not just culpable for its wartime inaction over the Holocaust, but for the centuries of tacit anti-Semitism that had led to it.

A millennium of insinuation had laid the blame for Christ's death at the feet of the Jews, despite Christ himself being a Jew. Until 1959, the term "perfidious Jews" was used in the Holy Week Liturgy. The trope of anti-semitism and the hostility of a thousand years, repeatedly beat a path back to the walls of St Peter's and the successive pontiffs who had enabled it through inference, disinterest or inaction.

None of that was addressed, and undoubtedly, with good reason.

John Paul II was a canny man. He knew that a well-timed, well-placed apology could do a lot of diplomatic heavy lifting – he also knew that to address the still-resonating failures of the

* The Hebrew term for the Holocaust

Vatican would be admit liability to the living. It was easier to apologise for things that happened long ago, than to seek redress for the Church's inaction over the Holocaust, whose victims were still remembered, mourned and loved. Whose survivors were still alive.

This, sadly, was typical of the Pope's 100 plus apologies. Sometimes the pointlessness was breathtaking. In 1992, he admitted that Galileo had been right all along – and all those threats of torture and years of imprisonment and denials of science had been regrettable. The Earth did indeed go around the Sun. But hey, we all make mistakes.

Seven years later, on a visit to the Czech Republic, he said sorry to the people of Prague for the death of Jan Hus, who was burned at the stake for heresy – in 1415.

In 2004 he apologised for the sacking of Constantinople – in 1204.

But there was never a whisper of remorse for the imprisonment and exploitation of thousands of girls in Magdalene Laundries in Ireland that had continued well into his papal reign. Not a word said about their many thousands of babies, the human plunder of religious sanctimony, who were forcibly taken from their mothers and given to "good Christian families" instead. Nor, for most of his 27-year reign, did he seek to address the endemic child sexual abuse perpetrated by priests, bishops and others – or offer comfort to the abused. Indeed, it was only, finally, in 2003, amidst a growing clamour of criticism surrounding papal inaction – that he addressed the matter:

"There is no place in the priesthood and religious life for those who would harm the young," he wrote, stating the obvious, in yet another nimble dodge.

Jan Hus never heard his apology, because he was 600 years dead. The Magdalene girls have yet to receive one, despite many of the victims still being alive. It's easy to say sorry when no sacrifice is required.

John Paul II's example kickstarted a fashion for meaningless apologies and the avoidance of actual ones.

In 1993, US President Bill Clinton was only too happy to tell native Hawaiians that he was sorry for the invasion of the islands in 1893, which nobody could remember, but he refused to apologise to Japan for the attacks on Hiroshima and Nagasaki in 1945 that killed a quarter of a million innocent people.

"The United States owes no apology to Japan for having dropped the atomic bombs on Hiroshima and Nagasaki," he said on the 50th anniversary in 1995. And in the years since, no subsequent incumbent of the White House has expressed any remorse for the use of the weapons.

That same year, Queen Elizabeth II put her name to a letter to the Maori people offering remorse for "colonial transgressions" in the 19th century. But the British state has never made amends for the massacre in Amritsar in India in 1919, which saw hundreds, perhaps over a thousand, unarmed men, women and children mown down. The forced castration and torture of Kenyans in the 1950s has yet to be addressed by the British government, beyond a diplomatic nod in 2013, when the then UK High Commissioner Christian Turner "recognised" that "abuses" had taken place and that the government "regretted" it.

The more recently events took place, the harder the apology is to make.

Tony Blair has never said sorry for the catastrophic invasion of Iraq in 2003 that led to an estimated 151,000 dead, but while prime minister, he did say sorry on behalf of "those who governed in London" for the Irish potato famine in the early 19th century.

That apology was mercilessly mocked in the right-wing media at the time, although perhaps, in this case, a little unfairly. The Irish Famine letter was part of a wider strategy of much-needed British rapprochement with Ireland. Blair was seeking to repair the long damage of Anglo-Irish relations and scars that were still fresh. To that end, starting with one of the greatest perceived injustices of all made sense. An important first step in efforts to address more recent grievances.

In 1998, in a climate of British Unionist anger and derision, Blair commissioned an inquiry into the 1972 Bloody Sunday shooting that saw 26 unarmed protestors gunned down by British paratroopers and 14 left dead on the streets of Northern Ireland.

The findings of the Saville Report were made public in 2010 and the new PM, David Cameron, duly stood up in the House of Commons and sought to lay to rest a deep injustice and apologise for the state execution of the victims.

"The conclusions of this report are absolutely clear," he told fellow MPs. "There is no doubt, there is nothing equivocal, there are no ambiguities. What happened on Bloody Sunday was both unjustified and unjustifiable. It was wrong."

Here was an apology that mattered. One that could be heard by survivors and the bereaved. It was a major step towards reconciliation.

There was something refreshing in this unabashed admittance of fault by the British state. But such unsolicited moments for still-resonating events are rare. Cameron also had much to gain from it. He had no skin in the fight. The events of 1972 had unfolded when he was five years old, and the Irish Troubles were largely over by 2010, when his government took power.

Accepting that the British government had failed and that the army was responsible enabled him to look like a different kind of Tory. Kind, compassionate – more ersatz Tony Blair than wicked Maggie Thatcher.

Much the same happened following the collapse of the Soviet Union with Presidents Gorbachev and Yeltsin both seeking to mark the new era with some well-timed political repentance, for the still-fresh crimes of the USSR.

In 1990, Gorbachev apologised for the 1940 Red Army massacre of nearly 22,000 Polish POWs in the Katyn forest near Smolensk. In 1995, under Yeltsin, a monument was erected in St Petersburg to the victims of Stalin's political repression.

Both men had more to reap than lose by distancing themselves from Stalin, not least because many of the relatives of the victims were still alive and could now vote.

This is not to say that all political apologies, nor calls for them are pointless – or cynical. The South African Truth and Reconciliation Commission, set up by Nelson Mandela in the post-apartheid years to seek restorative justice and conciliation for the country, is a case in point. There can be validity in seeking to redress the still open wounds of the near past. Or even the not so near past, because sometimes injustice lingers and the tremors of it can impact and resonate into another age.

The "trade" in African slavery, which John Paul II addressed so tentatively in Cameroon in the 1980s, is an obvious example. Many of the nations that were once key protagonists in that violation of morality remain in denial about it, despite the fact the injustice it predicated continues into our century.

The scars of slavery still run deep across the Americas, Europe, Africa and beyond. And unlike events in Mexico in

1520, this is painfully recent history. The last survivor of a slave ship, Matilda McCrear, who with her mother Gracie and sister Sallie was ripped from her homeland in Nigeria aged two and sold to a plantation owner, only died in 1940. Peter Mills, the last surviving American to be born a slave, lived until 1972. My life overlapped with his.

Centuries of persecution did not end with the abolition of slavery. Institutional racism and injustice still persist today. If you are an African American, you are still more likely to be shot, imprisoned or unemployed than your white neighbour.

Research conducted in 2019 shows that while making up just 14% of the US population, African Americans account for 23% of the 1,000 annual fatal shootings by the American police. One third of all US prisoners are black. White and black Americans use recreational drugs at about the same rate, but African Americans are four times more likely to get arrested for possession.

Poverty, injustice and social inequity still blight the black community in America, Britain and elsewhere.

And still the symbols of slavery linger.

In Britain, statues to slave traders and enablers remain in place. And any attempts to remove them are hotly contested. Of course, we cannot, in all sanity, blame the leaders of modern countries for the crimes of their forebears or for the monuments they erected, but we can and should hold them to account for failing to address the truth of it. They haven't, largely, because the debate has been deliberately opacified, with nationalist and Conservative politicians in particular still seeking to portray British Imperialism as a source of pride and Britain as the "good guy" in the slavery debate.

In 2015, the then Chancellor, George Osborne, claimed at the Conservative Party conference in Manchester, that his party ("we" again) had abolished slavery and, in the years since, many of his fellow party members, including MP James Cleverly and Tory peer Lord Hannan have repeated the claim.

In 2018, the official Twitter account of HM Treasury went even further, claiming that modern-day Britons had somehow ended 19th-century slavery. The logic was contorted to say the least.

"Millions of you helped end the slave trade through your taxes," the tweet gushed, stating that as the amount of money borrowed for the slavery abolition act was only paid off in 2015, "British citizens helped... end the slave trade."

Here then was the curious and bizarre rewrite in which "we" should be proud of our achievement in abolition of a trade that "we" had engaged in for almost 300 years. Patting Britain on the back for helping abolish slavery is a bit like congratulating a mass murderer for erecting a monument to his victims.

In May 2020, as the Covid-19 pandemic swept across the world, a series of demonstrations in support of the Black Lives Matter movement erupted in the wake of the killing of George Floyd in the USA by Minneapolis police. Soon the protests had spread to Europe and the focus of the demonstrations had broadened. We have seen already that in London Boris Johnson and others confected fears that statues, including the one to Winston Churchill, would topple.

In Bristol, however, one actually did.

Bristol is a city largely built on the profits of slavery and as the demonstrations went on, events culminated in the tearing down of a statue to Edward Colston – a 17th-century slave trader – and dumping it in the river. This should not have come as a shock. There had been objections to Colston's statue for years, but all attempts to remove it had been resolutely resisted by the society which had been set up in his name. The statue had little historic or artistic merit. Erected 200 years after Colston's death, even the Victorians had baulked at digging into their pockets to fund a project that elevated the memory of him. In the end, it was funded by the merchant who had proposed it.

But once it was torn down, the Colston effigy became an iconic battleground in "the culture war".

Nigel Farage, then leader of the Brexit Party, dubbed the protesters the vanguard of a "new form of Taliban". Conservative politicians lined up to condemn the "vandalism" and Sajid Javid, the former Chancellor, suggested that:

"If Bristolians wants [sic] to remove a monument it should be done democratically – not by criminal damage."

Some even sought to argue that this statue-toppling, like the confected fears over Churchill's Parliament Square monument, were an attempt to erase history. That without statues to slave traders we could never understand our past – and that the likes of Colston had to be seen in the light of their times and not judged by us.

But paradoxically it was in the uprooting of his statue that Colston's name and story became more widely known. Few people outside of Bristol had even heard of him before the event. Subsequent to the removal, most people had.

Direct action had given everyone a free history lesson.

When Colston's statue was eventually pulled out of Bristol harbour, it was placed in a local museum with proper context given on all sides. This is an eminently grown up and pragmatic approach to history – deeply at odds with both Obrador's attempts to castigate and apportion blame and the patriotic right's determination to preserve everything – unquestioned in aspic.

* * *

While a meaningful, unsolicited political apology might be rare, an unprompted offer of forgiveness for injustice, whether real or perceived, is virtually unheard of.

There can be significant leverage in victimhood. Long picked scars and carefully nurtured injustices can serve a purpose, and we can see it in Obrador's dead catting, the narrative of Brexit, the saga of the Falkland Islands, the Greek financial crisis, and independence movements in democratic nations across Europe. Almost without exception, such grievances are predicated on that same sense of a "paradise lost". The notion that an innocent people have been robbed of their sovereignty by malignant bullies.

In Britain, there is no better example than the Battle of Culloden (1746) the last land-based military engagement to be fought on British soil.

Nearly 300 years after the Jacobite forces of Charles Stuart – "Bonnie Prince Charlie" – were routed and slain, the event still matters. The simplified "paradise lost" version of events runs like this. In 1746 the Highlanders of Scotland rallied to the cause of the dispossessed heir to the Stuart dynasty in a last attempt to curtail English domination over their idyllic homeland. Men in kilts picked up their claymores* and headed south, only to be turned on by the duplicitous English and the supposedly "German" Duke of Cumberland who drove them back across the border and slaughtered them on the fields of Culloden.

The story lies at the heart of Scottish nationalist exceptionalism – the tale of an inherently virtuous people wronged, bullied and conquered by the English and their Germanic Hanoverian overlords. A conquest that was swiftly followed by the Highland

---

* A Scots broadsword – usually double-edged

Clearances, which drove the native people from their homes in what amounted to an act of ethnic cleansing.

It's a resonant tale and one that buys into every populist, nationalist cliché under the not-always-apparent Scottish sun. Like the narrative that Obrador sought to weave about Mexico, it seeks to reduce the complexity of actual history even as it serves very modern agendas.

If Culloden is a stew of fake history then Charles Edward Stuart is the meat and gravy at its heart.

Despite his place in popular folklore, tartan-wearing Bonnie Prince Charlie was about as Scottish as a McDonald's Happy Meal. His claim to be King of England and Scotland rested with his hapless grandfather, English-born James II – the man frequently dubbed one of the worst kings in history, in an admittedly crowded field, who having failed to learn the lessons of the Civil War, fell out with Parliament and lost his throne in the Glorious Revolution of 1688.

Charles, born in Rome to a Polish mother, was an heir to deep-rooted grievance. His father, James Francis Edward Stuart, known as the "Old Pretender", had tried and failed twice to take back his throne, and when he grew too old to do it himself, young Charlie was groomed to take his place.

Some in England and Scotland still toasted the "King across the water", but the majority of funding for the Bonnie Prince's lavish lifestyle and political scheming came from the French monarchy, then engaged in a protracted war against Britain. Charlie was what we nowadays call a "useful idiot".

Born with a silver chip on his shoulder, the Bonnie Prince's objective, when he set out to invade Britain in 1745, was fairly straightforward. He wanted to upset a nascent democracy and seize the British throne for himself.

Entitled Charlie had everything to gain from his adventure. Ordinary people from Land's End to John O'Groats did not. And it was they who were to pay the price.

Having landed in Eriskay in the Outer Hebrides in July 1745, Charles Stuart was welcomed by the anti-Hanoverian, Highland clan chiefs, who were only too willing to provide men and arms to support the insurrection.

The clan leaders who backed Stuart have somehow managed to escape the scrutiny of history. For many, they are seen as little more than benevolent benefactors, looking out kindly for the people in their charge – well-intentioned patriarchs wanting nothing but the best for their extended families and romantically engaged in leading a war of liberation against tyrannical "English" rule.

The truth is a bit more complex. The clan chiefs were also an elite and one that strongly objected to the 1707 Act of Union, which combined England and Scotland into the United Kingdom of Great Britain, not least because it diminished their own regional power. The Act removed the notion of the divine right of kings and replaced it with a progressive democratic contract between the monarch and the people. That undermined the clan chiefs' own "divine right" as feudal rulers and the clock was ticking down on their fiefdoms.

Clan chiefs liked things the way they were because it benefited them. They had a huge degree of autonomy and ran their clan kingdoms according to their own rules and practices. They didn't like or want outsiders meddling and had long sought to keep themselves apart from kings and queens, whether English or Scottish. Many ran their extended families in a manner that would put Don

Corleone to shame. The Highland Godfathers were forever sending their men to encroach on others' lands, steal their livestock and kill members of the other clans. Feuds were a way of life.

The "Ayrshire Vendetta" between the Cunninghame and Montgomery clans is a classic example. Lasting over 200 years, from the 15th century – to the very field at Culloden – this mutual antipathy saw repeated acts of murder and revenge perpetuated by both clans on each other, for reasons that are mostly shrouded in mystery.

These Highland "caterans"* pillaged and robbed as second nature and as Bonnie Prince's army later journeyed about Scotland and advanced into England, the Highland wing of his army grabbed all the spoils of war it could. The Jacobite pillaging and looting of 1745 remains curiously, almost deliberately overlooked by most histories. Perhaps because it does not fit the romanticised notion of noble Highlanders as popularised by Walter Scott and Rabbie Burns.

The clan system existed then to the benefit of its ruling chiefs and their families who gained, through notions of fealty, in taxes and labour at the expense of almost everyone else. The men who were sent to join the core of the Bonnie Prince's army – were there by obligation to fight in their masters' interests.

* * *

Things began well for the Jacobites. The Bonnie Prince had caught his enemy off guard and success came swiftly in Scotland. Having marched east and captured Stirling, the Jacobites moved on Edinburgh, seizing the capital, although not its castle, on the 17th September. Four days later, at the Battle of Prestonpans, Charlie's

---

* A band of fighting men belonging to a clan

"clan army" routed governmental forces in the first major event of the uprising.

The battle lasted less than 30 minutes and ended with remnants of the government's inexperienced army fleeing in terror. In this brief engagement, some 1,000 British soldiers had been killed or captured against 35 to 40 losses on the Jacobite side.

The defeat threw London into a state of panic. And matters weren't improved by soldiers' tales of a terrifying and seemingly unstoppable Highland army.

Thinking he had the upper hand, Charles Stuart set his eyes on his primary target – England – and more specifically London – much to the disquiet of his military advisers.

Assuring his generals that he had the guaranteed support of English Jacobites, and that numbers would be bolstered by 10,000 French troops invading to the south, they agreed to march 8,000 men into England.

There were initial successes. The Jacobites took Carlisle and were welcomed in Manchester, but in truth the uprising was already doomed. The promised supporters did not flood to the cause and the promised French invasion never took place. Worse still, many of the Highlanders had taken all the pillage they wanted and simply deserted the ranks. The insurgency had been left high and dry.

Reaching Derby in early December, Charles's military commander, Lord George Murray, called together the council of war and declared that they would have to turn back to Scotland.

The game was up. The diminished army retreated north where, at Culloden on 16th April 1746, events played out.

For some, this is the moment when perfidious Englishmen and brutal Hanoverians slaughtered innocent Scots in a violent massacre. The truth is rather more mundane.

Charles Stuart's soldiers were more than just the rebel "clan army" of popular mythology. Nor – as many think – were they all Catholic. Many of the prince's men came from the socially conservative, pro-Stuart, Episcopalian Scottish Lowlands, and his army was bolstered by French, Irish and yes, even some English Jacobites. A detachment of men from "The Manchester Regiment" was present at Culloden on Charles Stuart's side.

The majority of his force, at least by that final engagement, were reasonably well-drilled, well-ordered men and the majority carried muskets not claymores. Commands were given in English, not Gaelic.

They were supplemented by the remains of the less-ordered Highland soldiers who carried a variety of often makeshift weapons. These are the Jacobites of popular imagination.

Few of the men present were volunteers. None would have deemed themselves "freedom fighters". The vast majority had been raised by their clan chiefs who had an ancient right to demand military servitude from their tenants. Like the British Tommies of the Great War, the men at Culloden were compelled to be there and obliged to fight.

Truth is rarely as prosaic as literature and film would have it. Most people are not imbued with romantic motivations and grand ideals. The men who fought and died at Culloden on behalf of the Jacobite Charles, were, like so many other warriors through time, the hapless pawns of history. They were ordinary people obliged to give up their lives on the battlefield for the ambition and wealth of powerful elites.

The slaughter did not end on the battlefield.

In the aftermath of Culloden, the British army, under George II's son, the Duke of Cumberland, hunted down and killed the retreating forces with unremitting brutality, earning Cumberland the moniker "Butcher". At least a third of the Jacobite army were massacred – many in cold blood. The unbridled slaughter spilled out into nearby towns and villages and the horror of it carried through the ages. Some prisoners were shipped to London where they were publicly executed. Many more were taken from their families and transported to the colonies where they spent up to seven years as indentured labourers.

In time, the events at Culloden, like Cumberland's name, became infamous and the defeat was dubbed a massacre. But Cumberland's suppression of the Jacobites was no worse than any would have expected. Nor was it as bloody as portrayed.

By its end, the entire uprising had cost at most 4,000 lives on all sides. Horrendous yes, but slight in comparison to the English Civil Wars of the 17th century, which saw 200,000 die.

The "good guy and bad guy narrative" persists but is more than a little unfair. For a start the British government had not sought trouble, nor wanted to waste its time fighting an insurgence. But more tellingly, most people did not support this supposedly "popular uprising". If they had, then thousands would have flocked to the cause. They simply did not.

Blame for the loss of life at Culloden rests ultimately with the self-serving Charles and his aristocratic Jacobite supporters.

And having created mayhem, Bonnie Prince Charlie did what entitled people have done down the ages. He fled the consequences of his actions, leaving everyone else to clear up the mess. There's little honour in that. Or much that followed. Having left Scotland on a French frigate, Charles went back to France where the king swiftly grew tired of him and shoved him over the border into Italy.

As ballads and poems were written in his honour, the ever more boorish Prince turned into a violent, wife-beating drunk. Charles so regularly assaulted his wife Louise and the subsequent girlfriends and other women in his life that when he died suddenly in 1788, he did so alone. He was mourned by none who knew him. He had blown his wealth on misadventure, prostitutes and excess. All he left behind was a grotesquely obese, very un-bonnie, 67-year-old corpse. In the centuries that followed, his remains fermented in the crypt of St Peter's in the Vatican, while his legend grew and the falsehoods of Culloden – and its perceived aftermath – buried themselves deep within the psyche of the Scottish people.

Charles's defeat at Culloden is often conflated, for example, with the Highland Clearances. But despite being firmly woven into the narrative of the Jacobite Rebellion, the two events are broadly unconnected. The clearances were a result of the Agricultural Revolution – the transformation of the agricultural system, which involved the redistribution of land to make farms more compact and technological changes to farming – which didn't just affect the Highlands or Scotland.

As Scottish historian Sir Tom Devine points out in his book *The Scottish Clearances: A History of the Dispossessed*, it was actually the Lowlanders who suffered most.

This was less ethnic cleansing, more brutal capitalism. The misery visited on poor people by the Agricultural Revolution ruined lives across Britain. And for the most part it was greedy landowners and those self-serving clan leaders that were to blame rather than English capitalists.

But that is not how it is remembered. Perhaps it is easier to blame distant London and "the English" than to accept that you have been fucked over and betrayed by the feudal overlords who share your surname and who sent your ancestor to die for a lost cause.

Culloden, like Dunkirk, has become more than the sum of actual events. It is now central to a broader and bigger story and one which negates the truth of what followed. For quite swiftly most people north and south of the border accepted the Union was the future and moved on.

And inconvenient as it might be for those who would prefer it otherwise, in the years that followed, Scotland flourished.

The Union, which began in what Simon Schama has called "a hostile merger" ended in "a full partnership in the most powerful going concern in the world".

The marvels of the Scottish Enlightenment, which began in the middle of the 18th century, saw a vibrant intellectual atmosphere prosper in cities and towns as the doors of the nation were flung open to the world. The extraordinary intellectual climate, engendered in no small part by the peace, stability and prosperity that followed, led to an estimated literacy rate of 75% by 1750 – unparalleled anywhere in the world at the time.

The Act of Union granted Scottish merchant ships the protection of the mighty Royal Navy, allowing new markets to be exploited, and ended restrictions on trade between the two countries. From the 1780s onwards, Scotland began to modernise and to boom, and by the 19th century, the country was reaping the benefits.

The ship-building, textile and banking sectors flourished and became central to the success of Britain and her growing Empire.

Throughout the 19th and 20th centuries, unlike the citizens of Ireland, the majority of Scots did not question the Union.

That mood only began to shift in the years post-WWII, which saw shipping and industry decline and social deprivation take its place. Worse still, the government in Westminster did little to alleviate the problem. By the 1974 general election, the Scottish National Party (SNP) were polling at 30% and there were growing calls for devolution. The discovery of North Sea oil had led many to ponder whether Scotland might be able to go it alone.

Westminster's apparent uninterest and, at times, barely concealed contempt for Scotland made the terrain ripe for a populist nationalist resurgence, which started in the middle of the 1970s onwards. Scotland suffered more than most from industrial decline during this period. Unemployment in Scotland doubled in the second half of the 1970s and doubled again in the first half of the next decade. By 1986 it was hitting 18% a figure that compared unfavourably with a national UK average of just 11%.

Three years later, Margaret Thatcher enacted the unpopular "poll tax" in Scotland, a full year before it was introduced in England, and many Scots began to ask if they were simply "England's guinea pig".

The tax, eventually rolled out to the rest of Britain (but not Northern Ireland), was seen as deeply unfair, as it levied a single charge on people regardless of wealth or circumstances. By the end of 1990, more than a million Scots were refusing to pay, leaving local authorities in debt to the tune of hundreds of millions of pounds.

Scottish Conservatism had once been a major political force in the country. In 1955 the nation's 36 Conservative MPs had made up the majority of Scottish parliamentary seats at Westminster. Even in the Thatcher era, they were the second biggest party in

Scotland behind Labour. But within a decade of the poll tax, there were no Scottish Tory MPs in the UK parliament at all.

In an interview with *The Conversation* in 2014, Chris Whatley, Professor of Scottish History at the University of Dundee, summed it up.

"There is no doubt [that] the poll tax... bolstered support for independence, albeit indirectly. The Tory government under Margaret Thatcher helped strengthen the view that Westminster and especially Westminster under the Tories failed to understand Scotland and its needs and was therefore losing the right to rule."

The political climate was fuelling the rise of the SNP, but as it rose, the left-leaning nationalist party also appropriated history and increasingly nurtured perceived historical injustices by "the English".

By the 250th anniversary of Culloden in 1996, and with devolution looming, the SNP was no longer a fringe movement. The party had overtaken the Tories to become the de facto opposition to the Labour government north of the border, and fake history was on the march.

When it was reported that the Secretary of State for Scotland, Michael Forsyth, would be attending commemorations of Culloden, there were protests. Activists daubed the words "British Genocide" and "Murderers" at the battle site and soon the rage was spilling out into the media.

In the pages of Scotland's major newspapers, letter writers – including several claiming direct descent from those who had died in the battle – went full Obrador.

Writing to the *Daily Herald*, a John Hall of Stewarton unforgivably conflated the greatest atrocity in living memory with the Jacobite rebellion:

"Germany has apologised for the Holocaust and its leaders have laid wreaths at the sites of former concentration camps while Japan has apologised for war crimes also. The Culloden anniversary could be a suitable occasion for forgiveness and atonement."

Following further acts of vandalism and fears for his safety, Forsyth declared that he wouldn't be coming after all and, capitalising on the situation, Scottish Nationalist Party leader Alex Salmond went on the attack.

"It is probably very wise for Mr Forsyth to stay away since, [for] if he was representing a figure from the battle, it would most probably be Butcher Cumberland," Salmond told reporters, adding even more disingenuously that: "The Scottish National Party will be represented at the commemoration, but we have no plans to turn it into a political event as that would not be appropriate."

Salmond was deploying fake history for modern ends. But his narrative was built on very real, modern iniquities and a genuine feeling in Scotland that Westminster was ignoring its people.

Stirring up an ancient grievance can be a fabulous rallying cry. Picking at the scabs of deliberately misperceived history to enable an agenda may not be very Thucydidean, but it is a tried and tested formula that has worked time and time again through the ages. Again, there is rarely any benefit for ordinary people – forever deployed against each other whether on the fields of Culloden or on the modern battlefield of social media for other people's gain.

Setting fire to the world can seem more appealing than smoking the pipe of peace. It's a pity.

Political apologies and reconciliation can matter. With good intent, both sides can benefit to the greater good of all. There is perhaps no better recent example than the unlikely and enduring friendship between Ian Paisley and Martin McGuinness that began in 2007 and which lasted until Paisley's death in 2014. Paisley had been the most prominent figure in the Northern Irish Unionist movement and was a die-hard anti-republican "loyalist", who had once stood up in the European Parliament and denounced Pope John Paul II as the "Anti-Christ". McGuinness was the former IRA chief of staff and had presided over the organisation since the late 1970s. The two men were the bitterest of enemies, who for more than three decades, had represented opposing extremes as the ugly Northern Irish Civil war claimed 3,600 lives in violence, bombings, murders and state-sanctioned killing.

And yet, obliged to share power in 2007, a decade after the Good Friday Agreement had brought relative peace and stability to Northern Ireland, the two men became close. Indeed, they were so frequently spotted laughing in each other's company that they were dubbed the "Chuckle Brothers" after a popular BBC children's TV act.

Following Paisley's death, his widow Eileen praised McGuinness and paid tribute to the kindness, loyalty and friendship he had demonstrated towards her husband during his final illness. The former IRA commander was deeply affected by the loss and, speaking to Sky News, he paid tribute to his friend and their relationship.

"Despite our differences, I found him to be a charismatic and powerful personality. He always treated me and those who worked with me with respect and courtesy. The peace process and I have lost a friend," McGuinness said, sounding like he was holding back the tears.

The reconciliation did not end there. Despite having been responsible for the murder of her husband's beloved uncle, Lord Louis Mountbatten, Queen Elizabeth II agreed to meet McGuinness in 2012 and the two greeted each other warmly, with smiles and handshakes. Rather than perpetuating division and hate, they sought peace instead. This hugely symbolic act seemed, for many, to mark an end to The Troubles.

Several years later in a BBC interview, McGuinness paid tribute to the Queen – a woman who had once symbolised everything his movement stood against.

"I liked her courage in agreeing to meet with me, I liked the engagements that I've had with her," he said, adding, "I like her."

If only more people could follow the example. Seeking conciliation can be a thankless and time-consuming task. It requires time and goodwill. But more than that – a willingness on the part of leaders and players to set old enmities aside for the greater good of the people and show some humility.

But why waste your brief term in office on that, when you can throw dead cats around instead.

CHAPTER SEVEN

ABRAHAM LINCOLN BELIEVED THAT "ALL MEN ARE CREATED EQUAL"

Education and indoctrination

Are you sitting comfortably? Then I'll begin. Once upon a time there was a boy called Neptune, who loved playing on the shoreline. So, the gods decreed that he would become the "King of the Waves".

And his rule of the surf was so benign and dutiful that soon he had been promoted to "Ruler of the Sea" and was married off to a lady called Amphitrite – who, despite having a name that was impossible to pronounce, was wise and beautiful and everything a sea king could wish for. Together they had sea princes and princesses and the fourth child, whom they called Albion, was their favourite.

Now, as each child came of age, Neptune and Amphitrite would gift them an island, much as modern parents might get the kids an Xbox or trainers. When it was Albion's turn, they declared that as they loved him most, he would have the finest island of all, which – let's be frank here – was terrible parenting.

Now, in order to decide which island was supreme among the atolls of Earth, a mermaid (and merman) council gathered. And after a bit of merm-people debate, it was decreed that Albion would become the king of Samothea – a viridescent jewel at the very edge of the world. And thence having taken possession of it, he narcissistically dubbed it "Albion" and everything went swimmingly until he fell out with the Herakles (Hercules in Roman mythology), who killed him in a duel, presumably to the quiet satisfaction of Albion's neglected siblings.

Subsequently, the land was inhabited by giants of unknown pedigree, until one day, the Trojan Prince Brutus happened to be passing by, espied the island of Albion and decided to make it his own. The giants, who had just been getting on with things doing whatever it is that giants do, were none too pleased about that and resolved to eat him. But while they were chopping up the veg and boiling the pot, Brutus tossed their leader off the white cliffs – near what is now the A20 dual carriageway at Dover – seized power and renamed the island "Britain" after himself.

And that was the start, but by no means the end, of British history.

Some years after the giant-tossing, wise King Lear had a spot of trouble with his daughters and the nation was divided into three, and shortly after that the Romans turned up and gave everyone heating, roads and viaducts.

Subsequently, King Arthur pulled a magic sword from a stone and did the whole knights of the round table thing. Around the same time, Hengist and Horsa pitched up, betrayed Vortigern and created Angle-land, which does what it says on the tin.

But now England was Saxon, they needed a memorial to the heroes of Ancient Britain who had died fighting them. So, after a brief tête-à-tête with some fairies, famed wizard Merlin led an expedition to Ireland where he gathered up stones known as the "Giant's Dance" and transported them, using mind magic, to ships. Later, they were put in a circle on Salisbury Plain as that fitting memorial to the heroes of Ancient Britain, which later still became known as Stonehenge.

After that, King Alfred fought off the Vikings and then made peace with them before burning cakes at a cowherder's cottage and getting beaten about the head for it by the man's wife, who didn't realise he was a king.

Alfred learned a valuable lesson from his baking failure. It showed that you needed to keep an eye on the small things as much as the bigger picture. And he was so grateful that he made the cowherder a bishop.

King Canute was likewise inspired to demonstrate kingship with practical examples, most famously when he nearly got drowned in the North Sea, proving that kings can no more control the tide than they can the currents of destiny.

Shortly after that, Harold took one in the eye for the team and the Plantagenets came and went.

Eventually the Tudors popped up and then the Stuarts – but they lost the Civil War to the autocrat Cromwell – before staging a fabulous Vegas-style comeback with Charles II in the role of Elvis, only with much bigger hair.

Bonnie Prince Charlie blinged-up in tartan was very Bonnie indeed (yes you now know otherwise, but stick with the script). America gained independence – and eventually the map was painted pink and Britain became the greatest place in history and ruler of all the waves – as had clearly been their destiny.

Not that the road thereafter was entirely smooth. Ungrateful "cow worshipping" Indians tried to put a spanner in the works by rising up, and the Boers got the notion that South Africa belonged to them, despite the British having painted the map pink already. But order was restored and everyone lived happily ever after just in time for Queen Victoria to die in 1901.

The End.

The source of this deeply peculiar history of Britain, which if anything I'm downplaying here, is an iconic children's book called *Our Island Story* by Henrietta (H.E) Marshall, first published in 1905.

This 500-page hardback, beautifully illustrated with bold watercolours by A. S. Forrest, takes readers on a ride through history from – well, Neptune to the Edwardian age, in a readable if slightly patronising tone. Aimed at children aged 7–12 it became a staple of middle-class and upper-class English children's shelves throughout the 20th century.

Following her smash-hit debut, Marshall went on to write 14 further children's histories, including *Our Empire Story* (1908) and *A History of Germany* (1913), but none surpassed the success of *Our Island Story*. The book remained in print until 1953, the year of the Queen's Coronation and a year before rationing ended.

In "respectable homes" during the 20th century, the tome was many children's first introduction to history. Or at least "British history", which then seemed to be the only history that mattered. The narrative is one of inevitable imperial destiny. An island founded by the gods and then honed by time and fate. Everything has a purpose. The neatly defined, curiously inexorable events add to and improve the whole. Like those cringey 1980s American sitcoms, every episode ends with people learning things. And Britain's ultimate destiny is never, not for one moment, doubted.

If my brief summary makes it all sound slightly mad, that's because to most modern eyes it is all rather Python-esque. In the immediate post-First World War era, when Victorian presumptions about Great Britain were getting called into question, it even invited some well-deserved ridicule, and is said to have inspired Sellar and Yeatman's far superior 1930 commentary *1066 and All That*, with its ever prescient "compulsory preface":

"History is not what you thought. It is what you can remember."

An insight far more resonant than Marshall's own intro that tells readers:

"You will find some stories that are not to be found in your school books – stories which wise people say are only fairy tales and not history. But it seems to me that they are part of Our Island Story, and ought not to be forgotten, any more than these stories about which there is no doubt."

Some of those "stories" are so jaw-droppingly nuts as to put Sellar and Yeatman in the shade. The stuff about Neptune and Brutus reads like Geoffrey of Monmouth after a night on acid and cider. Monmouth is clearly her source material for the first half of the book. Hengist and Horsa, Arthur, Merlin, Robin Hood and Neptune are fictional characters but they all appear as actual historical figures.

The rest is twisted, edited and expunged in much the same way that Fake Family Sagas hone bullshit family myths.

The tragedy of the Irish Potato Famine, an event still well within living memory when the book was written, is bizarrely sentimentalised – presumably with the aim of not making the British look like uncaring cads.

"Rich people sent money and food to the poor, starving Irish, but in spite of everything that was done, the misery was terrible," we are told.

And while Marshall does veer into slightly more nuanced corners – not least when explaining the inequities visited on Catholics prior to the Catholic Emancipation Act of 1829, there's an ever-present air of "but despite all of that they all lived happily ever after".

When William Wilberforce abolishes slavery for example, the poor old plantation owners are unhappy because after all:

"They had paid a great deal of money for their slaves, and it seemed unfair that they should be made to lose it all." But once "we" the taxpayers had kindly compensated them "at last, all difficulties were smoothed away."

Our Island Story sees events almost entirely through the prism of kings and (some) queens. That was not unusual at the time, but the presumption becomes embedded that "we" are best ruled by monarchs – even bad ones – and if they're not available, a mash-up of Greek and Roman gods.

Many chapters have been entirely plagiarised from Shakespeare.

Richard III is rendered as a full-on pantomime villain. The story of Henry IV is quite literally told in two parts and features lengthy extracts of speeches from Shakespeare's plays, as if they are the actual words of Prince Hal and his friends, written down by scribes at the time.

Some chapters dance about the truth of events with such elaborate dexterity, that, to the modern reader at least, they take on a broadly comic note. A personal favourite is the one on William IV, who as the third child of George III and Queen Charlotte was never meant to be king. Unfortunately, the lack of any other available heirs and the ailing health of both of his brothers pushed him ever closer to the throne and, in 1815, it was decided that the 50-year-old prince had better be prepared for the gig and found a wife just in case the other two died.

This posed a bit of a problem, because William had spent much of his adult life happily living "in sin" with an Irish actress called Dorothea Bland, who went by the stage name of Mrs Jordan.

Dorothea had had a spirited early life and succesful stage career. Born into a bohemian theatrical family, she trod the boards in Dublin from the age of 13 but was obliged to flee to England following a scandalous pregnancy in her late teens. Pitching up in London in 1785, aged 25, Dorothea took a lead role in the scandalous musical comedy *A Country Girl* at the Theatre Royal, Drury Lane, where her talent for comedy was spotted.

She went on to become a major star, taking leading parts in Shakespeare plays, including Viola in *Twelfth Night* and Ophelia in a celebrated production of *Hamlet*. She cemented her fame by appearing in a number of popular, but now largely forgotten, contemporary comedies. Witty, smart and unconventional, she met the future king, then still the Duke of Clarence, in 1790 and, by 1797, they were living together in Bushy House, a large country residence in Teddington. Together they had 10 children and lived in something akin to domestic bliss for 21 years until the pressure on her common law husband to find a "suitable wife" became too much and the couple were obliged to separate.

H.E. Marshall doesn't mention Mrs Jordan – or William's colourful and, by royal standards, happy life. Instead, we are told that the former naval officer did a cracking job on the throne because: "British people have always loved a sailor, so they loved their sailor king."

The chapter ends, tantalisingly, with the line:

"Many other things were done during the reign of William IV, which you will find more interesting when you grow older."

And the story swiftly moves on.

Later – as the British sail around the Earth imposing their rule, no question of their motives is raised. The message is clear. They are doing the world a favour by colonising it, even if their efforts are not always appreciated.

When the Indians mutiny, the swine need to be taught a lesson. Order is only restored when Queen Victoria takes the government of India "into her own hands". Which never actually happened.

The one line mentioning the at least half a million Aborigines who were living in Australia when Cook turned up dismisses them as a "sparse population of native people" – despite their numbers exceeding those of the Europeans until at least 1850. By suggesting there's just a couple of people there wandering about with spears, the uncomfortable truth is brushed under the carpet.

As for the Maoris, well just about the only noble thing they do is to accept British rule and sign the Treaty of Waitangi in 1840, which confiscated their lands, for which Queen Elizabeth II was later to apologise in 1995.

Black Africans get but a passing mention, when the "habit of stealing black people" (aka slavery) is once again extinguished by the British. The African continent gets eight dreary pages, which prattle on about the then very recent Boer War, without ever mentioning concentration camps, or actual black Africans, or the logic of it all. The moral is that however ghastly that war was, or indeed anything else – at least (white, English-speaking) people ended up being friends in the end.

And notions of a collective colonial endeavour are hammered home throughout:

"Australia lies quite at the other side of the world from Britain, and when it is day in the one it is night in the other," we are told.

"Yet the people in the two islands are friends and brothers, and ties of love draw them together across the ocean waves."

"Children's Bibles" of the Edwardian era simplified the narrative of Christianity, cut out all the boring bits and played up the fun side of miracles and crucifixions with nice pictures alongside. *Our Island Story* did much the same with British history.

As the century advanced, the book became something akin to a standard text on British history for many families, and later still, as the Empire crumbled, *Our Island Story* became a comfort blanket that reassured Britons of their place as the major protagonists in history. Like Neptune's son Albion, Britain may not have been the first-born Empire, but it was undoubtedly the best and most favoured.

Much of the British children's literature that followed H. E. Marshall's bestseller was imbued with the same spirit.

Not so long ago, even as we ate bland food, tried to start our British cars and wondered what a tiramisu was, British culture – and particularly children's culture – was essentially homogeneous. With just four television channels available even as late as the 1990s, most people tended to watch the same shows, listen to the same music and read the same stuff.

Well into the 1970s, some (mostly middle-class) parents, including my own, bought their offspring *Look and Learn* magazine. It had a small and declining circulation when I was reading it and eventually folded in 1982. By then, its reach was no more than a few thousand nerdy kids of predominantly affluent parents, but the magazine painted that same reassuring H. E. Marshall vision of Britain at the centre of things, with bright and alluring illustrations throughout.

The same model was apparent in the hugely successful and far more ubiquitous Ladybird books that dominated children's literature in the late 20th century. These beautifully illustrated books, which sought to entertain and inform children, sold in their millions in their 1960s and 1970s heyday.

"Ladybirds" came in an iconic 11.5 x 18-cm hardback format and were read by practically everyone of school age from the 1960s onwards, not least because the "Key Words" series was used in primary schools in England and Wales to teach children to read. Peter and Jane – the breakout stars of those 36 editions – set the tone for the publications and, by dint of their pervasiveness, established a sort of standard for what Englishness was meant to be.

The world of Peter and Jane was safe, white and eternal.

Peter and James's social class was kept deliberately and curiously indistinct, but the family were otherwise imbued with a sort of idealised, utopian Englishness. They lived in an alternative post-war Neverland where everything was bright and clean, ordered and functional. Daddy smokes a pipe and drives to work in a shiny car that never breaks down; Mummy goes brightly about her day without the need for Valium, 40 Benson & Hedges, a midday gin or fear of impending nuclear war.

Glue-sniffing punks, race riots and the three-day week don't get a look-in.

At weekends, the family take trips to the coast with a shopping basket in bright, clean trains, untouched by graffiti and ripped-up seats, which always run on time and never break down.

Ladybird books were affordable. For years the price remained steady at 2 shillings and 6 pence – and 15p post-decimalisation. That's equivalent to about £2.50 in 2021. They were dished out as Sunday school prizes, picked up with pocket money – part of everyday life, essentially.

Beyond the world of Peter and Jane's nuclear family lay a broader horizon of hundreds of other Ladybird titles.

There was a nature series and a hugely popular set of "Learnabout" books, which taught kids among other things, magic tricks, knitting and how to use a magnifying glass to start a fire. There was also a "People at work" series that celebrated firemen, fishermen, policemen and nurses. Intentionally or not, these books hammered home that same "order of things" narrative that dominated *Look and Learn* and H. E. Marshall's *Our Island Story*. The policemen are stolid chaps on bicycles – or sometimes on motorbikes or in cars. They, like all men, are dependable, stoic, approachable. Women are in the kitchen. Or carrying baskets. And when allowed into the workplace it is merely to type, or in the case of "Women Police Constables", to reunite children with lost teddy bears.

A lot of people bought into it. A lot of people still do. Many a modern nostalgic will hark back to the days of "trustworthy plods on bicycles", who were never too busy to tell you the time.

In fact, the 1950s, 1960s and 1970s would actually witness a rash of high-profile cases against "bent coppers" who beat out confessions from innocent people and committed multiple miscarriages of justice. In 1950, the Metropolitan Police's handling of the case of Timothy Evans, a Welsh painter and decorator wrongly accused of murdering his wife Beryl and infant child Geraldine, led to him being hanged, despite him being completely innocent.

Sadly, Evans was far from the only victim of wrongful execution by the state. In 1952, Mahmood Mattan, a Somali-born fisherman, was arrested, charged with murder and executed on the testimony of one witness in Cardiff after the police bungled his case.

In 1957, the entire Brighton force fell under suspicion of bribery and racketeering. In 1976, the "Birmingham Six" were wrongly convicted and sentenced to life imprisonment for an IRA bombing campaign in the city which had nothing to do with the six men.

But there were no Ladybird books of police corruption. No "miscarriages of justice" series.

Bobbies on the beat in the Ladybird world were deemed to be incorruptible and dependable. Always there to tell you the time, just as firemen were permanently on hand to rescue kittens from trees and put out the fires you had just learned how to start with a magnifying glass in the Ladybird "Learnabout" series.

Fishermen were brave, handsome chaps in yellow oilskin raincoats – out in all weathers to catch a little fishy for a little dishy.

The map in the back of the Ladybird *The Fisherman* book shows "the North Atlantic Fishing Grounds" and seems to imply that the entire swathe of ocean belongs to Britain. British fishermen catching British fish in the British seas that Britain ruled.

Inside we are told that "some fishermen go to sea to catch whales" and that whalers have harpoon guns with bombs in the end of their spears:

"When the harpoonist sees a whale, he shoots a harpoon at it... the bomb explodes and quickly kills the whale."

Yes, even slaughtering whales with exploding shells was heroic, back when British sailors were doing it in yellow coats and big jumpers.

But, undoubtedly, the most lingering influence of the Ladybird books – and certainly the one that skewed two or more generations' understanding of history – came in the form of the "Adventures from history" series. That list consisted of 42 books covering the lives of 36 great men, one group of cave men and six token women.

Those lucky women were Queen Victoria, Cleopatra, Elizabeth I, prison reformer Elizabeth Fry, Joan of Arc and Florence Nightingale.

No black or Asian men or women made the cut. Cleopatra might have been an African queen, but there is an ongoing debate about her ethnicity. She was descended from a fairly incestuous line of Macedonian Greeks, which some argue makes her white, but matters are not entirely clear cut as nobody knows who her mother was and it is therefore possible that she could have been black. There is some evidence that she was the first in her line to speak Egyptian, which has given some weight to the suggestion that her mother may have been Egyptian herself. But the reasons for learning a language are many and the debate is inconclusive.

In Ladybird illustrations, Cleopatra is most certainly white and bears more than a passing resemblance to Elizabeth Taylor, who so famously played her in a 1963 Hollywood film.

Thirty of the history series books were written by one man. The grandly named Lawrence du Garde Peach OBE, MA, PhD, DLitt. who, after serving as an intelligence officer, wrote for *Punch* before becoming an established writer. Most of his work was on *Children's Hour*, the pre-war, daily 60-minute entertainment slot for young people on radio, and a number of largely forgotten films and plays. His final script in 1943 was a feel-good wartime caper, *Get Cracking*, starring ukulele superstar George Formby, which told the story of a Home Guard unit trying to get its hands on a machine gun. The film is remarkably similar in mood and style to *Dad's Army*, which came 25 years later. It is set in an idealised, rural England of thatched cottages and sleepy market towns and features people trying to get by and win the war. Soft-core, commercial propaganda that must have delighted the Ministry of Information.

Du Garde Peach's books played to that same mood. History is "Marshall-ed". It revolves around notable men (mostly) doing great things and baddies trying to undermine them. Many of the stories of kings seem, once again, to have been lifted directly from Shakespeare, or perhaps even *Our Island Story*.

Walter Raleigh throws his cloak in the puddle for Queen Elizabeth – despite the event being made up by an unreliable 17th-century cleric called Thomas Fuller. Famed minstrel Blondel gets his lute out to find his master, the imprisoned Richard the Lionheart, despite the story being fiction.

Even bad kings are somehow good because they enable the good kings who come later.

Peach indulges in many historical falsehoods. In the Bonnie Prince Charlie book (he seems to have been a big fan), we are told that:

"The Duke of Cumberland, with a true German's preference for comfort, occupied Aberdeen."

So the Duke is rendered German, despite being born and bred in London, and Charlie is somehow Scottish, despite actually being born in Italy to a Polish mother and resident for most of his life in France.

The dodgy history doesn't end there.

In the *Charles II* book, we learn that the Stuart king was "very poor" during his exile and that in later life "he used to look back with amusement on the times when he had even had to do his own cooking." Imagine.

It's not really true. A king's poverty is not a normal person's poverty. Charles lived in some luxury during his exile and rent-free, first in The Hague and later in a chateau at St Germain, with all other expenses paid.

Apart from the six titles they get to themselves, women are absent, unless they're queens in lieu of kings, having babies or dying. As with H. E. Marshall, some artful dodging is done. In the *Charles II* book, Nell Gwynn, his lover, mother of two of his children and one of the most fascinating people of the age, gets just one mention as "a well-known actress of the time".

There is no Ladybird book of the great 17th-century play-wright, poet, novelist and spy Aphra Behn, who rose above considerable contemporary obstacles to become one of the leading writers of her era. Her fame in life assured her a final resting place in Westminster Abbey in 1689, but, unlike her near contemporaries, her reputation was swiftly marginalised and forgotten like so many others.

Black people are rendered child-like onlookers (or savages) while great white men like David Livingstone (he was 5 foot 8, though not in the pictures) strut about making Africa better. The blanket whiteness of the entire series raised eyebrows even in the 1970s and, as their sales declined, Ladybird scrambled to render the books less imperial and partisan.

As the 1980s progressed, the Ladybirds and their fellow travel-lers did seek to evolve. By 1980, *Look and Learn* had taken a boldly Thucydidean plunge and, in the last two years of its imprint, the magazine ran a series entitled "What Really Happened", which sought to debunk fake history. But it was too little too late. Very few people were reading it by then and anyway, the damage had already been done. Most of us don't question the history lessons of childhood. We go through life for the most part believing what we were told.

The ubiquitous British children's literature of the 20th century undoubtedly had a huge and indelible impact on the psyche of the nation.

The false Eden embedded in Marshall, Ladybird and *Look and Learn* conjured up a Camelot of thatched cottages and perfect children where everything was neatly defined and where everyone knew their place. Britain was a land of great and decent men, of bobbies on the beat, loyal wives and happy fishermen – and the lie embedded itself in the minds of generations, like a parasitic worm. It was fantasy. But it was a beguiling fantasy and one that was later to come back and bite.

* * *

In 2010, 12 years after the closure of the Loughborough Ladybird printing factory, the Conservative Party returned to power, with their Lib Dem coalition partners, after 13 years in the political wilderness.

They came bearing a kinder and more compassionate conservatism. One that encouraged us to hug hoodies and worry about the environment. But beneath the veneer and spin was an agenda.

In the minds of many 21st-century Conservatives, there was much to do to right the wrongs of over a decade of progressiveness and general do-goodery. Michael Gove, the new UK Secretary of State for Education was, in particular, on a mission. As the former journalist unpacked his pencil case, he declared his intention to stamp out the invidious trends infecting modern teaching. Gove was particularly aggrieved with history lessons, which he and his libertarian allies on the Conservative right, believed lay at the root of so much of society's ills. There was a prevailing sense among Britain's right-wing think tanks that "proper history" had been ruined. Bearded, sandal-wearing lefties had upended Glorious Albion with their pernicious source-checking, materials and facts. It was time to return to the proper history, where great British men, in pastel colours, "discovered" African waterfalls, while grateful "natives" looked on.

Gove thought that children were being taught the wrong sort of history – a different kind to the one in the H. E. Marshall books. Stories that, frankly, made Britain look a bit bad. It was ruining everyone's fun and making the film *Zulu* look racist.

It was time to put things right.

The first victim of the cull was to be "world history". I mean, who needed such a thing when everyone knew that *Our Island Story* and *Our Empire Story* were the only bits that mattered? Hadn't everyone read their Ladybirds? Were they ashamed of the Empire? Were they unaware of all the great things "we" British had done before any of us were even born?

Gove sought a return to a Ladybird-like order, in which the timeline from Magna Carta to the end of the Second World War was not so much taught – as preached.

Some of the work had been done already. Five years earlier right-wing think tank Civitas had launched a campaign to get Marshall's deeply odd book back into print and on to school library shelves – and to that end they had been aggressively grooming various friends in high places.

On 20th July 2007, another think tanker, the historian Tristram Hunt, deliberately name-checked *Our Island Story* on *BBC Breakfast* and sales immediately rocketed, much to the delight of Civitas and its supporters.

Daily Telegraph readers, Gove-ite Tories and nascent Brex-iters from all sides adored the notion of the "Our Island Story

Movement", a term coined by the think tank to describe the ever more cultish mood. The book would right the slanderous accusations against the Empire and reassert Britain's place at the centre of things. Soon it was being gifted to schools and snapped up by nostalgic grandparents to pass on "the proper history" of Britain to the next generation. "The Movement" held writing competitions in which Year 6 and Year 7 pupils were asked to pen essays on how "British history had touched their lives". The winners received a tour of the Houses of Parliament with Labour MP Frank Field, who was later to become a key pro-Brexit figure.

None of this had anything to do with the teaching of actual history. It was about seizing the narrative. A counter-offensive to the progressive Blair years. These *Ladybird Libertarians* – raised on fake history themselves – were seeking to reimpose a nostalgic picture-book vision of the nation's past. It didn't matter that the history itself was wrong; what mattered was that people believed it to be true.

Like the breeze in the *Golden Hinde*'s sails, the wind was now firmly behind them. On coming to office, an on-message PM Dave Cameron cited *Our Island Story* as his favourite book in what was now a clear, cynical and concerted ploy to embrace a fictional past and to actively ignore truth and critical thinking.

Gove's then top advisor, Dominic Cummings, professed to be a fan of Thucydides. But, curiously, everything Gove, Cummings and their department did went directly against the teaching of the Athenian scholar. The past was reset to the cheering false narrative. The Ladybird Libertarians had taken back control of history.

Civitas later had a huge influence on the Vote Leave campaign and Britain's decision to Leave the European Union; none of this was unrelated. The EU posed an existential threat to the narrative of Britain being a major power and one of the big players in history because in the eyes of the true Brexit believers, throwing in our lot with Germans, Belgians and French people reduced "who" "we" were: a proud and independent "sovereign" nation. At the heart of that debate lay the same battle between the forces of progress and reason and those of deluded, sentimental, reactionary fiction.

One curious aspect of Brexit was that a number of significant Vote Leave Conservative politicians and influencers who forged its thinking had grown up abroad. Notable amongst them was Peruvian born Dan (later Lord) Hannan who became known as "the brains behind Brexit". Hannan once wrote that he had been raised to believe in a Britain that was a "byword for correctness, integrity and punctuality" but when he arrived here in the late 1970s, he found something altogether different. Late 70s Britain was failing badly. London and the great cities were shells of their former selves, still thick with soot and war damage. Industry was declining. Nothing worked. Nobody wore bowler hats. The nation and the capital looked nothing like the Ladybird books at all.

Hannan's tutor at Oxford, Roger Scruton, summed up his student's cognitive dissonance thus: "The expat mentality is [of] belonging to the old country and the inability to accept that it is changed beyond repair."

And when reading Hannan's book *How We Invented Freedom*, which formed much of the intellectual case for Brexit, the Utopian world of Ladybird books and H. E. Marshall never seem to be that far away. Hannan and many of his fellow Brexit cultists harked back to the Empire and a belief that Britain's place lay at the front of things in a partnership with Australia, Canada and the Commonwealth. It didn't matter that those countries showed no desperation to get on board with the project and were all doing "very well, thank you" without Britain bossing them about. To Hannanists, the British Empire was a good thing and people would soon leap at the chance of being part of Empire Part 2 once we came knocking at the door. That arrogance is summed up in the words of Boris Johnson who, in a 2016 *Spectator* article wrote:

"The problem [with Africa] is not that we were once in charge, but that we are not in charge anymore."

Cosplaying Edwardian MP and fellow Old Etonian Jacob Rees-Mogg went even further and wrote an ersatz *Great Men of History* in 2019 titled *The Victorians*, which suggested that 12 19th-century British male titans had built the modern world and that, frankly, the world had been better off for it.

Brexit's conceit, for the likes of Mogg and Hannan, was predicated on the myths embedded by those children's libraries. The idea that Britain's time at the top had been the best time in history and that those days would come again if we left the EU. "Europe" was holding us back, but once unchained, we could simply take up where we left off. This Ladybird Libertarianism was not rooted in economic or political sense or sanity, but rather in a fantastical and deluded belief in a British Neverland of order and honest bobbies, where Britannia quite literally ruled the fish. It didn't matter that this Arcadia had never existed. It mattered that people believed that it had. And that they'd willingly vote to get back there.

* * *

Mythologising the past, as we have seen already, is common to all countries. Just as all nations put themselves at the centre of the maps, so many long ago calculated the power of the narrative-driven children's book to weave a compelling lie about their nations. As we shall see later on, the Kim dynasty in North Korea calculated that children's literature was a means to indoctrinate the populace from the cradle up.

The Wiener Holocaust Library contains a catalogue of Nazi children's history books with bright illustrations and merry children waving flags, which if you were to half blink could come from almost any contemporary European nation of the 1930s or even later.

In America too, literature long conspired to weave a nationalist collective narrative. It's there in its first instance in Washington Irving's hagiography of Christopher Columbus, but US children's literature hammered the point home.

In 1917 H.E. Marshall did for the USA what she had done for Great Britain and penned *This Country of Ours*, in which she told the story of America from the Vikings to Woodrow Wilson's triumphant entry into the Great War – which was happening even as the ink dried on the paper.

As with all of her other works, the book is dedicated to a (possibly fictional) child, in this case "Peggy Stewardson" to whom she says:

"It is a book, I hope, which when you lay it down will make you say, 'I'm glad that I was born an American. I'm glad that I can salute the Stars and Stripes as my flag.'

This Country of Ours sets out a destiny narrative every bit as compelling as the one in *Our Island Story*. This is a tale of "paradise found". Big "American Dream" stuff.

Having got Columbus out of the way, American history really gets going when the English turn up in the early 17th century.

Marshall seems very taken with "swaggering" Captain John Smith, who is soon being saved from death by the Native American Pocahontas, who has to keep outwitting her "untrustworthy" father Powhatan to help the English and save their lives.

Actually, the well-worn story of Pocahontas saving Smith was probably made up by the captain himself, who seems to have plagiarised it from a popular Scottish ballad, "Young Beichan" about a Lord who is rescued by a Turkish princess. Smith seems to have been fond of the song because in his best-selling memoir he frequently claimed that he was saved from certain death by all manner of "native girls".

In Marshall's telling, the story of Pocahontas, whose real name was actually Amonute, is one of instinctive nativist innocence and purity. The beautiful girl defies the savagery of her birth to welcome Christian settlers to America and, in doing so, legitimises what follows.

Almost as soon as the English arrive, she is on their side and warning them against her terrible father who "would kill me" if he knew what she was doing.

The story becomes nothing short of a parable of Empire building. There is inherent raw good in America and Pocahontas represents it, but it needs the first white Virginians and later the Pilgrim Fathers to untap the potential.

Her subsequent kidnapping and ransom is downplayed and her forced conversion to Christianity is reworked as a necessity so that she might marry John Rolfe: "For was this beautiful savage not a heathen? That difficulty was, however, soon overcome. For Pocahontas made no objection to becoming a Christian," Marshall informs the reader.

Marshall is clearly uninterested in Pocahontas and her fellow people, beyond what they represent in the white European narrative of American history. Events are seen through the eyes of Smith and his companions; the unspoken assumption is that America is really theirs and, while the native tribes are useful in bringing them corn, really they have simply got in the way of things.

The Powhatan (the name of the indigenous people as well as the name of Pocahontas's father) were no loin-clothed savages, running about whooping and firing bows and arrows before retreating to their teepees with scalps round their necks. They were farmers and hunters, living settled lives on the Eastern seaboard of the North American continent in what we nowadays call Virginia. When the English arrived in 1607, at least 30 tribes were united under the rule of Powhatan in a complex federation.

They were also very far from unwelcoming. They extended extraordinary hospitality to the strange people who had come to their land and even helped them through the first winters, as their crops failed and as they struggled to adjust to their climate and survive.

If Smith is to be believed, then Amonute-Pocahontas even taught them how to sow tobacco, inadvertently sealing the doom of her people, along with millions of history's smokers.

Amonute-Pocahnontas, as far as we can tell from the reliable and available evidence, was a curious and intelligent woman. Her kindness, like that of her people, was to be repaid with maltreatment and quite probably rape at the hands of the English settlers. She was groomed and used by the English and subsequently paraded in England, where she died at Gravesend in 1617 aged 23.

Marshall's American book, like its prequel, wasn't big on nuance. It was flattering of white America, which ensured it remained in print for decades. Its tone chimes with a lot of contemporary American children's literature and in particular *Hazen's Elementary History of the United States*, first published in 1903, which was to become a popular standard of American classrooms and young Americans' book shelves in the 20th century.

It used to be said that Americans did everything bigger – and to dive into Hazen is to see that this applies to bad takes on history as well.

"Six hundred years ago, the whole continent of America was unknown to the white man…" we are told, but familiar only "… to the copper-colored races that hunted in its forests."

We're informed that "The Indians, who in the 15th century were the only inhabitants of America, were a savage people" distinct from the "brave English captains like Drake and Raleigh" and the "English Admiral" John Hawkins.

Both Drake and Hawkins were in fact slave traders, but that unsavoury detail is glossed over until, in 1619, when we are told that the Jamestown settlers had brought enslaved people with them, who the settlers: "… found ….so helpful in raising tobacco that more were brought in, and slavery became part of our history."

Slavery repackaged then as a sort of voluntary community service.

And so it goes on. Page after page of spin, usually with an accompanying picture of a man of note.

By 1831, we are learning about "Abolitionists" who:

"stirred up people by means of lectures and pamphlets. Some of their publications advised the slaves to kill their masters in order to gain their freedom."

It is true that the debate between violent and non-violent resistance did take place, but that same argument has dogged all freedom movements throughout the ages. Very few enslaved or oppressed peoples through history have gained their liberty as a product of non-violent revolution or insurrection. There are hardly any examples before the 1980s. Gandhi sought Indian independence through passive resistance and peaceful means, but violence still played a part, and the partition that followed at the end of British rule still saw millions killed and displaced. A handful of bloodless revolutions including the "Carnation Revolution" in Portugal in 1974 and the "People Power Revolution" in the Philippines in 1986, which removed President Marcos from power, took place in the post-war years. But it is not until the overthrow of Communist dictatorships in central and eastern Europe in 1989 that we see non-violent movements overthrow oppressors.

In the era of decolonisation, the people of many nations were "gifted" their independence by the British and others and often peacefully, but that was only because the former imperial powers were willing to surrender power.

American slave owners were not willing to do that and maintained their tyranny using the perpetual threat and practice of torture and barbarity. It is not surprising that such brutality stirred counter-violence. In August 1831, Nat Turner, an enslaved man in Southampton County, Virginia, led a rebellion. Turner believed God had sent him to deliver his people and became convinced that a total solar eclipse was a sign from heaven that he should act. On the night of 21st August, he led an insurrection against his slave masters and in the ensuing violence, 55 white people were killed.

The rebellion was ultimately unsuccessful. After going on the run for six weeks, Nat and his fellow rebels were captured and hanged. Immediately, the white apologists of slavery set to work writing articles and books that essentially went: "Look at these savages – and people argue that they should be free."

The incident made the Southern plantation owners fearful, and further tyranny was visited on the estimated three million slaves who lived under their rule. Slavery had been abolished in the North in 1804, but the reliance on free labour in the South and a culture of white supremacy meant that Southern states only hardened their position and doubled down in defending their right to oppress other people for financial gain.

Over the next 30 years, the issue came to dominate and divide the US political landscape. In 1854, the Democrats passed the Kansas-Nebraska Act, which allowed new states to decide on a basis of "popular sovereignty" if they wanted to have slavery in their territories. And a political crisis ensued.

By 1861, the new Republican Party had been formed, largely in response to the Act and the subsequent political fall-out. The Republicans were a coalition. For much of the 19th century US politics had been dominated by the Whig and Democrat parties. The Whigs were what might today be called "small c Conservatives" who stood for social order and religious do-goodery, but having provided four Presidents, the party collapsed in 1856. Out of it came the Republican movement in which the remnant Whigs teamed up with the Free Soilers, a group of social reformers, who were both ideologically and economically opposed to slavery. That economic case argued that slavery was unfair – not only to its victims, but also to white working men and entrepreneurs in the North who couldn't compete with all that free labour. As long as slavery existed, the South had an unfair competitive advantage.

In 1861 an election was held, and the new party won.

Enter stage left Abraham Lincoln, the first Republican Party President and arguably America's most admired and respected historical political figure.

Hazen sums it up in *Elementary History*, with the calm reserve of a screaming Beatles fan spotting John Lennon in the street:

"He was almost unknown to most of the nation, but now it seems to us as if God had raised him for the times."

However you spin it or seek to diss it, Lincoln's story undoubtedly epitomises the American Dream. His life was quite literally a rags to riches fairytale. Born in a one-room log cabin in the backwoods of Kentucky, he never received more than a year of schooling in his life and was almost entirely self-educated.

From the age of seven, his parents became "squatters", setting up a crude shelter on public land in southwestern Indiana before they eventually replaced it with a permanent cabin and bought the surrounding land. His mother died when he was nine. His beloved elder sister when he was 18.

Lincoln spent much of his early life helping his father run the smallholding and yet, despite it all, he educated himself and rose above poverty to become leader of the USA.

There is much to admire about Lincoln and much to question. He was a politician after all. But Hazen doesn't hold back as he goes full Ladybird Libertarian on the tale. And so, the familiar story of a great man, imbued with a noble spirit, taking on the South and leading the North to victory is trotted out.

It's not a "good and baddy narrative" though. In both Hazen and Marshall's books, the Confederate generals of the South get a surprisingly good press, with what Donald Trump might have called "very fine people on both sides" fighting out the war to its denouement.

Marshall describes General Robert E. Lee (the Confederate military leader) as "a noble, Christian gentleman" and a "great soldier", tapping into a broader myth of "he wasn't so bad really", which still pervades around the Southern military strategist. That narrative, that runs deep, suggests that Lee was a kindly Christian bloke who wanted everyone to be friends and that he only led the South to war to bring everyone back together.

However, this rather ignores his key role leading an army in a war that killed an estimated 618,000 people to protect rich white landowners' rights to keep slaves in chains.

Modern-day defenders of Lee – and particularly the ones who want to keep up the many statues later erected to him – have even claimed that he opposed slavery, but that case rests entirely on one carefully quoted 1856 letter, in which he actually claims that he only backs abolition because: "...it is a greater evil to the white man than to the black race."

Truth and examination have an unnerving habit of taking the shine off the halos of "Great Men of History" – and Old Abe is not the secular saint history would have us believe.

Yes, he led the North into a war whose principal aim was to liberate slaves. But his actual views on black people drifted with the times and his political ends. Because Lincoln, after all, was a politician not Jesus.

In that famous speech, on the eve of the Battle of Gettysburg, in 1863, Lincoln stated that the USA had been "conceived in Liberty, and dedicated to the proposition that all men are created equal", but for most of his life, he didn't really believe that himself.

In 1858, Lincoln stood against incumbent Democratic Senator Stephen Douglas in the Illinois Senatorial elections and challenged him to seven debates on the extension of slavery into the new territories. Douglas was an established figure and advocate of "popular sovereignty", the idea that white male Americans should be able to decide whether their territory and the other people in it should join the union as a slave state or as a Free State.

In the fourth debate in Charleston on Saturday, 18th September 1858, Lincoln said that he was: "not, nor ever have been, in favor of bringing about in any way the social and political equality of the white and black races."

He added that he opposed mixed race marriages, the black vote and the rights of black men to serve on juries. Uncomfortably, Lincoln also believed, very firmly, in "repatriating" black people to Africa.

In 1822, The American Colonization Society had begun sending free slaves "back" to Liberia, supposedly an African free state, but in truth a US colony that had been established on the west coast of Africa for the purpose.

The enterprise was a disaster. Freed slaves were no more "African" than Abraham Lincoln, whose ancestors had left Europe in the 17th century, was English, Irish or German.

Dispatched to a place they had never known and a country their ancestors had not come from on the assumption that they were naturally "African" because they were black – was not just rooted in stupidity but racist notions of what and who black people were.

Liberia was a disaster. There were clashes between the freed slaves and the local population, and in a depressing turn of events, black Americans – known as Americo-Liberians – became the colonisers and oppressors. The indigenous tribes-people of the region were not granted the same rights as Americo-Liberians until the 20th century.

Lincoln was a strong advocate of Liberian "repatriation" and broader "black colonisation". He hoped, in essence, to get the majority of black people out of America and these views understandably enraged black activists and abolitionists.

The Republican president saw the end of slavery as a moral issue, but this did not mean, at least for most of his life, that he viewed black people as the equals of whites any more than he wanted them in white America.

He was also a politician who shaped his message to suit the mood of the times. He was not an abolitionist. He thought change should come gradually and when he did eventually come around to the idea of extending suffrage in 1865 – he only wanted it given to black soldiers who had fought in the American Civil War.

Such nuances and paradoxes don't get so much as a nod in Hazen or Marshall. Their *children's histories*, like much of broader US history, conspired to exorcise black people from the story and elevate and bowdlerise the "great white men" who enabled it. Black liberation was another triumph of kindly, patrician "white people".

The great Republican social reformer, abolitionist and orator Frederick Douglass, who was also one of the first American politicians to back women's suffrage, certainly believed Lincoln was instinctively racist. And that was in spite of being a great admirer of the president.

In an extraordinary speech at the unveiling of the Freedmen's Memorial to black slaves, on 14th April 1876, Douglass – who was black – reminded his white audience, that Lincoln's motives had first and foremost been those of a "white president" who was "entirely devoted to the welfare of white men."

The Freedmen's Memorial hammers home visually what Hazen and Marshall put in their children's books.

Lincoln, the paternalistic and benevolent master, stands grandly above a cowering black man, dressed in rags, like some great religious figure granting him the gift of liberty. It is patronising, offensive and of course makes no acknowledgement of the role black people themselves played in the civil war. Abolition is "the white man's gift" given on white man's terms.

To be black is to be portrayed as being part of a homogenous mass of savages and victims whose destiny lies in the hands of their white masters for good or bad.

No Ladybird books were ever written about Douglass, nor does he get a mention in Hazen or Marshall. Nor did children's literature of the 20th century recognise the 200,000 black soldiers and sailors of the Northern Union Army who fought in the civil war. Despite facing bigotry from their own side, these men were engaged in the battles of Petersburg, Port Hudson and Nashville. By the war's end, 25 black servicemen had performed actions that would later earn them the Medal of Honor, the US's highest gallantry award.

While there are hundreds of biographies and films about Lincoln, there are none of William Jackson, a slave in the home of Confederate President Jefferson Davis, who at incredible personal risk gathered intelligence right in the heart of Davis's home. Davis was too arrogant and racist to realise that his "coachman" Jackson was listening to everything and making notes. In late 1861 Jackson escaped across the lines and provided high-quality intelligence on battle plans and supply lines. His contribution and that of many others, including the likes of Robert Smalls, the US's first black Congressman, were forgotten, deliberately, even as the Civil War narrative was weaved in children's books and the broader imagination.

And it wasn't just men.

Neither Marshall nor Hazen make mention of Harriet Tubman, perhaps the most famous black American to have taken part in the Civil War. Born a slave in the early 19th century, Tubman was so brutalised by her abusive captor (her slave master) that she was left with life-changing injuries. She eventually escaped her plantation and, having made it to Philadelphia, set up an escape line that enabled her parents and siblings and an estimated 70 other people to make it to the North.

During the American Civil War, she spied behind Confederate lines and later became a businesswoman and farmer before, belatedly, becoming renowned for her daring exploits. Her story has become a welcome part of the civil war story and in 2015, following a nationwide poll, it was even announced that her face would be put on the $20 bill, replacing Andrew Jackson, the seventh president.

Donald Trump, then campaigning to be president himself, declared the move "pure political correctness", telling NBC's *Today* show that Tubman should be put on the $2 bill instead. A note which, tellingly, no longer exists.

On becoming president, Trump and his administration deliberately dragged their feet on the issue of the $20 bill. Following his inauguration in January 2021, Joe Biden immediately moved to revive the idea and put her on the note in time for the bicentenary of her birth in 2022.

Harriet Tubman has become an icon in the US and a role model for many well beyond the African-American community. But even her story cannot escape the suffocating grasp of fake history. Dishonesty and exaggeration can affect all sides in the political discourse, and in the process truth can get distorted.

As Tubman's posthumous reputation grew, her narrative was pulled, stretched, rewritten and appropriated, much like that of any other great hero of history. Her best-known quote: "I could have saved thousands – if only I'd been able to convince them they were slaves" was trotted out during Hillary Clinton's presidential campaign of 2016 and has graced a million internet memes.

Unfortunately, there's no evidence she ever said it, and many African-American scholars have pointed out that the quote itself is a dangerous red herring. Rice University history professor, Dr Caleb McDaniel, writing on his blog in 2016, argued that:

"The corollary comes uncomfortably close to the paternalistic idea that those who somehow 'choose' not to be freed or don't 'know' they are slaves must tacitly consent to their own exploitation."

All of history's protagonists, good and bad, can be used by the opposing side to prove a point, but fake history is fake history. Just because "your" side are doing it doesn't make it right.

In his biography of Tubman, American academic Milton Sernett argues that she has become "America's most malleable icon", with all that entails. Certainly, the details of Tubman's life have frequently been blown out of all proportion with the number of people she is said to have saved frequently being exaggerated to well in excess of 300. A purported bounty of $40,000 supposedly put on her head is most probably a fiction.

Human beings need heroes. So, ordinary politicians become outsized gods, brave women escaping slavery become wonder women, and the blemishes and human failings of "great people" and the complexity of their stories get ironed out as their deeds get blown out of all proportion.

Black history and the lives of black women and men were long deliberately edited out of the civil war's history because they did not fit the mould of how white people wanted to remember events. That determined omission disgracefully traduced black Americans to onlookers in their own struggle and not "proper Americans" or even "proper human beings", but victims to be pitied. As the truth of events belatedly becomes part of mainstream history, it's essential that it is held to the same high standards of academic rigour and discipline as everything else.

Tubman's story, like all "great people" narratives of history needs to be properly examined. There can be no "free passes" in history.

Ladybird, Marshall, Hazen and others sought to elevate ordinary mortals to the status of gods to serve an agenda and to forge myths of American and British exceptionalism. That storybook legacy seeps deeply into the mindsets of political thinking and still defines the nations whose politicians and people devoured their books. Of course, it's possible to dismiss the literary detritus of childhood as "stories" and nothing more. Who after all would be stupid enough to believe in Merlin and his magical erection at Stonehenge?

What harm is there in the tales of Arthur and his sword, or even the reassuringly straightforward legend of good old Abraham Lincoln freeing black people from their bonds for purely altruistic reasons?

Well, the answer is *a great deal*. Truth matters, otherwise, like discarded munitions of armies, the bad history of youth can cause carnage many years after the storybooks have been put away. Out of myths great lies can prosper, vast conceits can be propagated and whole nations can go to war.

CHAPTER EIGHT

HITLER WAS A FAILED ARTIST

The power of creating your own mythology

It's 4:19 a.m. on 8th August 1918 and in the German trenches close to the River Somme, East of Amiens, thousands of men are still asleep. Overnight, a thick fog has descended and hugs the dugouts like a thick woollen blanket. The waxing crescent of the summer moon and the stars in the empty summer night sky above are invisible. Whispering sentries try to keep watch. But they can see no further than the sights at the ends of their rifles.

Little has happened along this part of the line for months. Little is anticipated. But one minute later, and all that has changed.

At 4:20, the French artillery opens up. Roused from their sleep, German soldiers stumble through the fog and chaos. The rumble of engines and creaking metal fuels the terror. Dozens of British Whippet tanks are advancing at speed, across no man's land, spraying bullets from their Hotchkiss heavy machine guns.

The German army has been taken by complete surprise. By day's end 30,000 men will be dead, captured or wounded. This is the start of the Hundred Days Offensive and the beginning of the end-game of the Great War.

Over the next two months, the unrelenting Allied advance continues. By 28th September the Central Powers have been pushed back to the Canal du Nord on the Hindenburg Line, just 24 miles from the German border.

Among the Canadians, Australians, New Zealanders, Belgians, French, American, Siamese (Thai) and Portuguese forces making up the Allied advance are the British 5th Battalion, Duke of Wellington's Regiment (West Riding) and in amongst its ranks is a private by the name of Henry Tandey, a 27-year-old former boiler attendant, from Leamington Spa.

Tandey is a battle-hardened, professional soldier. Twice wounded in the course of the war, he has seen action at every major engagement on the Western Front from Ypres, to the Somme, to Passchendaele. And despite his quiet demeanour and self-deprecating manner, he is a bona fide hero.

By Armistice, on 11th November 1918, he will have been mentioned in dispatches five times and won the Distinguished Conduct Medal and Military Medal. Today, he will go one better and be awarded the highest medal for valour in the British Army, the Victoria Cross.

On that September morning, the Duke of Wellington's Regiment overrun the strategically important village of Marcoing, east of Cambrai and by lunch-time have control of the bridge. Tandey and his comrades are securing their positions in the late September sunshine when suddenly, from across the canal to the north, the German Army counter-attacks.

Hundreds of well-trained, highly motivated Prussian Guards storm into the village, back across the bridge, and overwhelm the battalion's forward positions.

Tandey holds no rank, but takes charge anyway. Soon he is leading a charge on a German machine gun and knocking it out. Despite receiving a substantial head wound in that action, he refuses to withdraw. Almost single-handedly he secures the bridge, laying planks across a gap in the middle under heavy fire. Having done so, he leads a bayonet charge that scatters the enemy like skittles and takes back control of the village.

It is rare for one man's actions to turn the tide of any battle, but Tandey is that man. For his astonishing courage, he is awarded a VC.

But that is not the reason Henry Tandey will come to be remembered, nor the reason he features in this book. Instead, his life will become defined by a few brief seconds that follow on that fateful afternoon.

For as the German army retreats, a wounded and disorientated Tandey comes face to face, with a *Gefreiter* (lance-corporal) of the Bavarian Regiment of the Imperial German Army.

The enemy soldier is weaponless. Tandey is running high on adrenaline and his Lee-Enfield rifle has a full magazine. He lifts his weapon, puts his finger to the trigger, takes aim – and pauses. And in that brief moment, the future history of the world spins on the instincts of a former boiler manager from Leamington Spa. The *Gefreiter* winces and waits for the inevitable moment, but Tandey doesn't shoot.

Henry, you see, has a home-spun moral philosophy and key to it is a rule, that he never kills an unarmed man. The German poses no threat and Henry has taken pity on him. He lowers his rifle and gestures to the enemy to run.

Lance Corporal Adolf Hitler nods in gratitude – and flees into infamy.

* * *

"That man came so near killing me that I thought I should never see Germany again," the Nazi leader was to recall, 20 years later, as he pointed Tandey out to British Prime Minister Neville Chamberlain in a painting that hung in his study at the Berghof, his residence in the Bavarian Alps.

"Providence saved me," he said.

The work was a copy of a work by Italian artist Fortunino Matania, commissioned in 1923 by the Green Howards Regiment, depicting British soldiers at the Menin crossroads in 1914. In the bottom right-hand corner, Tandey can be seen carrying a wounded comrade on his back.

Matania had a Thucydidean obsession with accuracy, seeking out the real-life subjects of his paintings and bringing along toy soldiers, so that they could recreate scenes for him. This piece was based on that method but is actually wrongly titled, as it really depicts the village of Gheluvelt in the aftermath of the Battle of Ypres and not the Menin crossroads.

The original artwork still hangs in the Green Howards Regimental Museum in Richmond, North Yorkshire and many of the men depicted are named, including Tandey.

How Hitler got his hands on a copy is a serendipitous tale.

In the 1930s, one of Hitler's staff was a medical doctor, Otto Schwend, who, in 1914 had saved the life of a British officer, Colonel Maxwell Earle, of the 1st Battalion Grenadier Guards, at Ypres. Earle had been shot in the head and lost an eye, and most of his right ear and, having been left for dead, was almost literally brought back to life by the German doctor, who then became his friend.

In 1916, the Blimpish Colonel Earle was among a group of officers interned in Switzerland, in a curious arrangement that allowed wounded POWs to be transferred to the neutral country. By war's end nearly 68,000 British and Indian service personnel were living in curious military limbo, while the war was fought just a few miles away.

Earle regularly wrote to Schwend and was even visited by the German doctor before being repatriated in September 1917. The friendship outlasted the war and the rise of the Nazis, and in 1936, Earle sent Schwend a postcard of Matania's painting.

The doctor showed it to Hitler, who immediately identified Tandey as the man who had spared him in 1918. Further correspondence ensued and Earle arranged for a copy to be sent to Hitler, for which he received a letter from the dictator's adjutant*, Captain Fritz Wiedemann, who wrote that his boss:

"Directed me to send you his best thanks for your friendly gift which is so rich in memories."

This was the print that Hitler showed Chamberlain and, having done so, he asked the PM to convey his gratitude to Tandey on his return.

Chamberlain was in Germany to sign off the Munich Agreement. A disgraceful compromise which consented to the German annexation of the Sudetenland, at that point part of Czechoslovakia, without any say on the part of the Czechoslovakian government. The disgrace and dishonour of the deal purportedly led to Winston Churchill telling Chamberlain:

"You were given the choice between war and dishonour. You chose dishonour, and you will have war." But once again, the source of this famous quote is untraceable and it is likely another fake.

---

* A middle-ranking officer who assists the commanding officer with administration

Anyway, as news spread of Chamberlain's betrayal, bells rang joyously across Britain and people gathered at churches to give thanks to God that it wasn't "us" who were going to be invaded but some people who spoke a funny language to the east.

The British Prime Minister had another mission to fulfil. He had made that promise to the Führer about ringing Tandey. So, having waved the Munich Agreement at Heston aerodrome on September 30th and promised "peace for our time*", the PM hot-footed it to Downing Street where he got hold of Tandey's number and put in the call.

There are two versions of what happened next. In one, told to the *Middlesbrough Evening Gazette* after his death, Tandey leaves the dinner table when the phone rings and nonchalantly returns to explain that it was "just that Mr Chamberlain passing on thanks from Hitler."

In the other, Henry isn't in, so his nephew takes a note and leaves it on the side.

The story is one of the great "what ifs" of history: Henry Tandey – the English Tommy, who didn't shoot Hitler when he had the chance. It inspired Michael Morpurgo's novel *An Eagle in the Snow*. The History Channel made a documentary about it. There are dozens of YouTube videos, hundreds of articles and a thousand "alternative history" threads on the internet dedicated to it. With good reason. It's a cracking story. You might even have heard it before. And this far into the book, we all know what that means.

It never happened.

The two men could not have met in 1918. For while Tandey was at Marcoing, Hitler's regiment was 50 miles north and Hitler

---

* Not "peace in our time" as is frequently misquoted

himself was on leave, only returning to his unit on the 28th, the day of the engagement.

It is, of course, possible that at some point in the war and perhaps fleeing a battle, Hitler did come face to face with an enemy soldier, but the chances of that man being Tandey are very low indeed. Hitler appropriated Henry and threw him into his origin story on purpose.

Hitler was an avid reader of war literature and knew that Henry was the most highly decorated private in the British army. If his life was to be spared and his great destiny set in train, then only the best would do.

In the spring of 1943, the U.S. Office of Strategic Studies, forerunner of the CIA, commissioned psychoanalyst and Harvard professor Walter Langer, to create a "psychological profile" of the German leader. Over a period of eight months, Langer and his team threw themselves into the task. They studied everything Hitler had written, interviewed those who had met him and read every available interview the Nazi leader had ever given.

This was the first attempt to create a "psychobiography" of a political leader and the dossier remains a fascinating contemporary insight into the mind of the German leader. It is not without controversy, though. The *Goldwater Rule* – one of the guiding principles of US psychiatry – considers it "unethical" to analyse people without meeting them face to face. And seeking to "understand" Hitler is also problematic due in no small part to the scale of his crimes and infamy.

But Langer's research is the first attempt to understand the psychological motivation of the German leader and, given that it is a contemporary examination, unfettered by post-war thinking, it has value as a historical source. Declassified in 1968 and approved for public release in 1999, it makes instructive reading.

In the first section "Hitler as he believes himself to be", Langer seeks to examine the dictator from the perspective of his experiences in the Great War and in particular the incidents that gave rise to his belief that he was under "divine protection".

It was not unusual for men in the trenches to ascribe survival to providence. In his superb memoir, *Goodbye to All That*, the British poet Robert Graves, a veteran of the conflict, conjures up a trench life rich with superstition and amulets.

Contemporary British newspapers ran accounts of "ghost soldiers" warning men away from German regiments and even tales of angels at the Battle of Mons, who miraculously intervened to help British servicemen. Fake Family Sagas, including my own, are rife with the stories of relatives who were delivered from death by divine intervention, otherwise known as luck.

In a 1938 interview with British journalist George Ward Price in the *Daily Mail*, which Langer quotes in his report, Hitler recounted the following:

"I was eating my dinner, in a trench... when a voice seemed to be saying to me, 'get up and go over there.' It was so clear and insistent that I obeyed mechanically, as if it had been a military order. I rose at once to my feet and walked 20 yards along the trench carrying my dinner in its tin can with me... Hardly had I done so when a flash and a deafening report came from the trench I had just left. A stray shell had burst over the group in which I had been sitting and every member of it was killed."

Langer later concludes: "It became clearer that he [Hitler] was thinking of himself as the Messiah and that it was he, who was destined to lead Germany to glory."

In October 1918, while recovering from a gas attack, Hitler claimed to have had a vision while lying in his bed and later wrote in *Mein Kampf,* his autobiography-cum-manifesto, that: "I sensed now that I would liberate Germany, that I would make it, and I knew immediately that this would be achieved."

His redemption had purpose and the events in Marcoing fitted that religious narrative. It didn't matter that he had never been there. The story read like scripture. Hitler, bewildered and beaten, like Germany itself in 1918, had faced down the greatest warrior in the British army and been delivered to lead his chosen people to greatness.

What is tantalising about the Tandey story – and the reason it is still believed so widely, is that unlike the story of the cleaning lady finding Churchill's invasion plans, many of the elements in it are true. Tandey did all the things at Marcoing detailed above and was by all accounts a humble and decent man. And Hitler certainly owned a copy of that painting and claimed Tandey had gifted him his life.

Those elements have been taken and twisted to create an alternative narrative, while other entirely made-up events have been added by others to weave a "good story" narrative.

The story of Chamberlain phoning Henry is undoubtedly a lie. Probably a Fake Family Saga, told by Tandey's family, that has become accepted as fact.

Historian Dr David Johnson, who wrote a thorough 2013 biography of Tandey called *The Man Who Didn't Shoot Hitler,* dug into the BT records and discovered that, like most people in 1938 and indeed well into the 1970s, Henry didn't have a phone. Johnson doubts whether Chamberlain was ever shown the painting as the pre-war prime minister made no mention of it in his extensive diaries, letters or notes.

Whatever the truth, the urban myth, started by Hitler and propagated by others, swiftly came to be believed by both Hitler's supporters and enemies. In August 1939, the story was well enough known for the *Coventry Herald* to approach Tandey to ask him about it, but Henry wasn't willing to play:

"According to them, I've met Adolf Hitler… maybe they're right but I can't remember him."

But then a curious thing happened. A year later, following the bombing of Coventry which saw Tandey's own home hit, his "memory" of their encounter magically returned:

"I didn't like to shoot at a wounded man," he told the same newspaper, adding: "when I saw all the people and women and children he had killed and wounded, I was sorry to God I had let him go."

The Coventry Blitz, the most devastating attack of which took place on 14th November 1940, claimed 600 lives, injured 863 and destroyed the city's 14th-century cathedral along with 4,300 homes. Tandey was now buying into the myth and repurposing it, for his and his own country's ends. The lesson of this new British version of the story was clear: Henry, the representative of all that was good about Britain, with his innate decency and quiet bravery, had seen an act of kindness repaid with barbarism and the destruction of his home town. Britain must show no mercy anymore.

The story had as much truth as the one about the angels at the Battle of Mons, but it didn't matter.

Dr Johnson argues that Tandey should be remembered in his own right, as a hero of the First World War and that the Hitler story is a red herring which distracts from his real-life deeds. Unfortunately, by embracing Hitler's lie, Henry unwittingly legitimised a parallel reality and legendary tale that came to eclipse his own heroism.

Some stories are so good that people don't care if they are true or not, and the one of Tandey not shooting Hitler is just such a case.

Part of the reason for that, and uncomfortable as it might sound, is that very many people remain fascinated with Hitler and his iconography. There's a veritable Hitler cottage industry of films, books, documentaries and expertise. The TV schedules bulge with programmes about him and his fellow henchmen. Hitler's name sells advertising space on history channels – there's money in it and a large audience.

His notoriety feeds in part off our innate human thirst for good guys and bad guys. Hitler, like his nemesis Churchill, has outgrown reality. He is not really human anymore. He has become the cartoonish super-villain of history. A quasi-mythical monster, who inhabits the darkest reaches of our collective imagination. A figure who terrifies and revolts us even as he draws us in.

People like horror. Books about serial killers top the fiction charts. Films about psychopathic cannibals pull audiences in. Hitler occupies the same space as Hannibal Lecter and Rose West. But he is bigger than them all.

Almost 80 years after his death, his image is everywhere. His photograph adorns book jackets and magazines and, as with Churchill, there are endless biographies, films and documentaries to perpetuate his legend.

And that legend is the one ultimately formed by him. Disquieting as it might be to admit it, the worst despot in living memory retains an iron-clad grip on his own narrative.

The Nazis excelled at image management. From the carefully designed uniforms, produced by Hugo Boss who had joined the Nazi Party in 1931, to the stage-managed speeches and spectacles at Nuremberg, it was their intention to enthral and engage – in effect, to wow audiences. Hitler was moulded and crafted and presented every bit as carefully as a contemporary pop icon. And it is that artfully manufactured image of Hitler that lingers in our imagination and on our television screens.

Hitler has become what the poet W. H. Auden dubbed a "psychopathic God". A figure who seems to exist beyond the realm of humanity and one who is impossible to shake from our collective minds.

The real, human being Hitler – beyond the work of Langer and others – remains curiously absent in our consciousness. There is a reason for that: a prevailing sense that to seek to understand Hitler is to risk humanising him, which risks legitimising him. In an age where Holocaust denial is forever threatening to go mainstream and where revisionism seeks to excuse the Third Reich of its crimes against millions of innocent people, that is perhaps a legitimate concern.

But by failing to address the "human Hitler", we give space almost entirely to the "Hitler" who the lance corporal from Linz wanted the world to believe in.

His biographical account comes, in the first instance, from himself, in *Mein Kampf,* written in 1924 and printed in 1925. Some publications become more than the sum of their pages and *Mein Kampf* is just such a book. Few best-selling autobiographies have attained such infamy, despite being so little read, which is a great pity. Because to pick up *Mein Kampf* and open its pages is to set about debunking the dark mythos of Hitler.

In the version I tackled, translated by Irish journalist James Murphy in 1939, the author comes across as nothing more than an unhinged lunatic. That, frankly, might not surprise you. But what is far more intriguing is that this unhinged lunatic is as boring and self-obsessed as it is possible to imagine a person might be.

Mein Kampf reads like a very angry man shouting his life story through a megaphone. No edit is apparent in its 500 pages. And it is so tiresomely repetitive as to be almost unreadable.

The text seethes with a strange mix of misplaced arrogance, self-loathing and resentment for all that is clever or good. Again, that might sound fairly obvious – Hitler is not exactly renowned for being a humorous and engaging bloke – but it is staggering to discover quite how unengaging and furious he was. The text reveals a whiny man who hates the smart kids, the do-gooders, the French, the Jews and everyone else who failed to recognise his "genius" when he was growing up. In between the rattling of chips shuffling for space on shoulders, there is just about room for him to demonstrate his very obvious stupidity hidden behind faux intellectual guff. Here's a flavour, in one of his most famous anti-Semitic diatribes and I would challenge you to make it to the end:

The Jewish doctrine of Marxism rejects the aristocratic principle of Nature and replaces the eternal privilege of power and strength by the mass of numbers and their dead weight. Thus it denies the value of personality in man, contests the significance of nationality and race, and thereby withdraws from humanity the premise of its existence and its culture. As a foundation of the universe, this doctrine would bring about the end of any order intellectually conceivable to man.

The Hitler of *Mein Kampf* is strikingly similar to lofty modern-day racist trolls on social media. The sort of Twitter and Facebook users who write everything IN CAPITAL LETTERS and who block anyone who points out the dim-wittedness of their world-view.

You don't need Langer's assessment on hand to work out that here is an emotionally and intellectually stunted man – trapped seemingly forever as a put upon, hateful child whose father wouldn't let him draw. Early on, the 36-year-old Hitler spends paragraph after paragraph boasting about his achievements at school, over 20 years before. He brags about his talent for geography, aged 11, claiming this was one of the two academic subjects at which he excelled. The other being history.

It's like being accosted by a sweaty middle-aged man at a bus stop who wants to tell you about his SATS results at primary school.

His high school history teacher in Linz was Dr Leopold Poetsch, and from the pages of *Mein Kampf* spring the description of an individual who was less an educator and more a poisonous sophist – the noxious yang to my own teacher, Mr Higham's, yin:

"When we listened to him, we became afire with enthusiasm and were sometimes moved even to tears," Hitler writes.

Poetsch was an anti-Semitic conspiracy theorist, with a deep-seated hatred of the House of Habsburg. He believed the "Austro-Hungarian" Empire that the Habsburgs headed defiled the Germanic race by association not only with the Jews, who had enjoyed enormous prosperity and equality in Austria since the 1840s, but also with the "inferior" Slavs to the east.

Poetsch believed in a Greater Germanic Reich – that would see Austria and Germany unite – and he bought into the Aryan race mythology that was to later give so much work to those SS Ahnenerbe archaeologists.

His hatred touched a chord with the young Hitler, who tells us: "I learned to understand and grasp the true meaning of history," that "people of the same blood should be in the same Reich."

Which of course is not the "true meaning of history" any more than the one that claims that the original German people sprung from Atlantis, or that Britain was once gifted to Albion by the rulers of the sea.

Seventeen years after teaching Hitler, Poetsch was to educate another Adolf – Eichmann, who would later become one of the key architects of the Nazi Holocaust. As SS *Obersturmbann-führer*, he was to be jointly responsible for the false imprisonment, humiliation, starvation and murder of millions of innocent men, women, children and babies – simply because they were Jewish, gay or what he – the great Eichmann – deemed to be racially "inferior".

Eichmann, like Hitler and indeed the majority of the Nazi hierarchy, was a fundamentally stupid man, who thought he was the smartest guy in the room.

That same dull-witted hatred that imbued the "thinking" of all the major Nazi protagonists colours the pages of *Mein Kampf* and as this dull litany of loathing goes on (and on), and on, it's almost like Hitler is inviting us to despise him.

And yet, in time, in the popular consciousness, even his enemies came to view the book, if not as a sort of *Das Kapital* of Fascism, then at the very least as a Nazi manifesto. A Holy Bible of hatred. The Gospel according to Adolf. And thus a "dangerous book".

Even very bad and very boring books like *Mein Kampf* can come to take on a potent symbolism. They can become a crutch to prop up the credentials of people seeking legitimacy.

People who have written "iconic books" are deemed to be clever. And over the years, depressingly, *Mein Kampf* has retained that reputation. A sort of political witchcraft. Matters were not helped by it being banned in many countries for many years, lending it a menacing and intoxicating potency. Something akin to a fascist Pandora's Box.

It would be better not to hide it away but to read it instead. Because in doing so the true banality of Nazi thinking and the man at its centre is exposed like a naked Emperor. But despite being drivel, *Mein Kampf* was a bestseller in Germany throughout the 1930s and 1940s, shifting an estimated 10–12 million copies. Hitler grew rich on the proceeds, earning around $12 million in modern money – making him the wealthiest author of his era. He accrued a huge tax bill off the back of it, but, having abolished democracy, decided he didn't have to pay it and so he didn't.

Imagine anyone in politics nowadays doing such a thing.

Hitler hadn't set out to be a writer. From childhood, he longed to be a painter, despite his father refusing to acknowledge his son's "obvious talent for drawing", as Hitler describes it early on in *Mein Kampf*. And as with so many other aspects of his life we have continued to indulge that notion. The one of Hitler the "failed artist", an idea in which he wanted his contemporaries to believe. It is crucial to his mythos, despite not really being true.

Let's look at the evidence.

Following his father, Alois's, premature death, Hitler moved to Vienna and in 1908 tried to get into the Academy of Fine Arts.

Having submitted examples of his work, he passed the first round, only to be rejected on the second. When he applied again in the autumn of that same year, the board suggested that he enrol as an architect instead. Hitler had no interest in what the experts had to say, ignored their advice and stuck to painting – despite not being very good at it.

Vienna in those pre-war years had a thriving artistic scene and he walked the same streets as the modernist Secession artist Gustav

Klimt and Egon Schiele, whose daring, provocative work still fizzes with energy and the genius of originality 100 years on. None of those words has ever been used to describe Hitler's paintings.

In 1936, an American travel writer, John Gunther, who had seen an exhibition of the Nazi leader's works, described them as: "Prosaic, utterly devoid of rhythm, color, feeling, or spiritual imagination. They are architect's sketches: painful and precise draftsmanship; nothing more. No wonder the Vienna professors told him to go to an architectural school and give up pure art as hopeless."

Many who have appraised Hitler's work have used the opportunity to psychoanalyse him through it. As Gunther pointed out, most of the paintings are of buildings and urban landscapes frequently devoid of people, and this has led some to ponder, as Marc Fisher, did in *The Washington Post* in 2002 whether: "In these antiseptic street scenes [we] see the roots of Hitler's obsession with cleanliness and his belief that his mission in life was to cleanse Germany and the world of Judaism."

I approached Peter Fairbanks, co-owner of Montgomery Gallery in San Francisco and a former expert on the American version of *Antiques Roadshow*, to give me his commercial opinion on three of Hitler's paintings, *Mother Mary with the Child Christ* (1913), *The Ruins of the Cloisters* (1914) and *The Vienna Opera House (1912)*.

Fairbanks considered *Mother Mary with Child* to be more accomplished than the other two, which he judged to be of "minimal or no artistic merit" that would have no commercial value beyond association with Adolf Hitler.

This chimes with the conclusions arrived in a book by American author and former diplomat Frederic Spotts. In 2003, Spotts wrote *Hitler and the Power of Aesthetics* and in preparation approached an anonymous art critic and asked them to judge Hitler's paintings in a blind appraisal.

That critic noted, as had those at the Academy of Fine Arts in Vienna in 1908, that the buildings were "quite good" but that the works lacked passion and originality and "displayed disinterest in the human race".

Hitler created at least 1,000 paintings in his lifetime but of the ones available to view online, almost all are devoid of people. There's something a bit creepy about the world he conjures up. Like the Ladybird pastels in the Peter and Jane books, everywhere is orderly, everything is clean and nobody is about.

Hitler's tastes were conservative and insipid. As with his views on history, politics, philosophy and life, his ideas about art were predetermined as a child and immutable after that. Naturally, he blamed the Jews for creating the artistic landscape of the era in which he lived, writing in *Mein Kampf* that: "Culturally, he [the Jewish people] contaminates art, literature, the theatre, makes a mockery of natural feeling, overthrows all concepts of beauty and sublimity, of the noble and the good, and instead drags men down into the sphere of his own base nature."

He was repelled by Modernism. In his mind, his failure as an artist was not his but a conspiracy of modern artists and the Jewish establishment. That resentment fuelled an unceasing campaign against both. Once in power, he took revenge on all of the clever people who had conspired to disabuse him of his dream. In 1937 an exhibition of "degenerate art", organised by the Nazis to "educate" the public on "the art of decay", toured Germany, ridiculing great contemporary artists like Paul Klee and Kandinsky and bigging up Hitler's own ghastly tastes instead.

In a speech the previous summer he had declared his distaste for: "Works of art which cannot be understood in themselves but need some pretentious instruction book to justify their existence will never again find their way to the German people."

Hitler's favourite artists included Eduard von Grützner, who painted naff scenes of Bavarians drinking beer, or men like Matania, whose Ladybird book-like depiction of the Menin crossroads hung on his wall.

Having established a new aesthetic, Hitler banned "art criticism" and promoted kitsch artists who, like so many others in 1930s Germany, were only too happy to rally to the winning side and take the cheques.

To grasp Hitler's aesthetic taste, one only has to look at the grand, tacky, architectural blueprints for Germania – the giant, ugly city he planned with his architect Albert Speer. He commissioned vulgar public art and memorials to the dead and encouraged genre painting showing happy Aryan peasants and bold, broad-chested soldiers. All of it is tacky and obvious and lacks anything approaching an aesthetic.

Ultimately the legend of Hitler the failed bohemian artist persists, like his mythological encounter with Tandey, because Hitler wanted it to. The story of the neglected genius, who had been done out of his place at the Viennese Academy, eking out an existence selling his pictures to bourgeois tourists, was fundamental to his origin myth. The tale exemplified all that was rotten in Germany before his rise to power. Hitler's story of struggle embodied the spirit of the nation itself. Greatness cowed by the Jewish establishment – the great Aryan spirit cheated of its destiny by "modern" thinking and degenerate art.

In truth, Hitler's "career" as an artist wasn't exactly one of a frustrated, talented genius battling the establishment, but more of a spoiled layabout indulging in whimsical fantasy at his mum's expense. In Vienna, having decided he was now "an artist", he made no effort to get a job. Having failed to get into art school he was funded by money sent by his mother and an "orphan's allowance", and when that cash ran out, he took out a loan.

In 1913, he finally inherited part of his father's estate and, had the war not broken out, he would likely have squandered all of that money as well. He was a fantasist who preferred to blame his and his adopted nation's failings on greedy Jews, even as he himself grifted off his mother and lay in bed doing nothing.

That brief interlude in his life depicts Hitler less as a failed artist, more a failed human being. But we continue to indulge the myth because we like to buy into the "good story" in it. The "what if" inherent in his rejection by the Academy.

Both Churchill and General Franco painted and created a huge body of work. Their paintings were exhibited in their lifetimes and continue to be sold, and in Churchill's case, at much higher prices than Hitler's works. Of course, that has little to do with their actual merit and more to do with who painted them, but nobody ever defined either Churchill or Franco first and foremost as "an artist" – whether failed or otherwise.

In his *Life of Mao*, the author Philip Short recounts a story where the Sinologist and translator Arthur Waley is asked what he thinks of Mao's poems to which he replies: "Let's say they're better than Hitler's paintings but not as good as Winston Churchill's." It's a great joke, but many critics essentially agree with the analysis. In a comparison of the two men's work in a 2014 article for *Artylist*, for example, critic Paul Black wrote that: "There are few critics in the world of art that consider Hitler's work of any real artistic value aside from the generally historic."

But Black suggests that by contrast, Churchill, who only began painting at the age of 40, had some genuine talent.

Black applauds Churchill's evolving style over 40 years and suggests his paintings demonstrate a good eye, a curiosity, a willingness to learn and, crucially, a desire to take risks as he pushed the boundaries of his gift. "In Churchill's paintings there is a genuine sense of a strong amateur artist exploring his ability," Black writes. "In fact, Churchill's first word of advice to other budding artists was 'audacity'. So it would seem that to the victor go the art-critical spoils as well."

Hitler wanted to be an artist, but wanting to be something is not the same thing as being it. Wanting to be an astronaut and applying to work for NASA in that capacity does not make you a "failed astronaut" when the rejection email arrives in your inbox.

Embittered and resentful for much of his life, Hitler clung to and nurtured his grievance. He was one of humanity's natural "draggers down". Someone who sought to reduce everything to his level, rather than lifting himself up to some better purpose.

By degrading decency and championing hate, he could crown himself the King of Execration. By elevating kitsch art while demeaning modernism, he could likewise, in his own mind at least, promote his indifferent art to greatness while traducing that of the actual greats.

In 1936, seeking to pamper his ego further, his party brought out a leather-bound coffee table book called *Adolf Hitler: Bilder aus dem Leben des Führers*,* a sort of elaborate fan annual, which

---

* Adolf Hitler: Pictures from the Life of the Führer

included chapters on his views on architecture and his power as a speaker. The book also reproduced five of his paintings – all of them of buildings – with adoring accompanying notes by Goebbels that lavished praise on his talent. It seems that the state ban on art critics did not extend to Hitler's own works.

The banality was such that, as Paul Black notes: "It is surprising Germany didn't immediately give up on Aryan superiority" on picking up a copy.

It might seem a little trite to compare a mass murderer to a pop star – but Hitler was undoubtedly a celebrity, and one who excelled at self-promotion and performance. He was superb and compelling at projecting hatred in his ranting set-piece speeches, which formed the basis of his act and popularity. The paraphernalia and kitsch of Naziism was his set and he was the leading player in the show. In the central role of "Führer", he emitted a dark mystique and purpose that sent audiences wild. But the impact of his speeches at Nuremberg and elsewhere rested less on what was said and more in their delivery and staging. The vapid diatribes played second fiddle to the spectacle, the lights, the swastikas, the men in uniform and the moment.

Whipped to a frenzy, the adoring crowds were caught up in the rapture of the event.

Hitler believed wholeheartedly in his purpose but his script was unoriginal. Anti-Semitism was already rife in Germany by the time the Nazis emerged and had been for decades. It was no more novel than the idea of a "Greater Germany", which was already old hat when his history teacher was talking about it in his childhood. Even Hitler's famous speechmaking style was plagiarised. He had pinched it off Vienna's pre-war anti-Semitic mayor, Karl Lueger, who was famed for his violent, populist oratory and rising and falling delivery.

Hitler, the actor, played the role to a tee and revelled in being the centre of attention. But off stage, some who met him noted that he lacked much real-life charisma at all. The journalist, Dorothy Thompson, who interviewed Hitler for *Cosmopolitan* magazine in 1932, was unimpressed by her encounter, judging Hitler "startlingly insignificant" in the flesh: "He was formless, almost faceless, a man whose countenance is a caricature, a man whose framework seems cartilaginous, without bones. He is inconsequent and voluble, ill-poised, insecure. He is the very prototype of the Little Man."

The great American film director Orson Welles, who claimed that he too had met Hitler on a hiking trip in the 1930s, told the host of the eponymously titled *Dick Cavett Show* in 1970 that when they had met, Hitler had displayed "No personality what-soever... I think there was nothing there."

Historians have long postulated that one reason behind Hitler's irresistible rise was his unimposing presence in private. He was constantly underestimated by the ruling elite in Germany, who thought him unimpressive and pliable – someone who could be pushed about in the short term and pushed aside when no longer needed. In doing so, they underrated his talents for manipulation, his overarching belief in himself and his appeal to the mob.

By the mid-1930s, Hitler had long given up on his dream of being a great artist and wanted to be a great military commander instead. Much of his enduring infamy and dark legend rests on his presumed genius as a military strategist and his unbeatable way with armies and tanks. In fact, he wasn't that much better at commanding armies than he was at painting.

He was declared Führer of the German State in 1934 and was therefore the supreme commander of the German armed forces.

However, he increasingly wanted to assume direct control over the armies, so became Commander-in-chief of the Armed Forces in 1938 and, following the disastrous invasion of the USSR in 1941, Commander-in-chief of the Army, giving him a direct operational posting equivalent to that of a general. From that point, ultimate authority in matters military lay with Hitler. He sought to be a modern Napoleon, but he simply was not up to the task. He had never led an army and lacked competence to do so. During the First World War, he had been a junior non-commissioned officer who had run messages. His knowledge of strategy was gleaned entirely from books and articles.

He distrusted his senior officers, and perhaps with reason, because many of them thought he was in over his head. Hitler often clashed with his military commanders and, in the post-war years, those of his staff who survived sought to place all of the blame for Germany's military failure and collapse on the Führer. But then of course they would. In any analysis of Nazi Germany, it's essential to remember that not all of the killing and chaos was the fault of one man. Millions enabled it and Hitler himself was emboldened in his crimes and deeds by those who voted for him, supported him, propped him up and pampered his ego, including his military staff.

But by any measure Hitler was a bad military leader. He couldn't take advice. He was superstitious. He relied on instinct. He obsessed over tiny details, but was uninterested in complexity. He embraced confirmation bias and ignored the startling truth.

In June 1941, he deliberately invaded the USSR, sending three million men into Russia and creating a wholly unnecessary second front that was to cost Germany millions of lives and ultimately the war. Hitler had seriously underestimated his foe, the scale of the task and the weather. He had also, critically, invaded not as a liberator but as a tyrant. His purpose was to enslave and kill. There was no long-term plan beyond conquest, and the plan was predicated entirely on the belief that the Slavs were inferior and that the campaign would thus be short.

"You only have to kick down the door and the whole rotten structure will come tumbling down!" Hitler declared to his chiefs of staff as the invasion began. But the Russians hadn't received the memo and after initially being caught off guard fought back with a ferocity and determination that changed the course of the war.

German High Command calculated that victory was possible if they took Moscow, thus striking a decisive political and psychological stake into the heart of the Soviet Empire. But Hitler was more concerned with seizing industrial resources and defeating the Red Army in battle, and in the end, Moscow was never taken.

As events in Russia and beyond spun into a different orbit of scale and complexity, with new fronts opening and new enemies entering the fray, he refused to cede control to others. There was no way that one man could grasp it all, let alone command events that were going on thousands of miles away in places like Stalingrad or North Africa. But Hitler tried. And it made bad matters considerably worse.

The German war machine became a lumbering, wounded beast. There were huge delays in orders coming through and when they did, Hitler's instructions frequently bore no reality to what was going on on the ground. His desire to be in charge of everything and incompetence in the role was Germany's ultimate undoing and cost the country the war and millions of his own people's lives.

Hitler's personal ticks didn't help matters. Interviewed in 2014, one of his maids, Elisabeth Kalhammer, recalled that even

at the height of war, Hitler liked to stay up late eating his favourite snack, known as "Führer cake",* and watching cartoon films.
He rarely rose from bed before lunchtime and frequently stayed
under his blankets until 2.p.m.

As the Allies landed at Normandy on 6th June 1944, in the
first wave of Operation Overlord, German efforts to respond
were hampered because the Nazi leader was asleep and nobody
was brave enough to wake him. Without his say, no reinforcements could be deployed and the dithering cost the German army
valuable time and initiative as thousands of Allies poured ashore.

Having finally got up at noon, Hitler, relying on that famed
"instinct" and believing the Allied misinformation he'd been
fed, dismissed the attack as a diversionary tactic. He believed
the invasion would happen elsewhere and it wasn't until late
in the afternoon and long after the Allied forces had established a bridgehead that Hitler was convinced of the need to
do something.

Much of Hitler's reputation as a great military strategist rests
in the optics and the still resonating propaganda, like the images
of him poring over maps and prancing about beneath the Eiffel
Tower after the fall of France. The photos project him as an
indomitable military commander, and many people still buy into
it because – well – it's a good story.

His one undoubted success was the conquest of France in 1940.
But even that was more down to the planning of his generals, a
hefty dose of luck, and French and British incompetence, rather
than Hitler's military genius.

---

* Führer cake was made with apples and raisins. He insisted that it be baked during
the day and left overnight. Hitler was also partial to chocolate biscuits and scones.
A teetotaller – he drank a lot of tea instead.

As we saw with the story of Dunkirk, the legend of "unstop-pable Hitler" serves a wider agenda.

It is an oversimplification to say that WWII was caused as much by Anglo-French appeasement as it was by German aggres-sion. Appeasement made sense to many in the 1930s. People didn't want a war and didn't think Hitler wanted one either, and hindsight is a wonderful thing. Had Chamberlain and France PM Daladier not signed the Munich Agreement and had they instead stood up to Hitler, events may have turned out quite differently, but of course we don't – and can never – know that.

In the end, German victory in France in 1940 came in large part down to the failure of the Allies to effectively work together. Hitler got undue credit as a result. And it's much better to big up the enemy and claim that Adolf and the Nazis were unstoppable than to admit you failed. Like the story of Private Tandey, the narrative of Hitler's evil genius came to suit both sides and there-fore persists to this day, like so much other propaganda from the Second World War.

The curious and unhealthy fascination with Hitler and the Nazis continues, in films like Tarantino's *Inglourious Basterds*, and the work of Spielberg and thousands of documentaries and books. The narrative has been turned into the ultimate "goody and baddy" saga and one which too often buys into the "glamour and gore" of Nazism rather than decrying its inherent vapid banality.

We should seek to question why a bunch of racist oddballs and thugs wedded to a perverted and murderous delusion have been granted such a place in history. However much the cottage industry of history channels might wish you to believe otherwise, there is nothing that *fascinating* about Naziism itself or even Adolf Hitler.

Throughout time, narcissists have managed to chance their way to the top and commit mass genocide to satiate their inadequacy. Hitler sought to be remembered. We would do better to remember his victims instead.

* * *

Hitler was by no means the last inadequate human being to build a legacy on a bit of sharp image management and racial hatred.

Enoch Powell's daft-but-nasty "Rivers of Blood" speech demonstrates that it can happen anywhere.

Powell, a British Conservative MP who had longed to be Viceroy of India, replaced that ambition, in the post-war years, with a desire to be prime minister instead. But he had a problem. Other "lesser" men who were not as brilliant as he hadn't got the memo and kept getting the gig instead. By the late 1960s, Powell was a middle-aged man in a hurry.

In desperation, he fell back on xenophobia and bigotry and a bit of artful personal myth-making. Determining that he might be able to replace the incumbent Conservative leader Edward Heath, if he simply tapped into the worst prejudices of the masses, Powell delivered a famous speech on 20th April 1968, Adolf Hitler's 79th birthday, to the Conservative faithful in Birmingham.

The gist of the address was that unfettered immigration would lead to a race war. And, depressingly, it was a contemporary and enduring hit. Powell's speech was extremely calculated. He had tipped off the press and got the regional ATV cameras in and soon, in the pub saloons and TV studios across the country, people were nodding along to Powell's bigotry.

Enoch Powell was no skinhead in bovver boots. He came with sterling academic credentials. He was widely and popularly deemed to be an intellectual and a statesman. He was a classical scholar who had achieved a double first at Cambridge, and a brigadier in the army. A man able to evoke the "blood of the Tiber" and make clever allusions to Greece and Rome. This made his dog-whistle racism different – because he spoke posh and could quote Latin and gave hate a sort of intellectual integrity.

The speech lit a pyre under his ambition, but in the long-term his "words of warning" have persisted and arguably taken on that same "black magic" potency as *Mein Kampf*. The speech is still evoked with weary predictability by people who seek to use it as intellectual confirmation for the base racism of the mob. Many of his political admirers have tried to excuse him, arguing that the speech was "misunderstood" and that because Powell was so darn smart, silly people have sought deliberately to twist his words, when actually he was simply quoting Virgil, but it's nonsense.

If you read "Rivers of Blood", it's quite clear what the intention was. But what is even more startling, is quite how bad it is. The speech is nothing short of drivel. A hotch-potch of racist clichés, urban myths and old ladies complaining about black children shouting things through letter-boxes, along with dispiritingly stupid assertions such as: "In this country in 15 or 20-years' time, the black man will have the whip hand over the white man."

Back-of-toilet-door racism dressed in a Savile Row, pin-stripe suit.

Powell's speech, like Hitler's book, rests on a false esteem. Because people haven't read it, they imagine it to be something more potent and perhaps even dangerous than it actually is. In that, it has much in common with political manifestos down the ages, which have sat unread on bookshelves while at the same time giving wannabe despots the sheen of credibility. Gaddafi had his *Green Book*, Mao his red one. Both are made up of a series of rather insipid epithets, but both were published to give these men kudos and intellectual standing.

Mao's iconic tome includes penetrating observations like: "Diligence and frugality should be practiced in running factories and shops and all state-owned, co-operative and other enterprises." Thought provoking.

While the late Colonel Gaddafi's brilliant mind gifts us: "Women, like men, are human beings. This is an incontestable truth." So, so true.

Since coming to power, China's leader Xi Jinping has added to the canon of such great cut and paste political literature with two volumes of theory and collected speeches and quotes: the alluringly titled *The Governance of China volume 1* and its hugely anticipated sequel, *volume 2*.

Among Xi's great musings we learn that: "NBA games are very exciting to watch and have global appeal. They are very popular in China. I do watch NBA games on television when I have time." Right up there with "religion is the opium of the people", isn't it?

When not musing on basketball, Jinping's door-stoppers have introduced a world that didn't know it needed it to "Xi Jinping Thought", the new political theory of China. The books have been enthusiastically received by Chinese politicians, Chinese book reviewers, members of the Chinese Communist Party, Chinese bots on Twitter and, well, Mark Zuckerberg. The Facebook founder was so enthralled by Xi's thinking that he bulk-ordered copies for his employees. Only cynics would suggest that Zuckerberg, whose platform is banned in China, might have a vested interest in celebrating such a god-awful literary endeavour.

"Xi Jinping Thought" has all the entertainment value of the later *Police Academy* films, while lacking their essential originality. It argues that China is a great nation, which has lost its way and that only by reconnecting with its true (aka make-believe) history can it undergo a "great rejuvenation: that will see it return to glory.

Xi claims that China has a unique unbroken 5,000-year history and promulgates a notion of inherent purity and wisdom that Western countries don't have. He views that Western interference and thinking have corrupted the nation's destiny. This is exceptionalism in every way, except that once again, it is far from exceptional. Like the super-creepy, poorly constructed fake Disneyland outside Beijing, it is just the same old crap, unconvincingly repackaged.

Xi's flaccid catchphrase, "Never before, have the Chinese come so close to realising their dreams", is not so different to "Make America Great Again" or "Take back control". But based on conversations with Chinese nationals – even those who have lived in the UK for some considerable time – it seems that the idea is deeply embedded in the modern Chinese psyche. Chinese people – even very well-educated individuals – believe that their history is older than everyone else's and that it stretches back into time. And that Xi Jinping is the only man who can take it forward.

In Russia, Vladimir Putin has also found an intellectual prop in literature. Putin, whose own literary endeavours stretch no further than a co-written effort on judo, has revived the ideas of Christian fascist and nationalist Ivan Ilyin and has recommended his books throughout his presidency.

Ilyin's philosophy, as described by author and Yale historian Timothy Snyder, is "Russian Christian fascism" with an outlook summed up thus: "the world was corrupt; it needed redemption from a nation capable of total politics; that nation was unsoiled Russia."

This vision of Russian exceptionalism sells the belief that Russia needs to be reset and that this can only be done by eliminating history altogether and replacing it with superheroes uniquely attuned to the "Russian Spirit". And you can guess where the Russian president thinks he fits in that.

As with Hitler before him, who Ilyin explicitly admired, Putin has sought to drag others down to his own level, instead of raising the bar of ambition. In his book *The Road to Unfreedom*, Snyder sets out how Putin deliberately and successfully undermined democracies – including Britain, France and the USA – seeking to sow discord and discontent within them and encouraging separatist movements, even as he has done little to improve the lives of his own people, while making himself rich.

Estimates of the Russian president's wealth range between an estimate of $70 billion, given in evidence to the FBI by Russia analyst Stanislav Belkovsky, and a figure of $200 billion, given before the US Senate Judiciary Committee in 2016, which would make Putin the richest man in the world. Whatever the exact figure, the sources of Mr Putin's undoubted great wealth remain opaque.

Even as his regime has robbed the Russian people and violated international laws, Putin has been appeased by apologist politicians and commentators in the countries he targeted, suggesting that modern Western leaders could do well to watch some of those daytime TV programmes about the rise of the Nazis.

Populations, even in educated and advanced democracies, remain susceptible to fairy tales, much as their ancestors sought solace in lion-headed spirit animals. Strong men selling snake oil and quick fixes on the back of a dodgy, hackneyed but empowering narrative still have a depressing ability to beguile. And a book is a fantastic prop in building up the mythos.

In 1987, New York businessman Donald Trump, brought out his own one called *The Art of the Deal*. The autobiography-cum-business manual portrayed Trump as a genius of extraordinary, almost superhuman insight. A man who could broker deals, like no other.

It became a bestseller, cementing his reputation and turning him into the best-known property tycoon in the United States – if not the world. Trump was elevated in stature by the book, and even his critics bought the image of this All-American Tycoon, gifted with acumen and business brilliance.

Only, *The Art of the Deal* was a con. Donald J. Trump had not written a single word of it – and quite likely didn't even read it. Fake Publishing.

The real author was a guy called Tony Schwartz, who, having been approached to co-write the work, was staggered to discover that Donald Trump was an empty vessel of limited intelligence and very few ideas. On their first meeting, Trump gave one-word answers to Schwartz's carefully considered questions. With a mortgage to pay off, Schwartz began to panic. Eventually the two men brokered a deal. Tony would follow Trump around, eavesdrop on his calls and write the book, and Donald would get the credit.

Now I don't think it's giving up too much of a secret to reveal that most celebrity bestsellers aren't actually written by the celebrities that bear their name, but subsequent to publication Trump claimed it was his work and still does. In June 2016 while running for the White House he even told an adoring crowd in the lobby of Trump Tower: "We need a president who wrote *The Art of the Deal*."

It didn't matter that Trump hadn't written the book. What mattered was that people thought he had. This was classic self-promotion and myth making, and it was to sustain the legend of his business genius that would take him all the way to the White House.

In time, Tony realised he had helped create a monster and sought to distance himself from Trump. In October 2020 he told *The Guardian* that: "[his book] did help to create the mythology of Donald Trump and, unfortunately, I do think it played a significant role."

An even bigger part was perhaps played by the successful television series *The Apprentice*, which, like the Nuremberg rallies, magnified Trump's image in the minds of millions of Americans through some artful projecting. TV fashioned a fictional but enigmatic image of Trump as a big, bold, decisive, insightful and brilliant man. But it was an edit.

Unfortunately, in the blurred lines of reality, TV audiences didn't appreciate that what they were watching was a scripted reality.

It is said that Trump himself bought the deceit and began to believe he was *Apprentice Trump* – a brilliant businessman and self-made millionaire.

Actually, he was no more those things than Hitler was an artist. He was a privileged frat boy, who inherited his fortune from his father, who had inherited one from his. Even as "his" book sold in the millions throughout the 1980s, his businesses were haemorrhaging money. Between 1986 and 1994, he lost a staggering $1.17 billion.

The only arts Trump excelled in were vainglorious self-promotion and tax avoidance. In 2016, he paid just $750 to the US Internal Revenue Service. It was unsurprising that when handed the presidency he demonstrated that for all his bombast and hot air he was wholly and disgracefully unfit for the task. Despite portraying himself as a "can do" president, he did almost nothing.

In four years he failed to deliver on most of his key election pledges. His promised wall with Mexico was never built, Obamacare was not repealed or replaced, he failed to clear the national debt and instead increased it. He didn't build infrastructure, despite claiming: "It will become second to none, and we will put millions of our people back to work as we rebuild it."

When Trump left office in January 2021, his legacy was one of chaos, division and fear. The only growth industry in his term was conspiracy theories and – courtesy of his handling of the Covid-19 pandemic – the funeral sector.

Hitler sold himself as an all-powerful demagogue and failed painter; Trump portrayed himself as the world's greatest businessman. Both men progressed because enough people were willing to buy into the myth.

Schwartz now believes that *The Art of the Deal* could more appropriately be called *The Sociopath* – a title that would be perfectly fitting for *Mein Kampf* too.

Even the greatest democracies can be beguiled by self-serving conmen brandishing books that bolster their image and which create a mythos that makes people believe their leaders are something that they are not.

Of course, Trump was not Hitler. He was not responsible for the murder of millions of people, nor did he start a global war that killed 65 million people. But like Hitler, Trump's administration created "alternative truths" and normalised lying for political advantage. He also used the mob. By encouraging supporters to overthrow the election result by storming the Capitol in January 2021, Trump demonstrated that while times might change, democracy can ever be prone to the chancers and dissemblers of dangerous populism.

The United States has perhaps had a narrow escape.

CHAPTER NINE

IF NAPOLEON HAD WON, WE'D ALL BE SPEAKING FRENCH

Propaganda

In December 1986, my history teacher organised a field trip to the USSR and so myself and two dozen other sixth formers flew, on a half-empty Aeroflot jet, to Moscow.

The previous year, Konstantin Chernenko, General Secretary of the Communist Party of the Soviet Union, had died and 54-year-old Mikhail Gorbachev had replaced him. "Gorby" was the youngest Russian leader since Lenin – and different in every way to his geriatric predecessors.

Soon after taking power he was promising economic and political reforms – *perestroika* – and more openness and freedom of expression – *glasnost*. Many hoped a rapprochement between NATO and the Warsaw Pact nations would follow. For since the start of the eighties, the Cold War had been hot once more.

As my dad swore, under his breath, at our faltering Austin Montego, I would seek reassurance that we all weren't about to die in a cloud of nuclear dust and he would try to deliver it over the sound of the rattling engine. Ronald Reagan was building the Strategic Defence Initiative (SDI) aka "Star Wars" and it would keep us safe. Any ballistic missiles heading our way would get knocked out. All would be well.

I wasn't entirely reassured – "Star Wars" would take several years to build and what were we supposed to do in the meantime? Every diplomatic bump in the road had people talking about war and the fear of nuclear Armageddon.

The Soviet Union posed a real and existential threat to our way of life. The risk of being turned to toast by a Soviet nuke felt real. The people beyond the Iron Curtain seemed threatening. Our impression of Russians, forged by Hollywood films, was one of grim automatons eking out miserable lives in the permafrost of the East, while their masters plotted our downfall. "Nazi Communists" in all but name.

Having arrived in Moscow, much of it played to our prejudices. Lenin was ensconced in his mausoleum in Red Square. Menacing looking soldiers marched up and down outside. There were big bold statues of workers. The shops were empty.

We were misery tourists in Soviet Disneyland indulging in confirmation bias. Posing for ironic photos and – rather arrogantly – looking down our noses at it all. But then something curious happened. One afternoon, some local teenagers approached us outside our hotel. They were fairly cool – in fact, much cooler than us, and they wanted to listen to the music on our Walkmans. One of them told us about his cousin, a Red Army NCO, who sold military contraband to tourists. So, me and my friend met him in the car park and bought some army caps and a red flag that had been ripped off a pole.

He was a funny guy and not like an automaton at all. In fact, this went for all the Russians we met. There was no Ivan Drago to be seen. They were – to quote a cliché from *Dr No*, *Indiana Jones*, *Gladiator*, *Austin Powers* and, well, a dozen other films – "not so very different from us."

Every Wednesday at my school, we played soldiers. We would put on uniforms and march about and sometimes regular army officers would come in and talk to us.

One January afternoon, shortly after our return from the USSR, a young captain came in to do just that. He was a friendly guy with a relaxed demeanour and winning smile, and he declared that he didn't like nuclear weapons or arms races, but that they were a necessary evil to protect us from the threat posed by the Soviets until such time as "Star Wars" was built. Then he showed us a video. Being a soldier looked fun. You met girls, flew around in helicopters and blew up stuff to a thumping rock and roll beat.

The promo ended and the captain began talking again in earnest, when suddenly a guy dressed as a Red Army soldier appeared at the back of the hall and started heckling him. "You imperialist British pigs are powerless capitalists!" he shouted – or rather words to the effect because quite obviously I can't remember his exact phrasing, so this is a fake quote – sorry. Anyway, you get the idea – the two men exchanged carefully scripted insults, with the British Army officer dispelling everything the "Russian" (his colleague) was saying.

It was a pantomime in all but name with the captain in the role of anti-Soviet Prince Charming and the "Russian" as Blue-beard. Or possibly Rasputin. And as the nonsense dragged on, it dawned, like an eco-light bulb slowly coming to life, that this was not some benign talk by a visiting lecturer. We were – quite obviously and explicitly – being exposed to propaganda.

Until then, I had believed, with the insularity only a British public school can instil, that such ghastly things didn't happen here. That in the land of Spitfires and warm beer we played by the rules of cricket and fair play. But here before me was stark bollock naked evidence to the contrary.

I'd like to claim I got up and walked out in disgust and that the path to this book began there. But I was a respected member of the Upper Sixth. A member of the Chapel Committee no less. So, I sat meekly in my seat and when it was over, I slunk off, thinking, perhaps, about those teens on the streets of Moscow, but more likely wondering what we were having for dinner.

"It's easier to fool people than to convince them that they have been fooled," wrote the great American Mark Twain and, certainly, the first rule of propaganda is that the target audience must be gullible enough to believe anything they hear – or read. The second is that an attractive lie is always better than the ugly truth, and the third is that even if people realise that they're being brainwashed, they willingly buy in anyway.

The term *"propaganda"* was coined by Pope Gregory XV, who established the Congregatio de Propaganda Fide (Congregation for Propagating the Faith) in 1622 to promote Catholicism in "heathen" places. The move sought to counter Dutch and British protestants proselytising their faith as their Empires expanded. Gregory hoped that by spreading Catholic missions about the place he could fight Protestant fire with Vatican fire and so he carpet-bombed Africa and Asia with catechisms and monks.

Of course, the notion of propaganda long predates the term.

The 15 m x 25 m Behistun inscription is generally accepted to be the first extant example. Dating from c. 515 BCE, this giant slab and accompanying carvings, stands 100 m up the side of a sheer limestone cliff and brags about what a great King Darius the Great of Persia is. Unfortunately, once it was finished, the platform built to make it was removed so that nobody would be able to tamper with it or deface the inscriptions. That meant that nobody could actually read it for the next 2000 years, unless of course they had a 100-m long ladder or a pair of very powerful binoculars.

So, the Behistun inscription was very much "early steps" in the information war and, great as he was, Darius clearly wasn't much of a forward planner in getting the message across.

It isn't the first surviving example of propaganda, either. A much older candidate is a 10,000-year-old cave painting in Morella la Vella in Spain that depicts archers fighting a battle – proof positive that people were marking victories and likely exaggerating successes as far back as the Mesolithic era.

Propaganda in its purest sense is defined in the OED as: "The systematic dissemination of information, esp. in a biased or misleading way, in order to promote a political cause or point of view."

This means that the Homeric epics are propaganda, as are all religious texts and even those long-forgotten fireside myths that gave us the Lion Man. As long as humans have existed, they have undoubtedly sought to big up their own achievements and deceive others.

By the era of Alexander the Great, inaccessible carvings and cave paintings had gone and recognisably modern techniques were being deployed. The "Great" men and women of history didn't just happen – they had to work at it. And, like his father Philip II, Alexander (born 356 BCE) appreciated the importance of "brand". He was to become a master of image management and spin.

Despite their growing military and cultural prowess, in the closing 500 years of the last millennium BCE, the Macedon rulers of the Argead dynasty had a brand problem. The other Hellenic Greek city states viewed them as little more than barbarians. To the people of Athens, the Macedons were not "proper Greeks" at all, but more upstart oiks and yokels – unsophisticated rednecks who kept infringing on their territory.

To counter the horrid insinuations, the dynasty propagated a myth that they were descendants of Herakles, son of Zeus and paragon of the Greek virtues of courage and physical strength.

Coins featuring Alexander deliberately conflated his image with Herakles and, while that of itself was not new, what was novel was that the same picture was used throughout the Empire. This innovative conformity of design forged a brand identity every bit as potent as the Apple logo or Che Guevara and sold Alexander as a "product" as the coins traversed his Empire.

Sex sells. And though, like Zoolander, Alexander may have just had the one look, it was a very good look indeed. A haunting, wistful, slightly upward gaze complemented by luscious flowing locks of hair. This BCE Blue Steel has been mimicked ever since and stolen wholesale by every teenage heartthrob from Byron to Rudolph Valentino, from David Bowie to Bruno Mars.

Following his father's assassination in 336 BCE, the hot young ruler sought to consolidate Philip's achievements while eagerly looking East towards further expansion. Unfortunately, the Greek states of Thebes and Athens had other ideas. They hated Macedonian rule and were even less thrilled when, following an uprising, Alexander put thousands to the sword and sold everyone else into slavery – apart from the descendants of his favourite poet, Pindar.

Alexander's super objective was to invade the great Persian Empire of Achaemenid, but crushing all these rebellions was draining his time and resources. So, he hatched a cunning plan and repurposed history for his own political gain. What a novel idea.

To get the other Greeks onside, Alexander claimed his invasion of Persia had nothing to do with his own ambitions and everything to do with revenge on their behalf for the failed Achaemenid assault on their territory 100 years previously. That invasion had witnessed the legendary last stand of 300 Spartan warriors at the Battle of Thermopylae, an event that was a big deal in 4th century BCE Hellenistic Greece. It spawned poetry, epigraphs, songs and notions of "Spartan Spirit" – a sort of pre-Common Era Dunkirk.

And, as with Dunkirk, events had been massively romanticised and mythologised. The "300 warriors" thing was bullshit for a start as the Spartans had as many as 10,000 other allies at the battle. But this myth of "The Few" was a great story and people were wedded to it and so Alexander took advantage.

Having overrun the great Persian City of Persepolis, built by Darius the Great – Alexander razed it to the ground. According to Greek historian and senator Arrian of Nicomedia, who drew on eyewitness testimony, the motive was clear: "Alexander burnt up the palace at Persepolis to avenge the Greeks because the Persians had destroyed both temples and cities of the Greeks by fire and sword."

By selling his victory over the Persians as revenge, Alexander got the Greeks on side, made his victory theirs and, critically, didn't have to waste time policing them.

By his death, aged 32, in 323 BCE, Alexander commanded a vast Empire that stretched from the Adriatic Sea to modern-day Pakistan. The whole, bonded together by some adept politicking and a forged sense of common unity, ruled beneath his beguiling, heroic image and perceived charisma. Unfortunately, having unified the whole conceit on his cult of personality, as soon as he was gone, it was over and the Empire swiftly fell apart.

Although undoubtedly a superb field commander, strategist and highly capable political leader, Alexander was not always what might be deemed "great". He was short-tempered and vengeful. He frequently killed people and laid cities to waste, simply because they got in his way. He could be reckless and, ultimately, because he lacked foresight and didn't appoint a successor, most of his achievements rapidly turned to dust.

Those that lasted – most notably the unification of Greece and the propagation of Greek culture and ideas – were really extensions of his father Philip's achievements. It was Philip II who had conquered Greece and he who had subsequently united it under the League of Corinth, spawning the Hellenistic era. The plans to invade the Persian Empire were Philip's too.

But who ever heard of Philip? It's Alexander the Great who everyone remembers and much of that is down to his and his propagandists' genius. His name and his image persist because, when not looking incredibly hot, he was the first great master of spin and self-promotion.

Create your own myth and – as we have seen with Hitler and Churchill – that myth will persist and guarantee your place in the history books. Even if the truth is quite different to the legend.

* * *

Alexander's methodology was so effective that it was copied wholesale by all the great Empire makers who followed. It was the Romans who dubbed Alexander "Magnus" (or Great) and the first Emperor Augustus unapologetically pinched the look, the act and the gestures for himself, just as Napoleone di Buonaparte, Corsican-born scion of minor Tuscan nobility, was to later lift all of that from Augustus.

And it was undoubtedly Napoleon who built our notions of modern propaganda, on the shoulders of the greats. In 1797, aged just 28, Napoleon was already commanding the French army in Italy.

He had got there through dedication and reputation – but he had also got there through some artful manipulation. Like Alexander, Bonaparte knew how to plug into his people and forge a legend. He was an adept user of the era's social media, although, as the internet and cinema had yet to be invented, all he had was art, portraiture, fashion, music and the press. This was the age of Romanticism, and Napoleon projected himself, in the words of Stanford Professor Albert Guerard, as the "romantic ideal incarnate".

In late 18th-century France, there was a craze for metal medallions and, realising the importance of iconography in getting yourself noticed, Napoleon commissioned a series of five that depicted his victories in Italy on one side and himself on the other as a Roman-cum-Alexander warrior, with laurel-wreath crown – a figure at once romantic, heroic and imperial.

As his star ascended, he courted artists willing to portray him as a dashing revolutionary figure. The first work in this vein, *Bonaparte at the Pont d'Arcole*, painted by his favourite artist-propagandist Antoine-Jean Gros in 1796, shows him going "full Alexander". As Napoleon leads his troops through the thick of battle, flag in hand – his long hair cascades behind him while his sword bears the inscription *Bonaparte, Armée d'Italie* – lest anyone should wonder who he is.

Over the two decades that followed, Gros and other favoured artists pushed their man and sponsor. And like Barbie or Action Man, we see different versions of the same product. We get to see Napoleon the man of action, the man of the people, the glorious Roman Emperor, the latter-day Hannibal crossing the Alps and even the hard-working bureaucrat in his study, in the wee small hours of the morning, hammering out the fine details of the Napoleonic Code. If you've ever seen a photo of a politician, poised with a pen at a desk or riding a horse, or sitting in a tank – it's arguably in part down to Napoleon.

He also harnessed music. Mighty, bombastic stuff with bloodthirsty choruses about crushing France's barbaric enemies and freeing enslaved people from the tyranny of everyone else. In fact, not so very dissimilar to "Rule, Britannia!" Songs such as "Chant du Départ", whose words were penned in 1799, the year Napoleon seized power, give a flavour:

Tremble, enemies of France
Kings drunk on blood and pride
The sovereign people shall advance,
Tyrants descend in graves to hide!

Which is all well and good until you remember that "sovereign" people means "men", seeing as women had no rights in 1799 and indeed didn't get the vote in France until 1944, and "white", because, despite the Revolution having abolished slavery, Napoleon re-established it in 1802.

Tunes aside, Napoleon's greatest propaganda innovation was to harness the power of the press. As he stormed through Italy in the dimming light of the 18th century, he wooed the existing domestic newspapers, even as he set up his own. By 1797, he could count on no less than six mouthpieces that promoted him as the man of the moment, while attacking his critics. Two of those, the *Courrier de l'Armée d'Italie* and *La France vue de l'Armée d'Italie*, were his own. Ostensibly military newspapers, distributed to his troops, between articles about life back home, Napoleon – the hero – was sold extremely effectively. Copies bolstered his support among his troops and made their way back to the capital, where other papers sucked up his many real – and frequently exaggerated – victories, printing them unexpiated.

Quite literally fake news and all curiously modern. In a sense, the paintings and medallions were his Instagram, the music his YouTube, the papers his Twitter and Facebook.

Literacy was high in late 18th-century France – at least 65% of the adult population could read (much higher still among men) and Napoleon took advantage. He was the only guy who could end the chaos; a strong man who could pull fractured, post-revolutionary France together. He was a figure apart from the affairs of Parisian politics – a man of the people – who would make France great again.

Napoleon's propagandising efforts were so effective that he went viral and the "Cult of Bonaparte" went way beyond the territories of France. Even in Britain, he was seen as something of a superstar. The writer William Hazlitt called him the "greatest man in modern history".

Elizabeth Vassall Fox, wife of the Lord Privy Seal and Whig Politician Henry Fox, was nothing short of a Napoleon super-groupie and, having met him, put up a bust of the French leader in her garden at Holland House. Byron wrote poems about him, Scottish aristocrats commissioned paintings of him, Beethoven wrote his third symphony in his honour and called it *The Bonaparte Symphony* – before angrily changing his mind when Napoleon crowned himself Emperor in 1804, erasing the dedication from the score.*

The problem with turning yourself into an icon is that you then have to live up to the image you have created, and living gods rarely stand up to scrutiny in the flesh. Lady Fox might have gushed with praise after first meeting the future emperor, writing to her sister about his "neat ears", but others were less impressed. Just as the "real life" Hitler left *Cosmopolitan* journalist Dorothy Thompson cold, so Napoleon failed to live up to his hype.

Bavarian artist Albrecht Adam, who painted him in 1809, later recalled:

"There he sat on his little white Arab horse, in a rather careless posture, with a small hat on his head... no one would have recognised the personage as the mighty Emperor – the victor of Austerlitz and Jena before whom even monarchs must bow, if they had not seen him represented so often in pictures."

Novelist Paul de Koch, who saw Napoleon in 1811, described him as: "yellow, obese, bloated, with his head too far down on his shoulders."

Following his capture at Waterloo, the defeated General was taken into exile aboard HMS *Northumberland* to St Helena where Major-General Sir George Bingham, who had been put in charge of his guard, wrote: "His tout ensemble not at all giving an idea that he had been so great or was so extraordinary a man."

Of course, most people and most of his admirers never met the man at the centre of the myth – they just saw the iconography and

---

* A rare case of a "good story" actually being true. Beethoven was so angry that he stabbed through Napoleon's name leaving a hole in the score.

read about him in his newspapers, and that was all that was needed in the pre-moving image age. Once a celebrity has a committed following, they are almost impossible to dethrone in the eyes of their adoring fans.

Not that it didn't stop the British trying. Taking a leaf out of Pope Gregory's book, the government fought fire with fire and in doing so even mimicked Napoleon's methods. They secretly funded their own French-language newspapers including *L'Ambigu*, the *Courier de Londres* and the *Courier d'Angleterre*, all of which were ostensibly run by émigré refugees from revolutionary France but all given heap loads of Exchequer cash and free licence to attack Bonaparte.

As this counter-propaganda and misinformation filtered into Europe through back channels, Napoleon mounted a rear-guard information war. He began by complaining to the British government and, when that failed, exerted influence in Batavia, Hamburg and Saxony to stop distribution. Like a later populist leader, he denounced the attempts to counter his own fake news as "Fake News". Simultaneously he tried to get at the editors and journalists behind them and with some success. Several were lured back to France; others were bribed into silence.

But not Jacques Régnier. Régnier was a "Creole colonist" and he hated both the French Revolution and Napoleon with a passion. That loathing stemmed from events in 1791, when black slaves in the French colony of Haiti had risen up under the leadership of African-born Jean-François Papillon and revolutionary fighter Georges Biassou. Napoleon was later to seek to regain control over the island and reimpose slavery, but following a protracted war of independence, in 1804, the French were defeated and Jean-Jacques Dessalines, born a slave, became the first black president of the first republic in South America and the Caribbean.

By then, an embittered Régnier, who had been dispossessed, first by the revolution and then by the uprising that followed, had long ago moved to France and was writing for the Jacobin (radical republican) journal *Cosmopolite* when the Reign of Terror erupted in 1793. That year of carnage saw the two dominant political factions of revolutionary France turn against each other in an orgy of bloodshed, beheadings and arrests – often on spurious charges.

Régnier's publisher was executed, but Jacques dodged the guillotine and languished in jail instead. Following his release, in 1795, he fled to England. Having provided intelligence to the authorities, he found work as a propagandist, got thrown into prison for debt and found salvation when, in 1802, he was rescued by the owners of the *Courier de Londres, who* offered him the job of editor.

Seething with indignation, self-pity and an ever-expanding grudge against France and Napoleon, Régnier set to work and was to become perhaps the most highly effective anti-Napoleonic propagandist of the era.

Unlike many of his contemporaries he remained unbribable. This was in part because he was being paid more by the British than the French could offer but also, critically, because like many of the most notorious propagandists of history, he was driven by ideology, bitterness and revenge. He had lost his home, his land and his fortune and had nearly lost his life – all thanks to the revolution – and he blamed it and later Napoleon for his misfortune. His personal, ideological hatred of the target made him untouchable.

Régnier's stint as an anti-Napoleonic influencer ended with the Battle of Waterloo in 1815. But in the years leading up to that, his efforts in spreading dissent and disinformation from Spain to Sweden, Russia and beyond in his newspapers and pamphlets played a pivotal role in the information war against Napoleon.

Britain proved fertile ground for others who were ideologically opposed to Bonapartism, and "lone wolf" privately funded propaganda was rife. *The Revolutionary Plutarch*, which was published in 1804 purportedly by "A Gentleman Resident in Paris" but probably written by Lewis Goldsmith, an Anglo-French publisher and writer in London, is a prime example. Goldsmith went from Napoleon superfan to anti-republican polemicist and the book accused the Napoleonic regime of sickening human rights abuses.

The Revolutionary Plutarch was an early example of "atrocity propaganda" – the deliberate spreading of fake, often violent and pornographic accounts of crimes committed by the enemy to discredit them. Attention-grabbing violent and sensationalist content remains a powerful method of spreading fear and disinformation in the social media age, and things were little different in 1804.

The book claimed there were 132,000 French secret police in Paris alone out of a population of 600,000. It described in some detail the Chambre d'Enfer (Chamber of Hell) at the headquarters of the secret police, where prisoners were tortured, raped and had their limbs pulled apart on the rack. Most of it was made up but the best propaganda latches onto some elements of truth that can then be used to give it a degree of credibility. The 1790s Reign of Terror had been real and, in many minds, it still defined the French Revolution. Likewise, the secret police did exist.

Under the leadership of Joseph Fouché, dissent was brutally stamped out. Paranoia was rife, agents provocateurs widespread and arrests and disappearances common. But the idea that there were 132,000 spies in Paris was obvious fabrication. Goldsmith also popularised the idea that the guillotine sat at the centre of everything in Napoleonic France and portrayed daily life as one of heads rolling left, right and centre in an orgy of perpetual violence.

Used in France until 1977, the guillotine came to be seen as the apotheosis of the inherent barbarity of the regime and French revolutionary bloodlust in general. But it has also attracted its fair share of fake history. Curiously, Joseph-Ignace Guillotin, who gave it its name, was opposed to capital punishment and only encouraged the use of mechanised execution because he thought it less barbaric than hanging. Death by decapitation had long been the preserve of the "elite" because it was swift and less painful, so bizarre as it might sound, the guillotine was viewed as a "progressive notion" in 18th-century France.

Despite giving the device its name, Guillotin didn't actually invent it or play a part in its construction. The device we call a "guillotine" had existed in some form or other for centuries and the earliest examples are found in, er, England. The "Halifax Gibbet" had been used as far back as the 13th century and contemporary woodcuts show that it looked and acted just like a guillotine. The device had been used well into the 17th century but its use was forbidden by Cromwell, and it was dismantled in 1650.

Obviously, the English propagandists kept quiet about that and played up the barbarity of the "French" instrument of death instead.

Guillotin's family were so embarrassed by the association of his name with the implement that following Joseph-Ignace's death, they lobbied the Parisian government to change the machine's name, and when that failed, they changed theirs instead. Poor old Guillotin's good intentions have gifted him a place in infamy.

A common belief about the peace-loving Monsieur Guillotin is that he was executed by the very contraption he had popularised. The story was so widespread even in the early 19th century that the story appears in the first English language mention of the guillotine in an 1818 update of *Johnson's Dictionary* by the Reverend Henry Todd, just four years after the inventor's death. It's a "good story" but quite untrue. He lived to a ripe old age and died of natural causes.

Films and popular culture have embedded a widespread belief that well into the 19th century the French were toppling heads like skittles while braying "sans-culottes"* cheered on. But while public executions remained a source of public spectacle from the 1830s, the state guillotine was removed from the centre of Paris to La Sante prison and its usage pared back. The excesses of the Reign of Terror, when 16,000 people had died, many beneath that blade, never came back to haunt Paris. Indeed, contemporary records show there were actually three times fewer executions during the Napoleonic period than there were in England and Wales. And that, despite France then having a population three times larger.

We believe otherwise because Régnier, Goldsmith and their ilk were very good at propaganda and promulgating stories of terror and execution. That many British people still perceive Napoleonic France as an unending tale of violence and sorrow is a testament to their work. Which is not to say that the spectacle of executions in France ended with the removal of the guillotine to La Sante Prison. Incredibly, public beheadings continued in Paris long after they had ended elsewhere in Europe and the last took

---

* French revolutionary working class

place in June 1939, when German serial killer Eugen Weidmann was decapitated in front of a braying and whistling mob. The crowd of onlookers included a 17-year-old English student called Christopher Lee who was so appalled by the spectacle that he later wrote in his autobiography: "I thought I would die myself."

Even that was not the end of it. The last execution carried out by the guillotine in France came, behind closed doors, in September 1977 when convicted murderer Hamida Djandoubi was decapitated. The machine's 189-year history finally ended four years later when France abolished the death penalty.

Napoleon's legacy, like that of the revolution that bore him, is complex and fraught with contradictions. For some he was – and remains – the romantic embodiment of the French Enlightenment, the champion of religious freedom and a progressive to the tips of his bicorne hat. A man who defined the very best of the ideals of his age. The promulgator of the Napoleonic Code, which codified laws and which acted as the bench-mark for many modern democracies. The instigator of educational reforms that laid the foundation for those in Europe and beyond. A military genius and populist beloved of his people, whose star still dazzles brightly 200 years after his death, even in Britain.

To others, he is a self-aggrandising brigand. A gangster and petty despot who beguiled the ignorant masses and who sought to reimpose slavery and tyranny. A man who espoused great ideals even as he trampled on the sovereignty of other nations. A hypocrite who spoke of democracy and liberty but who ruled as an autocrat and an emperor.

The truth, as ever, lies somewhere in between.

Napoleon's achievements in education, law and religious freedom should not overshadow the fact that his ambition caused the deaths of between three and six million people – many of them his own. An estimated 1.8 million French and allied soldiers died in the invasion of Russia alone. The ultimate pawns of history, sacrificed for their emperor's ambition. Napoleonic France was undoubtedly a dictatorship, but then in the early 19th century the great enemy Britain was hardly a democracy either.

In 1800 less than 5% of the adult population could vote and those who were allowed to were all rich men. Most cities and towns had no MPs at all. There was no such thing as a secret ballot and frequently there was only one candidate standing in any given constituency. Ordinary people and even affluent middle-class people had no say in their government at all.

Britain was very far from being some benign patriarchy. Governments of the era were quick to crush dissent and radicalism as the Peterloo Massacre of 1819 demonstrates. On that day, in August 1819, hundreds of people, who had gathered to protest against economic inequity and call for reforms to suffrage that might allow them to vote, were charged by sabre-wielding hussars who killed at least a dozen people and wounded hundreds more.

Napoleon's conquests might have cost the lives of millions of his people, but the British didn't have to even engage in foreign misadventure to sacrifice theirs. The Irish Potato Famine in the 1840s might have started courtesy of potato blight, but the loss of upwards of a million lives was very much down to incompetence, inefficiency, callousness and disinterest on the part of Westminster politicians and the ruling elite.

As for accusations that Napoleon was "depriving other people of their liberty", well in the same era, British Imperial ambition was coming into its own. The British establishment viewed their people near and far as subjects. In France, the Napoleonic Code, for all its flaws, judged the French (male) population as equal citizens. And yet in Britain at least, the notion of "despotic Boney" persists, while the early 19th-century British rulers, despite their failings, are viewed as benign and well-intentioned men.

Much of the reason for that paradox rests in the still pungent propaganda of the era that so effectively ingrained itself in the British psyche. Arguably, the most potent freelance assault on Napoleon of all and the one that has helped define our enduring false image of him came from contemporary cartoonist James Gillray.

Following Nelson's defeat of the French fleet at the Battle of the Nile in 1798, Gillray drew a famous cartoon depicting the General throwing a hissy fit. In later take-downs, he portrayed Bonaparte as "Little Boney" – an angry, diminutive Frenchman in ill-fitting boots. In truth, Napoleon was around 5 ft 5 in tall (1.69 metres), which was actually slightly above average height for a Frenchman in the early 19th century, but attacking a leader's stature is a tried and tested means of debasing him. There is no weapon so effective as mockery and Gillray's vicious caricatures did more to demythologise Napoleon than anything else.

With so much disinformation flying about, it's not surprising that so much of it persists. And likewise, as the British eventually defeated Napoleon, many of the generally accepted ideas and propaganda that came out of that victory at Waterloo persevere. Prime among them is the line attributed to Wellington, that "Waterloo was won on the playing fields of Eton." Understandably, Eton College is very proud of that, but in fact Wellington never said it. He hated his old school, and when he left Eton in 1784 there were no playing fields anyway.

The English claimed Waterloo as "their" victory and even named a train station after it, but in fact the Battle of Waterloo – won on the fields of Waterloo in Belgium – was achieved by a broad alliance of nations and classes and not just a bunch of English public schoolboys.

Half of the Iron Duke's forces came from Belgium, Saxony, Hanover and Holland. Of the remaining 23,000, around a third were Irish, another third were Scottish, leaving approximately 8,000 English – making up just 6% of the forces of all nations present. There may have been a handful of Etonians present – but they were hardly the deciding factor.

The other cliché bequeathed to us by that battle is: "If Wellington had lost at Waterloo, then we'd all be speaking French." A fantastic example of a spectacularly stupid notion gaining general currency, despite being obviously and quite palpably wrong. Had Wellington been defeated at Waterloo, it would not have been the end for Britain or her allies. It would simply have been a lost battle in an ongoing war. Wellington and his armies would not have surrendered but withdrawn. This was Napoleon's final throw of the dice and nobody else's.

And even if Napoleon had somehow managed to turn the tide of events and surmounted the pile of cards that were stacked against him and one day invaded Britain, it is very unlikely that the people of these islands would have started adopting French. Napoleon conquered Holland, much of Italy, a good proportion of Germany and great chunks of Poland and Spain. But all of those places retained their native tongues.

And if the assumption inherent within the idea is that defeated nations always end up speaking the language of the conqueror – then the opposite would be true. The French would all be speaking

English and nothing else. And in case you are an English native speaker and have never been to France, then please take it from me – they don't.

* * *

Human beings have prospered in great measure as a species because of their inherent sociability and willingness to cooperate, but, unfortunately, throughout history that has made us all susceptible to liars, conmen, bad relationships and people who write great CVs.

Anyone who ever passed a job interview or got laid is first and foremost a successful propagandist. All of us spin and lie for advantage.

Social media influencers are a superb example of the art. Like all great propagandists, the best use a base reality and build an alternative truth on top, selling the best of what they are. The most successful politicians of our age do it too, building their reputations on social media platforms that bypass mainstream media and inject the message straight into the veins of the world's smartphones. That's not always a bad thing. Social media can counter propaganda too. In dictatorships and failing democracies, smartphones have enabled anti-government voices to fight back with counter-narratives and counter-propaganda and of course, not all propaganda is bad. Even state propaganda can be benevolent.

Take Britain's iconic "public information films". From the 1960s onwards, these shorts warned of the dangers of playing near water or railway tracks or of crossing the road. Soon, children believed that if you so much as strayed near a pond or a station you'd drown (or be cut in half by a train).

It was exaggerated but it was hugely effective. In the late 1970s, 2,000 children a year were dying as a result of injuries caused by accidents in the UK. By 2011, the figure had plummeted to 140. Since 1983, accidental deaths by drowning have fallen by a third. That was not exclusively down to public information campaigns, but their role in increasing awareness had a hugely beneficial impact.

Government information is propaganda. During the Second World War, the propaganda ministry was even called the Ministry of Information. But most British people don't think it happens *here*. The very term "propaganda" conjures up thoughts of Goebbels, Hitler and Soviet Russia. If we think of British or American efforts, we – mistakenly – believe them to be somehow benign – or honest.

In truth, throughout the 20th century, the UK excelled at the dark art of disinformation and message control. Four days after the declaration of war in August 1914, Herbert Asquith's government passed the Defence of the Realm Act, which effectively gave the government the power to arrest journalists or editors who undermined the war effort. Most fell into line, as did writers and artists who officially and unofficially threw their weight behind the great war effort. As the war dragged on, though, the government deployed more sinister methods.

In 1915, as recruitment faltered, the Bryce Report on "Alleged German Outrages" was published. This 48-page, seemingly meticulously referenced government booklet detailed "German atrocities". It set out the Kaiser's use of women and children as human shields and terrified readers with the "murder lust and pillage" of the enemy. The Germans didn't play by the rules. They fired shells at hospitals and executed civilians. They even chopped off children's hands to cow the populations of places they invaded.

Lord Bryce was a hugely respected figure and the publication caused a sensation. When it was printed in America, it added to the growing clamour of voices calling for US intervention in the war. The Germans were out of control monsters – they needed to be stopped.

The "atrocity narratives" that had been so effective in countering Napoleon were being used again, and once again, there was just enough truth to render it credible. It was meticulously referenced, after all. The accounts of hands being cut off were in fact rumours, spread by fleeing refugees and completely made up. The Bryce Report shared them anyway.

Keeping the lies credible and emotive was a hugely effective strategy and one that stirred admiration in no less a figure than Lance Corporal Adolf Hitler of the Bavarian regiment.

The notion of a barbarian, barely human enemy, whose savage men were sent forth by equally savage Prussian generals, was far from fair. For a start, the German High Command treated their men better. German soldiers tended to enjoy more comfortable and better equipped trenches and, while the British Army alone shot 306 of their own people for "cowardice", the Imperial Army executed just 25.

The credulous subjects of the British Empire, drawn to simplistic narratives and comforted by confirmation bias, bought the version spun to them wholesale and many continue to do so. Germany were the baddies – the war was entirely their fault – and their atrocities a matter of record. "We" were the goodies.

There were atrocities, of course, but they were carried out on all sides. There are no truly innocent parties among the combatant nations of the First World War. By the outbreak of the Second World War, things had changed in the propaganda war, not least because the Nazis had made things easier for their enemies. Hitler and his henchmen were palpably bad people, wedded to an obviously evil doctrine and quite open about their intentions to commit mass murder and invade sovereign lands. They had in fact become the imagined enemy of the Great War.

The British Ministry of Information had a lot of material to work with and fought the propaganda war on many fronts. Even as they ridiculed the enemy and played up fear of it, British "Home Front" propaganda artfully spun the "Blitz Spirit" and notion of plucky little Britain standing up to the mighty Nazi war machine.

The British also developed "black propaganda" – a methodology stretching back to the anti-Bonaparte papers of the Napoleonic era, which involves spreading disinformation from another country. In 1941, British Intelligence set up fake radio station, GS1, and once again used pornography as bait. German soldiers were lured in to listen to "Der Chef", a charismatic self-professed "Nazi loyalist", who simultaneously claimed he wasn't "a real Nazi" while ranting and raving about Hitler's shortcomings and providing lurid accounts of the leadership's sexual proclivities. Hungry for truth and sensing that they were getting it from "Der Chef", the Wehrmacht troops tuned in en masse. This was not the "mainstream media" fed to them by the Nazi propaganda machine – it was "the truth".

The clandestine station was a hit and cemented its credibility by attacking the British and Americans and even killing off the host in a dramatic final programme. Everything the German soldiers heard was being broadcast from London and "Der Chef" was a former pulp fiction writer by the name of Peter Seckelmann.

The whole "fake news" package was so effective that debriefed enemy combatants were astonished to discover the deceit that had been played on them, and the German High Command spent considerable time and money on trying to block the signals.

British efforts contrasted with the far less subtle German technique of simply broadcasting into enemy territory in English – a methodology that made unlikely stars of the American Nazi propagandist Mildred Gillars aka "Axis Sally", and William Joyce, otherwise known as Lord Haw-Haw. Gillars was popular with allied audiences because, despite her repulsive views and fear-spreading, she was funny. After the war she was sent to prison for 12 years. Joyce was shot.

Where the Germans got it wrong was in the blunt nature of their approach. By comparison, British disinformation was cunning and engendered an emotional response in listeners who trusted it. And in that it was similar to that of the undisputed masters of the art – the Russians.

The term "disinformation" was first coined in 1923 when Josef Stalin set up the Special Disinformation Office in Moscow. This was part of a wider strategy of "active measures", both internally and externally, which the Soviet Union conducted to destabilise other countries, to stir discontent abroad, to weaken and divide enemies and, where necessary, to rewrite the past.

The efforts began first at home. Under Stalin, enemies and even former allies were literally erased from history. Nikolai Yezhov, a loyal lieutenant of the Russian leader, later fell out with him and almost immediately his image disappeared from pre-existing photographs, along with Trotsky, Kamenev and Khalatov – all key Bolshevik figures in the early days of the revolution. The Russian propaganda machine created an "alternative truth".

On that same Russian Intourist* trip I took with my school in December 1986, we were shown around the Lenin Museum in Moscow and, having been led from exhibit to exhibit in which we had searched in vain for images of Trotsky, we asked our guide where he was. To this our visibly ruffled guide replied that: "Trotsky does not matter to us. He is irrelevant." That would be Leon Trotsky, architect and military commander of the Russian revolution in November 1917, original member of the Politburo, creator of the Red Army. Irrelevant.

The Russian word *"dezinformatsiya"*, people were told, was taken from the French *"désinformation"*, and is itself an example of the art. By blaming the French for the term, it made them look untrustworthy.

This was part of the brief of the Special Disinformation Office, to 'spread false information with the intention of deceiving the public.'

The best disinformation, like the best propaganda, blends real narratives with fake ones, playing to existing rumours and urban myths, or perhaps playing to the prejudices of a target audience by creating an "attractive lie" and feeding existing fears.

In the Cold War, there was much for the Russians to play with. Throughout the 1950s the CIA experimented on its own people. It put thousands of soldiers in the field to "observe nuclear detonations", when really it was testing what would happen to the men. "We were basically used as guinea pigs," one survivor told *Vice* magazine in a 2018 interview. "There's no other word for it."

From 1953 onwards, the CIA administered LSD to mental patients, prisoners, soldiers and even its own employees to see what the effects would be.

---

* The state-run travel agency for foreign tourists visiting the Soviet Union

Between the 1930s and 1970s, the US Public Health Service secured the cooperation of poor African American sharecroppers in the infamous "Tuskegee Syphilis Study" on the promise of offering them free treatment for "bad blood". There was no intention to treat them at all. The unethical study was set up with the sole intention of "observing the natural history of untreated syphilis". The lingering distrust of many African Americans for the US state and in particular healthcare and vaccinations stems, understandably, from that event.

And it wasn't just America. Distrust of the West within the West was a thing long before the Russians turned up. All the USSR needed to do was to weaponise it.

Following the creation of the KGB in March 1954, the Special Disinformation Office became a particularly active and effective tool in spreading anxiety and discord in the West. Former KGB general Oleg Kalugin, who ran disinformation campaigns in the US and elsewhere in the 1970s by posing as "Press Officer" of the Russian Embassy in Washington, later described the process as: "Not intelligence collection, but subversion: active measures to weaken the west, to drive wedges in the western community alliances of all sorts, particularly NATO, to sow discord among allies, to weaken the United States in the eyes of the people of Europe, Asia, Africa [and] Latin America."

The USSR found fertile ground in the anti-nuclear movements, fringe parties of the far left and even in the moderate mainstream left-wing parties of the West. There were many others jaded by the Second World War and sceptical of Western interventions at Suez, on the Korea peninsula and especially in Vietnam who came to view their own governments suspiciously.

The conspiracy theories spread by the USSR had a willing and susceptible audience – and many of their campaigns were so effective that the whispers they started still persist today. You may at some point in your life have even believed one or two.

Within days of the assassination of John F. Kennedy in 1963, the Special Disinformation Office was spreading a myth that he had been killed by rogue elements of the CIA, working in harmony with the Mafia. Subsequently, they also covertly funded a bestselling book propagating the theory. They repeated the trick five years later following the murder of Martin Luther King, and in the violence that followed the assassination, they actively tried to stoke up a race war in the US.

Many of these Soviet-era "big lies" have gone on to have afterlives of their own. Many people still whisper darkly that Kennedy was "killed by the CIA", that mass vaccination programmes are a cover for something else and even that the fluoridation of the US water supply was somehow a means of mass control.

Most notable of all Russia's "active measures" was Operation Infektion, a scheme in the 1980s that managed to convince a good number of people in the West that HIV/AIDS had been deliberately created in Fort Detrick, a US weapons lab in Maryland.

Through a letter from an anonymous "American scientist" to *The Patriot*, a covertly funded Indian newspaper, the lie was disseminated around the world with nudges and winks from Moscow-backed media outlets. It was incredibly effective and even today there are people who murmur cladestinely that "AIDS was created in a US lab" despite there being no evidence for it.

The willingness to believe that "AIDS" was a virus created by the US government was predicated in no small measure on the truth that the US state had experimented on black men and used servicemen as guinea pigs.

Throughout his period in office, Thabo Mbeki, South African president between 1999 and 2008, used the Fort Detrick conspiracy to cast doubt on the science of HIV.

On his 2005 single, "Heard 'Em Say", US artist Kanye West raps: "I know that the government administers AIDS". Useful idiots both but far from alone in believing and encouraging the lies.

The "they made it in a lab" narrative is still used to discredit the other side – and not only by the Russians. It resurfaced during the Covid-19 pandemic – when the US and Chinese governments both spread rumours that the other side had created the virus in a laboratory and then infected rival nations with it for their own nefarious ends.

The prevailing mistrust feeds not only the myth of lab-made AIDS, but more worryingly a mistrust of vaccination programmes in general, particularly in the black community. In December 2020, Pew Research found that just 42% of African Americans were willing to have a coronavirus jab compared to 63% of white and Latinos and 82% of Asian Americans.

The fear has been consistently stoked by the Russian disinformation machine with "anti-vax" narratives being a staple of English-language Kremlin media channel RT. But it only works because people are willing to believe it and because "freelance" conspiracy theorists are willing to push the agenda on Twitter, Facebook, TikTok and other social media platforms. In the digital age, people are ever more prone to fall for big lies – and the misinformation is easier than ever to disseminate.

On 4th March 2018, former Russian Intelligence agent Sergei Skripal and his daughter Yulia were discovered, vomiting, on a bench in Salisbury. On examination, it became clear that they and a police officer, Nick Bailey, who had gone to their aid, had been poisoned with a nerve agent, Novichok.

The obvious suspect was the Kremlin. It was well established that critics of Mr Putin had an unfortunate habit of dying, and the attack in Salisbury bore striking similarities to that against Alexander Litvinenko in November 2006. Two Russian nationals, Anatoliy Chepiga and Alexander Petrov, both agents of the Russian military intelligence unit the GRU, were identified by the Bellingcat investigative website as having been present at the scene in Salisbury.

And yet, despite there being more smoking guns than on the fields at Waterloo, many simply refused to believe it. The Russian disinformation machine found eager supporters in the British media and political elite, and some even suggested that the British had done it instead.

In all of this, Russia's hugely effective glossy propaganda machine RT played a significant role. Managing to position itself as an "alternative voice" telling the "real news" and beamed via satellite into TV sets across the West, the channel excels at convincing people that day is night and night is day. The legacy of 70 plus years of tried and tested formulas, it is polished, accessible and mixes "truth" with agenda to devastating effect.

The Russian state also employs thousands of "Twitter trolls" whose job is to spread disinformation with varying degrees of success online.

Putin's modern disinformation campaigns have caused havoc. Their work is visible in the election of Trump, Brexit, the migrant crisis, the pernicious anti-vax movement and countless "separatist" movements in Europe as well as Calexit and Texit – the respective independence campaigns for California and Texas. These last two went curiously silent during Trump's four years in office, not least when it was revealed that the organiser behind Calexit actually lived in Siberia. But as soon as Trump was gone both campaigns began to start up again.

The hand of Russian state media disinformation is also visible in any number of health scares, not least the widespread suspicion of "Western" 5G and, since 2020, the fairly bonkers rumour that super-fast broadband might even be responsible for Covid-19.

A BBC investigation in 2019 found that both RT and its sister channel Sputnik repeatedly attacked 5G roll-out in the West, inviting in "experts" who were actually conspiracy theorists and promulgating baseless theories that "bees are dying under 5G poles". The fear tactic works.

Simultaneously, Russia has used its media to portray its own, Chinese-built, 5G systems as superior and itself as a major global superpower while having a GDP ranking roughly akin to Spain's and significantly lower than Italy's.

Big lies and disinformation work and all sides do it.

Take Ronald Reagan's shiny Strategic Defence Initiative or "Star Wars", which my father used to console me with in the 1980s as I worried about approaching Armageddon. Even as it was used as a bargaining chip against the USSR, it never actually existed, nor had any hope of existing. The technology hadn't been invented and the cost of even trying would have likely bankrupted America. Classic disinformation. But the Russians bought into it as willingly as the many who wanted to believe it.

"It's easier to fool people, than convince them that they have been fooled" as Mark Twain once said (and yes, I've quoted him already). The epithet is everywhere – on the internet, in school text books and even in dictionaries of quotations. It's a great quote. Typical of Mark Twain. The only problem is – the words are not his.

CHAPTER TEN

GENGHIS KHAN WAS A PITILESS BARBARIAN

The Importance of Being Enemies

Nation states need enemies. In the absence of them, even the greatest empires can lose their way – and in the second century BCE, Rome did just that.

At the climax of the Third Punic War in 146 BCE, after a three-year siege of Carthage, the Roman general Scipio breached the walls of the city and his men flooded in. Six days of brutal close-quarter combat ended with the Carthaginian general Hasdrubal surrendering beneath the Temple of Eshmun, the city's most sacred site. As he did so, his wife*, appalled at his cowardice, took her sons' hands and walked into the burning embers of the temple never to be seen again.

Rome's triumph was absolute and the aftermath was unforgiving. Carthage was reduced to rubble, most of its people killed, the rest taken into slavery. The very ground was cursed.

But as Scipio watched the desecration, tears filled his eyes and, turning to his friend and mentor, the Greek historian Polybius,

---

* Her name is sadly unknown to us

who was conveniently on hand to cover the event on behalf of history, said: "A glorious moment, Polybius; but I have a terrible foreboding, that eventually the same fate shall be pronounced on our own land." Scipio then quoted Homer: "A day will come when sacred Troy shall perish – and Priam and his people shall be slain."Rome didn't fall in a day. In the years that followed, trade flourished, the Empire expanded and the Pax Romana, a 200-year period of relative stability across the Mediterranean, brought peace and prosperity. But even as it did so, some – including, most vocally, the historian Livy – began to feel that it couldn't last and started to propagate the idea that the Republic had lost its sense of purpose and needed to return to what it had been before. By becoming something bigger, its earlier spirit was gone. The Romans needed big personalities who would take back control and turn back the clock on the moral decay.

In destroying Carthage, their last great nemesis, the Romans had nobody to fight but themselves. In the absence of an enemy, Rome was having an existential crisis.

The United States, forged out of mass immigration, has always defined its sense of self or that "imagined community" through its sense of "the other". The savage native "Indians", the brutal colonialist "British Empire", Nazism, and latterly what Ronald Reagan deemed in 1983 to be the "Evil Empire" of the Communist East, all served that role. America's enemies defined who America was and served the notion of that "imagined community".

But with the collapse of the USSR, following the fall of the Berlin Wall in 1989, the USA found itself suffering much the same dilemma that had faced Rome two thousand years earlier. The sole, remaining, superpower was now Batman without the Joker, twiddling its gloved thumbs and wondering what to do with its utility belt and fancy car. Or to break from the metaphor – its armies, missiles, fleets and airpower.

In lieu of an adversary worthy of its talents, the US declared an ultimately unwinnable war on "drugs" and looked around for another enemy, which came eventually out of a deep blue sky on the morning of September 11th 2001.

Ten years after that fateful day, which saw the loss of 2,977 innocent lives, academics at Drew University and the University of Illinois published a study called *The Expulsion from Disneyland* on the social psychological impact of 9/11 on the American people. Much of it is what you might expect. The nation had suffered an unprecedented assault on its territory. Certainties had been upended. People were afraid. Nothing felt safe anymore and, seeking to make sense of it all, millions of Americans fell back on the comfort blanket of nationalism.

On Tuesday, September 11th 2001, US supermarket giant Walmart sold an astonishing 116,000 Stars and Stripes flags in one afternoon. Hundreds of thousands of Americans were responding to the still unfolding event by unfolding flags. By Wednesday, September 12th, the store had sold 250,000 more and, by Thursday morning, the company had completely run out of stock.

Soon the flag-waving had given way to hate-mongering. In the absence of a tangible enemy, Americans began lashing out at proxies and, in the months following the attack, there was a 10-fold increase in racially motivated crimes against Muslim Americans and anyone who could be mistaken for one. Alongside it came a dramatic shift in public opinion, particularly on issues of freedom and liberty. Polls showed a clear majority of Americans now willing to forego civil rights to "beat terrorism".

But not all of it was bad. Many US citizens reported that they were reassessing their values and priorities. Loved ones suddenly mattered, and 60% of people said that their personal relationships had improved as a direct result of the attacks. Altruism increased. Blood donations surged and between 2001 and 2002, charitable giving was the highest recorded in American history.

The re-emergence of a bona fide enemy had given the US a renewed purpose and a sense of unity.

9/11 also paid dividends for those in charge. George W. Bush, at that point president for just eight months, had a sliding approval rating sitting at about 50%. By October, in the immediate aftermath of the attacks, he was riding the wave of nationalism and, without doing very much of merit at all, was now the most popular president in US history, with a rating of 90%.

The Bush administration had obviously not willed the attack, despite what those conspiracy theories might say. But Bush, as leader, undoubtedly benefited. As the US-led attacks on Afghanistan and Iraq and as the hunt for Osama bin Laden intensified, one thing was clear: the "war on terrorism" had given the country renewed purpose. The "enemy" was back.

Fifteen years later, Donald J. Trump used the same narrative to get himself into the White House, promising that he would not only make America "great again" but also "safe again". By 2016, the unpopular wars in the Middle East were a bit "last decade", so Trump conjured up a new threat: foreigners.

Trump promised a "beautiful wall" to keep immigrants out... of immigrant America. He would fend off the threat of Chinese capitalism and protect American jobs. He would ban Muslims from entering the States and stop terrorism forever. In the meantime, he would bring the boys back home from Iraq.

The troops never did come home, nor was that wall ever finished, but Trump did sign Executive Order 13769, which for two brief months prevented people from Iran, Iraq, Syria and a selection of other "Muslim countries" from entering the USA. He also launched a trade war with China, which cost the US an estimated 300,000 jobs and reduced American GDP by 0.5%.

None of it made any sense but that wasn't the point. His core supporters, struck dumb by Facebook and Fox News, believed that Trump was keeping the US safe and that was all that mattered.

Over the next four years, Trump's entire Presidency was to become defined by enemies. The list included Facebook, most of Asia, the CIA, FBI, Hillary Clinton, the media, the IRS, Mitt Romney, the relatives of deceased US military personnel, Canada, France, former employees, former *Apprentice* contestants, former *Apprentice* contestants who were former employees, the EU, most global media agencies, the "establishment", sanity, Fox News, clever people, good-looking people, intelligent women, women who objected to being groped, Barack Obama, NASA, the Mayor of London, mail-in ballots and, of course, the dreaded "Antifa".

During his last months in power, the President warned constantly about the threat this last organisation posed. In June 2020, he claimed on Twitter that he was seeking to outlaw Antifa altogether and classify it as a terrorist group. In September 2020, he claimed that they would "attack your homes!" if he wasn't re-elected the following month He even warned that they would "hide voter fraud in your kids' Halloween candy".

This is all the more incredible when you consider that Antifa doesn't actually exist. The term means "people opposed to fascism". It is a sensibility, not an organisation. Declaring war on it, is like declaring war on salad. And looking at Mr Trump, it's tempting to believe that he might well have done that too.

* * *

Fear of "other" looms large in our tribal collective conscience and is there to be tapped into. The amygdala region of the human brain contains a reflex which is associated with emotional processes and which hardwires us to fear unfamiliar things, and studies show that these instincts are hard to shift. This might explain, if not excuse, the lingering xenophobic tendencies in some people and also why bigotry remains such a potent political tool. It also elucidates why voters in countries like Britain remain happy for their governments to spend billions on aircraft carriers and nuclear submarines that will likely never be used, even as people come to rely on food banks.

Notions of what constitutes an enemy can be summed up in the handy little acronym which I have dubbed "BETS".

B is for *Barbarians* – uncivilised "wild people" coming over the horizon and destroying everything in their path. In the old days, these were the Vikings, Goths, Mongol hordes and the Kaiser's army. Nowadays, "asylum seekers", "Muslims" and "terrorists" have taken their place.

E is for *Enemies within* – from fifth columnists, to EU fanatics, globalist bankers, Antifa, Brexiters, Democrats and Greens – depending on your sensibilities. Their aim? To destroy everything for reasons that remain obscure.

T is for *Traditional enemies* – never to be trusted. They drive on the wrong side of the road, eat funny food and remind us too much of ourselves. Think the French and Germans, Oxford versus Cambridge, or the people of Yorkshire and their Lancastrian neighbours.

S – stands for *Schrödinger's Foe*.

Erwin Schrödinger was an Austrian physicist, who posited the thought experiment where a cat in a sealed box, who may or may not be exposed to radioactive poison, can be considered to be both living and dead at the same time. The Schrödinger tag – as popularised on social media – has subsequently come to mean any paradox where two seemingly anomalous agendas are at work.

So, "Schrödinger's immigrant" is both coming here to take all the benefits *and* steal your job. "Schrödinger's Foe" is any enemy at once posing an unimaginable threat – while simultaneously being comical, inept and stupid. The 19th-century contemporary characterisation of Napoleon Bonaparte as "Little Boney" is classic "Schrödinger's Foe". So too, as we shall see, are modern depictions of the leaders of North Korea.

The further we travel from home, the more cartoonish our perceptions of "other" become. For some Europeans, pretty much everything east of the Bosporus is "Schrödinger's Foe" *territory*.

Iran may have a rich cultural heritage, an ancient system of etiquette known as "taarof", and a youth literacy rate of 98% that ranks it alongside most of the advanced nations of the world – but the "cleric and veil" view of the country reduces it to a fundamentalist backwater full of shouty people waving guns. It's a depressingly similar case for pretty much every other "Middle Eastern" country and, by the time we reach Central Asia, things have just got worse. Kazakhstan, the ninth largest country on Earth, has been so thoroughly *Boratised* that few in the West take it seriously at all. While it would be a considerable exaggeration to say that the nation is a thriving democracy where the LGBTQ+ community can go about their lives without fear of persecution*, the country is a growing regional power. Since 2002, the nation's GDP has seen a six-fold increase and poverty has fallen sharply. This is no nation of mules and dirt tracks, but it nevertheless remains the butt of a thousand bar room jokes and memes thanks in no small part to Sacha Baron-Cohen's comedy creation and Western ignorance.

Its neighbour to the south, Turkmenistan, fares no better. Google the country and one of the first stories to pop up is one about how President Berdymukhamedov erected a massive statue of himself riding a horse in 2015 and a gold statue of his dog in 2020. The nation's on-going political failure and appalling human rights record are brushed under the carpet as we dismiss the country as little more than a live action *Simpsons* episode.

Perceptions don't change much in most Western eyes, the further east you travel. China is now acknowledged as a major emerging superpower, but it is still broadly looked down upon in the West. And in the wake of Covid-19, things aren't improving. Research carried out in 14 countries including the UK, France, Germany and Australia in November 2020, showed that 73% of respondents had a negative or "very negative" view of the People's Republic.

Some of this was understandable – a result of perceptions of China's handling of the coronavirus outbreak and increasing scrutiny of the country's many human rights abuses. And then there's the treatment of the Uyghur minority and reports of internment camps, where "reeducation" and even state-sanctioned executions have taken place. Likewise, the cover-ups and attempts to conceal the government's failure over coronavirus.

---

* Same-sex relationships are legal in Kazakhstan and the age of consent is 16. But the LGBTQ+ community still encounter hostility in the wider community and many gay Kazakhs feel obliged to hide their sexuality.

However, much of the broader well of resentment and fear of China is undoubtedly rooted little more than in bad old-fashioned Sinophobia (the fear or hatred of China).

China, like Japan before it, may be modernising and changing, but the West still views it with a mixture of fear and contempt. Its people are all too frequently defined by racist clichés and false perceptions, with much of that rooted in a broader lingering suspicion of "Men from the East". None of this is new.

In 1945, Frank Capra, later to direct *It's a Wonderful Life*, made a film for the US Army called *Know Your Enemy: Japan*, which ticks just about every stereotype in the "BETS" box.

The Japanese are portrayed as "barbarians", uncivilised and primitive but also as "Schrödinger's Foes" – stupid and vicious at the same time. Remarking on their short stature "5 feet and 3 inches", the narrator explains that these "brother soldiers are as much alike as photographic prints from the same negative".

They are also *Enemies within*. Japanese hairdressers in California didn't speak to their customers prior to Pearl Harbor, we are told, because they were engaged in a mission of mass eavesdropping for their spymasters. Mata Haris all, with their combs, scissors and fiendish way with curlers making notes behind the hairspray about US naval deployments.

Know Your Enemy: Japan ends with US marines storming Iwo Jima and raising the Stars and Stripes in a famously staged propaganda stunt. The message is clear. Good has triumphed. The monster crushed. What it doesn't show, because the film was released on the day it happened, is "Fat Man", the second nuclear bomb to be used in warfare, falling from the Bockscar B-29 bomber and eviscerating the city of Nagasaki 30,000 feet below. The device wiped Nagasaki off the map, killing 35,000 men, women and children in the blink of an eye.

Post-war politicians, historians and journalists conspired to push the narrative that both bombs "shortened the war". And that the barbaric Japanese were willing to fight to the last man and so they were necessary. But if that was the case, then why did they surrender after the deaths of just a few thousand people? Doesn't make sense does it? And that's because it's fake history.

From May 1945 onwards, the Japanese actively sought peace terms and a path out of war. In June, Emperor Hirohito was asking his government to come up with "concrete plans" to end the war. The Russians were viewed as a potential mediator. In July, the Potsdam Declaration, issued by the Allied powers, called for Japan's "unconditional surrender".

However, Hirohito was still deemed to be a descendant of God and his position crucial to the preservation of Japanese society. Unconditional surrender was not an option, because descendants of gods aren't in the business of throwing in the towel. The Japanese stalled and while they did, the Americans planned the endgame.

The US was also itching to try out its new superweapon – the atom bomb – and wanted to send a signal to the USSR. Washington was fearful of how its ally Stalin might behave after the war. Truman wanted to show the power he had at his fingertips. If he could demonstrate that the new weapon could destroy entire cities, the Soviets might park their silly ideas and play along to his tune.

This was acknowledged at the time. In 1946, Admiral William F. Halsey, commander of the Third Fleet, claimed that the scientists had a "toy and they wanted to try it out", adding it "was an unnecessary experiment [and] it was a mistake to ever drop it."

The case of necessity has persisted because the Allies were meant to be the goodies. And goodies don't incinerate children. Consistent opinion polls in the years following 1945 have shown that the message got through. Between 80 and 90% of Americans still deem the bombing justifiable. History is as much written by the spinners as the winners. American actions have been justified ever since.

None of that lets the Japanese wartime leadership off the hook. The Japanese army was guilty of some of the most egregious atrocities of the Second World War (and the era that immediately preceded it), which stand comparison with those of Nazi Germany. As it overran Asia in the late 1930s, the Empire of the Sun butchered opponents and enslaved millions.

Even before the Second World War started, it was committing atrocities. In December 1937, during the Second Sino-Japanese War, the Japanese army murdered between 40,000 and 300,000 unarmed soldiers and civilians in the Chinese city of Nanjing before embarking on a rampage of rape, butchery, torture and looting.

Subsequent to its entry into the Second World War, it treated prisoners and conquered lands with savage disregard, even as it disingenuously claimed to be the "liberator from Western Imperialism". Over 200,000 women were forced into sexual slavery to work as "comfort women" and an estimated 6–10 million prisoners and slaves were worked to death between 1937 and 1945. More than 100,000 Chinese, Indonesians (then inhabitants of the Dutch East Indies), Filipinos and Koreans died building the Burma Railway (also known as the Death Railway), made famous in the epic David Lean film *The Bridge on the River Kwai*, along with 12–13,000 soldiers of the British Commonwealth.

For all of the above – and more – malice towards the Japanese lingered for decades afterwards. Many old soldiers, including my own father, were willing to come to terms with post-war West German recovery but were far less forgiving of the Japanese. It was one reason why my dad held out for so long against Japanese technology and he was certainly not alone in that.

Much of the animosity was predicated on the belief that Japan had never apologised for its actions during the Second World War. But, as early as August 1945, Emperor Hirohito was seeking forgiveness from former enemies and Japan continued to issue apologies for the next 70 years – although not always to the satisfaction of the nations it had traumatised. Matters were not helped by former Japanese soldiers and figures on the political right maintaining that there was "no need" for any apology, which understandably enraged survivors of Japanese atrocities and the families of the dead.

But as we have seen – political apologies can frequently become meaningless. The further we recede from an event, the less merit one has. If the perpetrators are gone and the victims too, how sincere is any late act of atonement?

Much of the resentment aimed at Japan, China and their neighbours stems from bad old-fashioned racism and the Western psycho-terror known as the "Yellow Peril", that 19th-century racist notion that Eastern Asians are inferior, monkey-like, sexually lascivious and savage. The term was coined in 1897 by Jacques Novicow, a Greek-Russian Francophile, but intolerance towards Chinese and Japanese people has far older roots.

The 19th-century fear of the "Yellow Peril" and antagonism felt by "European Americans" who claimed the Chinese were "taking their jobs" led to the US Chinese Exclusion Act of 1882. This law actually prohibited immigration from China and removed the rights of Chinese people resident in the US to claim citizenship. Depressingly, it was not until the Hart-Celler Act in 1965 that bars on immigration from certain nations were lifted.

"Yellow Peril" has never gone away. During the coronavirus pandemic, the National Republican Senatorial Committee issued a 57-page long document, which argued that calling Covid-19 "the Chinese Virus" was not racist.

Trump repeatedly sought to lay the blame for hundreds of thousands of American dead at the feet of the country and claimed in July 2020 that the Chinese government was "fully responsible for concealing the virus and unleashing it upon the world."

Like all the best propaganda, there was a hint of truth. The virus had originated in China and the Chinese government had engaged in a cover-up. But that did not excuse Trump's failure to take the pandemic seriously or his government's abject failure in tackling the crisis.

The "Yellow Peril" was a useful scapegoat. Adding weight to the belief that the virus was created in a lab in Wuhan, or emerged as a result of East Asia's feral culinary ways.

Many memes laid the blame for it on pictures of someone eating a bat. It didn't matter that the photo had been taken years before the pandemic even started – few paused to check if it was true. The Chinese, with their weird habits and funny customs, were to blame for the crisis – it was obvious – and there was a picture on Facebook to prove it.

* * *

Pull at the thread of "Yellow Peril" hard enough – and you go all the way back to Genghis Khan.

Everyone knows the story of Genghis Khan. The raving madman, who burst out of Mongolia in the 12th and 13th centuries and bolted West, East, South and everywhere in between, pillaging and laying waste to everything in his path.

The 12th-century Persian chronicler Rashid-al-Din Hamadani, quotes Khan's motivation in his two-volume history *Jami-al-ta-warikh:* "The greatest happiness is to scatter your enemy, to drive him before you, to see his cities reduced to ashes, to see those who love him shrouded in tears, and to gather into your bosom his wives and daughters."

Hardly great PR for anyone seeking to restore his reputation.

The Mongols' notoriety went before them. They didn't like cities – so they sacked them and slaughtered everyone inside. That made city-dwellers rather reluctant to open their city doors when Khan's men started knocking, so Genghis Khan essentially invented biological warfare and catapulted plague-ridden dead bodies over the parapets.

The Mongol hordes were astonishingly proficient at murder. Entire regions were depopulated, and it is claimed that in his lifetime, Khan was responsible for the deaths of 40 million people, reducing the world's population by as much as 10%. That figure includes a reported 1,748,000 people, who were beheaded in a single hour following the siege of Nishapur in the Persian Empire in 1221.

The scale of the killing was such that climate change reversed. In 2011, Julia Pongratz and colleagues at the Carnegie Institution's Department of Global Ecology, published findings suggesting that this mass reduction in the global population saw forests regrow and carbon dioxide absorbed. Although, it's unlikely that Genghis Khan will be replacing Greta Thunberg as an icon of the green movement any time soon.

Summarising his legacy in 1748, the French philosopher Montesquieu wrote that he: "Destroyed Asia, from India even to the Mediterranean — and all the country which forms the east of Persia [was] rendered a desert." Which all begs the simple question: "Why?"

If you are seeking to conquer the world and make yourself powerful and wealthy, why would you want to lay waste to it? It makes no sense. Dead people don't pay taxes. Scorched earth isn't a bounty. Barren fields don't grow crops. By his death, in 1227, Khan had not only built the largest land Empire in history – but held onto it. It's hard to do that if you're a pitiless barbarian with just a small number of chaotic men doing nothing but killing and pillaging.

The scale of Khan's territorial gains is breath-taking. It dwarfs anything achieved by Alexander the Great and stretched as far west as Ukraine, covering most of Russia. It even encroached on modern-day Austria, Bulgaria, Hungary and Poland. To the south, it overran all of China and created the great Yuan dynasty under his grandson Kublai Khan.

The vast measure of it all was ultimately untenable and it later fractured into four. But even the remnant pieces were enormous. By 1294, Kublai Khan was ruling an estimated 23,500,000 sq km of land – an area one and a half times bigger than modern-day Russia.

None of that could have been achieved if the Mongols had been the marauding barbarians of popular imagination and their leader Genghis Khan a murderous lunatic.

Before his rise to power, the tribes that roamed Mongolia had been bedevilled by in-fighting. Khan, born Temujin, the son of a minor nomadic chief who was murdered in his childhood, managed to unite them. And he did so less through brute force and more through diplomacy and guile. By 44, he had been proclaimed "Universal Emperor" or "Genghis Khan" and, shortly after that, he set about conquering the world. Over the next 20 years, Temujin overran Northern China, Central Asia and the great Persian Khwarazmian Empire.

The Mongols were superb horsemen. They moved fast and lived off the land. Sixty per cent of the force was made up of "light cavalry", which could easily outwit and outmanoeuvre the heavily armoured knights of 13th-century Europe. They had better kit and superior weapons, including a mysterious thing called "gunpowder" which they used with devastating effect.

But their greatest weapon of all was their terrifying reputation. Like Alexander before him, Khan was a master propagandist, who managed to instil fear in the hearts of his enemies before he had even turned up. Rather than fight him, many states immediately capitulated. The Mongols preferred it that way. If territories surrendered peaceably, Khan demanded tribute, incorporated them into his Empire and then pretty much left them to their own devices. If they didn't, he would show no mercy and set an example that ensured that the next city would simply give up. And this was no bad thing.

Khan was a far sighted and accommodating leader, and his Pax Mongolica (the name given to the period of relative stability during the 13th and 14th centuries) brought trade and prosperity. He was inclusive with regard to newly conquered lands. He was also meritocratic for the time – it was possible to rise to the top on ability not connections. His Empire also allowed an unparalleled degree of religious tolerance.

At the same time, merchants had hitherto unprecedented freedom of movement. With the Mongols controlling the Silk Road, safe travel was made possible between East and West for the first time in history.

The Mongolians were innovators. They created the first paper money and set up a pony postal service, known as the "Yam", with relay stations across the Empire. At its peak the Yam could deliver a message over a distance of 300 km in a single day. Khan's administration introduced a standardised system of decimalised weights and measures and a universal set of laws known as the Yassa.

It would be a bit of a stretch to claim they were tree-hugging hippies. The Mongols were undoubtedly ruthless, but no more so than their contemporaries, and the scale of death was clearly exaggerated. Take the executions that followed the defeat of Nishapur in April 1221. If 1,748,000 people had really been beheaded in a single hour, then more than 29,000 people would have needed to have been executed per minute. Which rather smells, quite frankly, of Mongolian horse shit.

It is undeniable that between the 13th and 14th centuries, the populations of China and Eurasia depleted dramatically, but the exact causes remain unclear and weren't all down to Genghis who died in 1227 . Quite likely much of it was due to bubonic plague and a significant global weather phenomenon of the time, the Dantean Anomaly, that started in 1315 and ended in 1321 the year Dante died. This period saw crop failure and climate change along with mass migration and famine.

Other causes of the massive population fall might simply be down to bad bookkeeping in the aftermath of events. Super-spreading census-takers don't tend to fare well in bubonic plagues.

Although they lived over a thousand years apart, there is an obvious parallel between Genghis Khan and Alexander the Great. But while Alexander has enjoyed consistently good press since his rock star young death, Khan is still viewed with what one historian dubbed "awe and disdain". Perhaps we prefer our Eastern enemies, that way. A comical and fearsome "Yellow Peril". "Schrödinger's Foes". From Khan to the Japanese to the Kim dynasty in modern-day North Korea.

Trying to pen anything sensible about North Korea (DPRK) poses an immediate challenge to a writer, because so much about the regime seems just plain mad. For a start, two of its current leaders are dead. The Eternal President Kim Il-sung (henceforth Kim 1) died in 1994, while his son, Kim Jong-il (Kim 2), the Eternal General Secretary of the Workers' Party, died in 2011.

Kim 1 was responsible for coming up with the state philosophy, *Juche*, which guides the DPRK people's lives. *Juche's* four principles are:

Juche – the nation's self-reliance ideology
Chaju – political independence from other states
Charip – the power to make our own economic decisions
Chawi – military independence from other countries

Everything in North Korea is done the *Juche* way. They even have the *Juche* calendar, which begins on what the rest of the world calls 1912, but seeing as that's the birth year of the Eternal President, it's called Year One.

At the symbolic heart of *Juche* lies *Paektu*, the highest and most sacred mountain on the Korean peninsula and birthplace of Dangun, the founder of the nation and the offspring of a bear woman and the son of god. Dangun was once viewed as a "fictional" figure, but Kim 2 put that right in 1994, by sending state archaeologists out to find his mausoleum and prove he was real. You are unlikely to be astonished to hear that they were successful.

Koreans are told that Kim 2 was born on Paektu in 1941, while his father was leading the resistance to the Japanese from a secret base. More likely he was born in the Soviet Union.

The Kims' divine right to rule is based on the belief that they, like Dangun, have "Paektu blood" – a unique strain, gifting them divine powers including *"chukjibeop"* – the ability to fold space and time. It was this superpower that allowed Kim Il-Sung to defeat the Japanese and it has inspired poems, books and the popular song "The General Uses Warp" with its catchy reprise:

Mount Paektu's strategies
Are Divine strategies
The General uses warp

Since Kim Jong-un (aka Kim 3) came to power, the whole "use the force" thing has been downplayed and state newspaper *Rodong Sinmun* has even candidly suggested that: "If there is a 'chukjibeop', it is the people's 'chukjibeop'."

Monuments to the greatness of the Kims dot the land lest anyone forgets who they are. There are 40,000 statues of Kim Il-Sung alone in the country and in the three years of mourning that followed his death, plans were devised to erect over 3,000 Yeong Saeng (eternal life) Towers in his honour. The one in the capital, Pyongyang, is over 90 metres tall and straddles six lanes of motorway.

Even as it glorifies its leaders, the DPRK vilifies its enemies. Hatred of Japan is written into the constitution and an Orwellian state of perpetual war exists with its neighbour to the South.

The Kims, like all the greatest enduring dictators, have made themselves demagogue protectors. Thousands of paintings commemorate them. One of the best known is of Kim Jong-il riding a great white stallion across the snowy landscape of Paektu in an image plagiarised wholesale from Napoleon crossing the Alps.

Children's literature is central to the theory of *Juche* and critical to their brainwashing. As Kim 2 wrote: "Only our style of children's literature can contribute to bringing up our children into pillars of Korean revolution armed with the Juche idea."

If you believe the propaganda, Kim 2 was a prolific author. It's claimed that he wrote 1,500 books before he'd even completed university and, as he was a bit of a frustrated luvvie, many of his published works set out his thoughts on theatre and cinema. The punchily titled *Let Us Produce Revolutionary Operas That Are High in Ideological and Artistic Quality by Strictly Applying the Principle of Creating Revolutionary Operas of the Type of the Sea of Blood* (1971) is typical.

Kim 2 also wrote operas. Or, more likely, he told composers to put his name on their works. In the 1970s, six key works firmly put the "Juche" into opera. The best known is *A True Daughter of the Party*, a work later described by Kim 2's biographer as "better than any in the history of music".

If you buy into the Kim 2 myth, you believe that he was much more than the world's greatest statesman, poet and composer – he also invented the hamburger (in the late 1990s). Koreans call it a *Gogigyeopbbang* and also believe that later in life the Beloved General created the *Cheese Gogigyeopbbang*, which is served in *Samtaesong* (Three Big Stars) restaurant chains across the capital city by attractive women dressed in tartan uniforms.

Kim 2 was also the greatest golfer in history. Following the completion of the Pyongyang golf course in 1994 and, despite never having played before, he turned in an astonishing round of

34 under par. No photos exist but we know it's true because the man in charge of the course said so and the Kims never lie. Or go to the toilet. Those with Paektu blood have no need.

When Kim 2 died, the whole country famously started sobbing and images of thousands of North Koreans weeping and banging their fists on the ground went around the world.

Believe the state machine and you will soon buy into the notion that Kim 3 is every bit the man his forebears were. Paektu blood meant he could walk at three weeks and that he was a crack shot at five. He's also unimaginably brave. One of his first acts as leader was to retrieve the half hour stolen from the country by the Japanese in 1919.

Oh, and brilliant, because under his direction, DPRK's world-beating scientists found cures for AIDS, cancer and Ebola and discovered that garlic, onions and honey could ward off Covid-19.

Like any great ruler, Kim 3 also has his playful side. As East Asia's very own Simon Cowell, he gave the world the fabulous all-girl pop band Moranbong and their best songs, including "Fluttering Red Flag", "We Can't Live Without Our Great Leader's Care" and the smash-hit single "My Country is the Best".

It is impossible to gauge how much of this stuff is believed by ordinary people. Foreign visitors are tightly controlled. The internet remains almost non-existent and communication across the 38th parallel is nigh on impossible. The all-pervading fear that grips any totalitarian state means that the nation's citizens are fearful of expressing their doubts even in private.

Human rights activist Park Yeon-mi, one of the country's best-known dissidents, has said that her parents raised her to keep her opinions to herself – in the knowledge that anyone could be listening. Having escaped DPRK with her mother aged 13, Yeon-mi became not just a vocal critic of the regime, but also an advocate for the people she had left behind.

In a Q and A session with *Guardian* readers in 2014, Park said: "We need to realise that the people in North Korea are just normal people like you and I. Yes, [they] are brainwashed and live a different life to ours, but they are still people, so we must avoid dehumanising them."

It's a point that cannot be understated. The North Korean people – the faceless pawns in the giant chess game of 21st-century global politics – are the biggest victims by far of the Kim regime. Held back and imprisoned in what amounts to a colossal state prison, they are still broadly viewed with a mixture of mockery and curiosity by Western commentators who still, seemingly, cannot bring themselves to see East Asian people as anything more than "joke people".

On the evidence of defectors like Park Yeon-mi, it is likely that they are not as dim-witted as many would like them to be. Likewise, to mock the Kims is to underestimate them. Unhinged lunatics don't build lasting empires. Hapless fools can't keep a tight grip on the lives of 25 million people for more than 70 years.

Kim Jong-un is not as daft as Western perceptions paint him, and nor is his state propaganda. Kitsch as it might be, it is very effective indeed. I can't speak for Kim 2's literary oeuvre because I haven't read it, but the operas are not nearly as ghastly as you might think. *A True Daughter of the Revolution*, which (at time of writing) can be watched in its entirety on YouTube, is curiously stirring. It's blunt and obvious, perhaps, but it has energy, style, musicality and – in the opinion of this critic at least – some degree of theatricality. The staging is not so removed from long-running West End musicals *Les Misérables* and *Miss Saigon*. It would be a stretch to claim that *A True Daughter of the Revolution* is the smash-hit London musical waiting to happen, but if it wasn't a eulogy to one of the worst dictatorships on Earth, you might be forgiven for tapping your foot along to the tunes.

Outwardly, the DPKR is built to instil awe in its own people and visitors. Pyongyang's huge statues, buildings and monuments are the set; the vast choreographed displays, the musical numbers; the people themselves, the extras; and Kim Jung-un – the central protagonist and hero of the tale – pitted against the capitalist enemy outside.

This stuff was done by Hitler, of course, and with good reason: it works. So, we underestimate North Korea at our peril. The grip is tight, the fear is real, the control is total.

Tales of North Korea's atrocities against its *enemies within* are legion. In 2013, two years after coming to power, it was reported in South Korean newspaper the *Chosun Ilbo* that Kim Jong-un had executed Hyon Song-wol, the lead singer of that all-girl band Moranbong, after she had been caught selling videos of an orgy she had filmed and featured in... and some bibles. The paper claimed she had been executed with a machine gun "while the Wangjaesan Light Music Band... looked on."

Later that same year, Kim 3 purged his uncle and former deputy, Jang Soeng-thaek. Soeng-thaek was branded "a wicked political careerist, trickster and traitor for all ages" before apparently being thrown naked to a pack of deliberately starved dogs who ripped him apart and fed on his bones.

In 2016 it was reported that Kim Jong-un had executed two high ranking officials with "anti-aircraft guns" after one of them had fallen asleep in a meeting and the other had had the audacity to suggest some new policy ideas. Across the world, newspapers and TV stations dutifully picked up the stories and reported them with an anomalous mixture of horror and glee.

None of it was strictly true. Kim's uncle had in fact been shot. The "pack of starving dogs" narrative had been made up by a popular Chinese social media satirist called Pyongyang Choi Seongho, but it had seemed so credible that it was picked up by Hong Kong newspapers and later the influential Singapore-based English-language newspaper *The Straits Times*. The story spread and, eager to fear the madness of the "Schrödinger Foe", many people believed it.

The source of the story about the use of anti-aircraft guns seems to stem back to South Korea's intelligence agency and is probably made up. At least one of the individuals who was allegedly killed was later spotted on state TV. As for Hyon Song-wol, she is alive and well and pursuing her music career, while dabbling in a spot of international diplomacy. The Bibles and Orgy story and her execution are fake news.

Without doubt the rumours of atrocities serve a deliberate purpose at home. Like those attributed to Genghis Khan, they demonstrate the ruthlessness of the Kim dynasty, striking fear into dissenters and dissidents alike and keeping enemies or wannabe dissenters at home in line.

Further abroad, Kim Jong-un may be seen as a sort of elaborate joke heading up a comedy country. But there's nothing particularly funny about it. The threat posed is real, not least for his neighbours. North Korea has been working towards the creation of a nuclear warhead for a decade, and analysts fear they may have already succeeded. The reason that threat is not taken so seriously in Europe is because it's "in the East" and therefore "far away".

Life is also far from comical for ordinary North Koreans, living in fear and abject poverty. Inside the country, summary execution is common. In the 1990s, mismanagement and neglect on the part of the leadership caused food shortages in the country, which turned into a famine that killed millions of people.

The Database Center for North Korean Human Rights, established in 2003 to highlight human rights abuses in the state, estimates that 87% of the country's many thousands of executions since the 1990s are carried out in public. Almost all without due process and mostly within the many prison camps that dot the dictatorship.

The only things thriving in the DPRK are the Supreme Leader's expanding waistline and the swelling labour camps. And yet, at the same time, North Korea – like all enemies through time – offers us, its adversaries, a number of sobering Thucydidean lessons.

The great German poet Hermann Hesse once wrote that: "If you hate a person, you hate something in him that is part of yourself. What isn't part of ourselves doesn't disturb us."

And, strange as it might sound, North Korea is far from unique in its peculiar excesses. Fake history, like gullibility, is not the preserve of the DPRK.

Across the world ruling elites have become ever more prone to historical negationism – the act of deliberately rewriting history or falsifying the past to suit modern agendas. For example, under Putin, Russian schoolchildren no longer learn about the 1939 Molotov-Ribbentrop Pact and thus the bit where Russia divides Poland between itself and Nazi Germany.

Much the same is going on in Poland. In 2018, a law passed by President Andrzej Duda made it an imprisonable offence to suggest that Poles were complicit in the systematic mass murder of Jews during the Nazi occupation. That is a complete whitewash of history since there are multiple documented cases of collaborators in Poland throughout the war who actively enforced Nazi anti-Semitic policies.

Further to the south, Bulgarians have increasingly expunged the history books in active denial of 500 years of common heritage with Turkey, while Turkey in turn has passed laws forbidding discussion of the Armenian genocide. At least six journalists have since been prosecuted for trying.

You need only look to Britain's distorted view of its past to see the same resonances here. The Orwellian DPRK might be engaged in perpetual wars with Japan and South Korea, but so too are we. The only difference being that while the Kims talk war, the USA and Britain have actively fought them from Iraq to Afghanistan and beyond. And the parallels don't end there.

To many in the West, those memes of North Koreans weeping at the death of Kim 2 are hilarious. They epitomise the "crazy North Koreans" and, yes, the exaggerated mourning does look very bizarre indeed. But so too is the footage of the 1997 funeral of Princess Diana. You don't have to turn up the volume to take in the full and frightening wail of people who never knew her personally, weeping loudly as her funeral cortege leaves Kensington palace and passes them by.

Royalists in particular might baulk at comparisons between the Windsor dynasty and that of the Kims, but both were born from power grabs and the same conceits of divine right and "special blood".

The notion of Paektu blood is no more risible than the blue variety. The undue reverence, fawning attendants and the practice of bending double before the "great leaders" are not so very different in either country. Both the House of Windsor and the House of Kim are ultimately grounded in long-past-their-sell-by-date notions of feudalism. Ultimately, we deem "our" unelected leaders OK for no other better reason than that they are "ours".

And the same goes for all those crazy monuments. Turkmenistan might have a giant statue celebrating a dog breed, but in London there's a huge memorial to "animals that died in war" featuring elephants, donkeys, horses, dogs and camels. In Salford, Manchester, there's a bronze statue to the Blue Peter dog "Petra" that died in 1977, just a few months before France's final execution by guillotine. Sure, these examples in England aren't covered in gold leaf, but they're still sentimental and fundamentally bizarre statues to animals that only serve the purposes of those who put them up.

Then there's the architecture. Any trip to fascist-chic Washington is not complete without a visit to Lincoln's memorial, featuring a colossal statue of the 16th American president, housed in a vast Neoclassical temple that would not have looked out of place in Soviet Russia or Hitler's Germania. There may be many, many more tributes to the Kims in North Korea, but in the US, there are 200 statues to Lincoln alone and dozens to Washington, General Grant and others. These monuments have become sacred. Question them or indeed any of the statues in Britain – even ones to slave owners, and you will be accused of "rewriting" or "erasing" history.

As for that crazy North Korean *Juche* philosophy that calls for exceptionalism, self-reliance and political and military independence – well, what's the difference with Brexit, which seeks exactly the same? And we can hardly mock North Korean school books for propagating myth after myth about the country's past and its great leaders when members of our own government spent years promoting *Our Island Story* and other Ladybird Libertarian narratives of war and Empire.

In recent years the Democratic West has turned ever more towards strong men with big personalities. Donald Trump literally rewrote his origin story, just like Kim 2 did. For years Trump said his grandparents were Scandinavian, despite both of them having been born in Bavaria. When he became president, he began insisting that his own father had been "born in a very wonderful place in Germany", when actually he'd been born in New York.

Truth didn't matter to Trump. He had no time for it if it didn't fit his agenda. And in a Western democracy, he should have been held properly to account for the lies and indeed all of his more egregious actions while still in office. After all, "that" is what makes us different to the likes of the Kims – or so we are told.

For the most part, he simply got away with it.

By November 2019, *The Washington Post* estimated that Trump had told a whopping 14,000 lies since taking office. When not rewriting his own history, Trump rewrote America's. In a speech on Independence Day in July 2019, he claimed that during the War of Independence, Washington's forces (in 1775) had had air supremacy and "taken over airports" – a full 128 years before the Wright brothers achieved the first controlled powered flight.

In September 2020, he launched an attack on American history teaching, telling a Washington conference that children had been brainwashed by "decades of left-wing indoctrination".

He stated that American children should be taught that "they are citizens of the most exceptional nation in the history of the world" and that "toxic propaganda" was teaching them about slavery and civil rights instead.

The Trump dynasty saw themselves as defenders of America – protecting it from its enemies. And yet, like the Kims, the greatest threat to the nation during those four chaotic years – was Trump himself. The true *enemy within*.

One nation's propaganda and fake history is another nation's source of amusement or fear. We would do better to look inward more, even as we fret about those "Schrödinger's Foes" to the East.

THE GOOD OLD DAYS WERE GOOD

Long before the Wright brothers took to the skies, people were falling out of them.

In the 9th century, Arab polymath Abbas ibn Firnas strapped on some wings, jumped off a hill and crashed. A hundred years later, Kazakh lexicographer, Ismail ibn al-Jawhari, took off from the roof of a mosque in Nishapur in Persia and died. A few years later, a monk called Eilmer of Malmesbury stepped gracefully from the roof of his abbey and broke his legs.

In June 1785, Frenchmen Pierre Romain and Jean-François Pilâtre de Rozier became the first recorded fatalities of a modern-day flying accident, when their balloon crashed and killed them both. Things went quiet for a bit until 1896, when Austrian gliding pioneer Otto Lilienthal died while demonstrating his plane. After that, everyone started dropping like flies.

French pilot Eugène Lefebvre became the first person in history to die piloting a powered plane, in 1909. He was swiftly followed by the original members of the world's first aerial display team, the

"Wright Fliers", all of whom were killed failing to do so efficiently between August 1909 and New Year's Day 1910. That same year, Charles Royce (of Rolls-Royce fame) died in Southbourne, Dorset, when the tail snapped off his plane – making him Britain's first air casualty. Edith Maud Cook, the first British woman to fly a plane, was killed in – you guessed it – a plane crash in 1910.

Other pioneers to perish in air crashes included, in 1912, Harriet Quimby, the first woman to fly across the Channel, followed by American circus star Sam Cody, the first man to fly in Britain, who was killed demonstrating a new plane in 1913. In 1915, Lincoln Beachey, the first man to perform a loop the loop, was killed in 1915 having just done a loop the loop. In 1919, three more innovators were killed: John Alcock, the first man to fly across the Atlantic, Swiss flyer Oskar Bider, the first man to fly across the Alps, and Raymonde de Laroche – the first woman to get a pilot's licence, who died after crashing an experimental aircraft in her native France. Bessie Coleman – daredevil, media star and air pioneer, who was also the first black person and first native American to gain a pilot's licence – lasted longer than almost any of her contemporaries. But she too died in an accident, during an air-show in Florida in 1926.

Clearly what was needed was for someone to invent the parachute.

Actually, parachutes existed. And had done since 1783 when Frenchman Louis-Sébastien Lenormand successfully demon- strated one by jumping out of a tree. But later developments had not been without incident. In 1837, in a once-celebrated episode, a 61-year-old English watercolourist called Robert Cocking, who had never been in a balloon before, released himself from 2,000 metres up above Greenwich in his unique, cone-shaped prototype. Having detached himself from the balloon, his elegantly decorated contraption demonstrated all the air resistance of a falling elephant on a steam locomotive – and he tumbled dramatically earthwards before ending up five miles away in Lee. Cocking didn't paint any more watercolours after that.

Chastened by the memory of these disasters, it is unsurprising that there were no recorded parachute fatalities in Europe or the US for the rest of the 19th and first decade of the 20th centuries.

All of that changed with the invention of the plane.

The problem for those trying to use parachutes in evacuations from aircraft, was that early planes flew fast and low, not high and slow. Even the Wright Flyer that took off at Kitty Hawk in 1903 moved at 48 km/h. Six years later, planes were hitting 70 km/h. By 1911, they were belting along at 133 km/h. And all the while, the casualties were mounting up.

France – the true birthplace of aeronautical innovation – was scene of much of the carnage and, to put the gravediggers out of work, a solution was urgently sought.

In November 1911, a mysterious benefactor, 'Monsieur Lalance', wrote a letter to the Aéro-Club de France offering 10,000 francs (approx. £120,000 in 2021) to anyone who could develop and demonstrate a parachute, weighing no more than 25 kg, that could be used for safe evacuation from a plane at low altitude. The competition attracted attention from enthusiasts, scientists and eccentrics, and even an Austrian-Czech tailor, by the name of Franz Reichelt. Franz had emigrated to France in 1898, been naturalised as a citizen in 1909, changed his name to François the same year and promptly grown a magnificent moustache to underline his Gallic credentials. He was also ahead of the curve.

Long before the competition was announced, he had been at work on a parachute design. He knew sod all about air velocity or how parachutes work, but he more than made up for it in enthusiasm. He had even taken an early prototype to the Ligue Aérienne (the French National Air League), who had the first and last mots* on all things aerial in Belle Epoque France. But they had rejected it as unsafe and sent him home, suggesting his time would be better spent making clothes and sewing buttons.

Franz had no intention of doing such a thing and, imbued with a surfeit of self-belief, set about trying to prove the experts wrong. The significant financial reward was undoubtedly a factor. The lure of fame was another. Franz had dreams. He didn't want to be an anonymous émigré sewing merchant – he wanted to be somebody. He wanted to be a contender.

So, throughout the winter of 1911 he dedicated himself to the task and was soon fitting his invention to mannequins and throwing them off the five-storey roof of his factory. But unfortunately, the elaborate parachute system he had come up with failed, failed and failed again. On every single occasion, the tailor's dolls simply clattered depressingly to the cobbles below.

Clearly what was needed was a bit more height and, sitting on the banks of the Seine, in the 7th Arrondissement, was the best parachute testing site in the world. Franz began lobbying the Parisian authorities for permission to use the Eiffel Tower. His persistence paid off and eventually he was granted permission – on the condition that he use a dummy.

Any inventor expects a "fail rate" when testing new equipment, and as Franz set off for the tower on the frigid morning of Sunday, 4th February 1912, his was an impressive 100%.

---

* French for "word"

Franz had promised the Parisian authorities that he was going to use a mannequin, but on the day the only dummy he brought along was himself. Having posed for photographs and brushed off the concerns of friends and well-wishers, he ascended to the first tier of the tower with a cameraman in tow. Footage shows him grandly mounting an insubstantial wooden chair, on top of a slightly wobbly table and speaking to two concerned onlookers in hats. As it's silent, we don't know what they're saying but we do know that around this time he told an official: "I want to do the experiment myself and without sleight of hand, as I intend to prove the worth of my invention."

After a brief moment of hesitation, at 8:22 a.m. precisely, he jumped. Three seconds later, he was dead.

Photographs splashed across the front page of Parisian daily newspaper *Le Petit Journal* show gendarmes, in the immediate aftermath, posing next to the large hole he left. Through reckless disregard for his own life, Franz had found the fame he craved, but not of the kind he had sought. As the event was filmed, he became the first person in history to be captured demonstrating the consequences of what we now call the Dunning–Kruger effect.

This particular cognitive bias, named after social psychologists David Dunning and Justin Kruger, who identified it in 1999, occurs when people of limited knowledge, competence or ability wrongly imagine themselves to be extremely proficient at something of which they patently are not.

Dunning based the study on the case of a bank robber, McArthur Wheeler, who, having read that lemon juice rendered things invisible to sight, applied some to his face and went off to rob two banks. He was so confident it would work that he even waved at the CCTV cameras as he walked in and out and, when later arrested, famously exclaimed, "But I wore juice!"

His logic was so demented that a professional opinion was sought and, after examining the prisoner, the state psychiatrist gave their unforgiving conclusion. McArthur Wheeler wasn't mentally ill – he was just very, very stupid. But his monumental stupidity was twinned with an innate and wholly unjustified belief in his ability.

Franz Reichelt displayed the same "illusory superiority" 90 years earlier. It was clear his parachutes didn't work. He had been told it was useless by the experts at the Ligue Aérienne and even seen it with his own eyes. But Dunning-Kruger convinced him otherwise.

Franz Reichelt believed he was an expert in parachutes, when in fact he knew nothing at all – and the consequences killed him.

Dunning–Kruger is not the preserve of the innately stupid. All of us are prone to it.

A 1983 study in the US and Sweden asked drivers to rate their proficiency behind the wheel compared to average road users. A whopping 93% of Americans and 69% of Swedes put themselves "in the top 50%", which is of course a statistical impossibility.

Other studies into "illusory superiority" have shown that most people overestimate their IQ, their immunity to bias, their popularity, their ability to remember things and even their proficiency in bed.

A 1977 study found that 94% of US university professors believed themselves better teachers than their peers – again a statistical impossibility.

Anecdotally, an awful lot of people who think they can sing well very clearly cannot.

Prior to the EU referendum, voters on both sides claimed they understood the full complexity of the relationship between Britain and the European Union, when even most of the experts and career bureaucrats did not. The full extent of that relationship only really became clear when the UK spent four years trying to leave without doing itself permanent damage. In the months that followed full departure in January 2021, Twitter was full of videos of bitter fishermen claiming they had made a mistake in backing it and that they hadn't realised the consequences.

At its extremity, Dunning–Kruger goes some way towards explaining far bigger things than Brexit. The grotesque phenomenon that was Adolf Hitler was due in no small measure to his own illusory superiority and the willingness of others to buy into his lies. The Nazi leader believed himself a genius – adept at art, brilliant at thinking and the only man in history (apart from Genghis Khan) who would be able to successfully invade Russia. None of those things were true.

"People who lack knowledge, lack the knowledge to realise they lack the knowledge," as David Dunning himself said in a 2019 interview on YouTube channel *The Damage Report*, perfectly summing it up. And the Dunning–Kruger effect is equally important in understanding the true nature of history.

Many people prefer to wallow in the consolations of superficial understanding and commonly held notions that feed existing world views. It's less effort to latch onto lazy tropes like "taking back control", the "Blitz Spirit", the Dunkirk narrative or even the comfort blanket of Fake Family Sagas than to seek the truth and embrace complexity. Why challenge the bedrock of our collective national consciousness when it comforts us to indulge in fairy tales instead?

History is nuanced, complex and, quite often, frankly unsatisfying. The truth of events doesn't always live up to the legends we believe and the "good stories" we are drawn to. The slick packaging of urbane populist narratives, forged by the likes of H. E. Marshall or Nigel Farage, are easier to digest and sometimes more appealing than the facts.

People want to believe that the inventor of the guillotine was killed by his invention, that Christopher Columbus was a great adventurer whose sailors thought the Earth was flat, that the brave British Tommies were saved from Dunkirk by a fleet of "little ships", and that Winston Churchill was a man of destiny and the greatest Briton who ever lived. Why ruin it all with horrid facts and inconvenient evidence that suggest otherwise?

But truth does matter. In the age of the internet when anything can be fact-checked at the click of a button, there is no excuse for anyone to buy into lies and myth.

Like a juicy *Gogigyeopbbang* burger, we might love indulging in the comforting "E-numbers" of phoney nostalgia, but it is detrimental to our collective health. At its extreme, fake history can be the pyre upon which nations and democracy self-immolate.

It's reassuring to think that your country is "the best" – and that *your* history is richer and more resonant than anyone else's. Some actively seek to keep us believing that way and many more pawns are only too willing to buy in. It suits politicians and documentary makers to play to the narrative. It makes for great "and finally" segments in news programmes. Fake history is the bedrock of "imagined communities" and "conceits of we". It makes up the lifeblood of exceptionalism – it is the bullshit compost on which populism thrives.

* * *

Every age looks back in envy.

Middle-aged Upper Palaeolithic cave dwellers in the Swabian Alps no doubt banged on endlessly about the "good old days" as they handed round that Lion Man. The Greeks looked back to the era of the gods, the Romans to the Greeks, the British Empire to the Romans and so on and so on.

For many modern English people, the lost, lamented Eden is the eternal summer of Edwardian England. That glorious age when men played cricket and women wore white cotton dresses, while a grateful world rested under the congenial eye of the Empire. An idyll that was rudely interrupted by those horrid Germans launching a messy continental war.

Core to Brexit was a belief that if we believed hard enough and clicked our Union Jack slippers together, we might overcome everything in between and perhaps get back to it. That rewrite would have us believe that pre-1914, England was a safer, kinder, more ordered place. A land where kindly Downton Abbey-type aristos ran everything while grateful villagers lived out their days in thatched pubs drinking cider. In truth, Edwardian Britain was very far from a utopia.

Life expectancy was 48. The country was notionally "the greatest democracy on Earth", but women couldn't vote and neither could around 40% of men. Infant mortality was high. Approximately 10% of babies died before their first birthday. And, despite being the centre of an Empire on which the sun never set, 25% of British people were living in poverty, with 10% in such abject poverty that many children didn't have shoes, let alone enough food to eat.

The "Great Britain" of my grandparents' youth had no national health service and no universal old age pension. If you were poor and got sick, you had a significant problem. Some charitable hospitals existed but unless you were lucky enough to live near one you had to pay – or hope for the best. Or die.

In the absence of vaccinations, most people who died prematurely did so of what are now preventable diseases. Health and safety legislation was rudimentary, and workplace deaths and accidents were commonplace. Hundreds of thousands of families had livelihoods dependent on hard labour in dirty and dangerous occupations like mining. If you weren't killed or maimed earning a crust underground, pneumoconiosis (aka black lung) would likely shorten your life.

Most children left school at 12 and went into unskilled and poorly paid work. Holidays didn't exist. If, like my maternal grandmother, you worked as a scullery maid in a big Downton Abbey-type home, you had no days off except for Sunday mornings when you were expected to attend church. If you got ill or pregnant or married you lost your job. If you caught the eye of the master of the house, or one of his sons, you lost your job.

Women in all professions faced the same ruin. Women teachers were not allowed to marry and so would drag out engagements, and it was not until 1946 that married women had the right to work as teachers without fear of losing their jobs. The same "marriage bars" applied to the Civil Service into the 1970s.

But, bad as things were, it was all a huge improvement on what had gone before, just as terrible as you might like to believe things are now. Despite pandemics and Brexit and all the other woes of the 21st century, we live in a significantly better time than our ancestors. Our age is one of unparalleled equality, liberalism, human rights, employment rights, prosperity, security and peace. A world my grandparents could only have dreamed of.

Social attitudes have shifted more in the last 60 years than in the thousands that preceded them. It's staggering to consider quite how recently so much of the change has come.

My grandfather's post-traumatic stress, a result of his experiences in the First World War, went undetected and untreated for his entire life. Nowadays, awareness of mental health has become the norm – and increasingly is not viewed by most of us as something to be hidden away.

Society has become significantly more open-minded. Attitude surveys show that the majority of British people (71%) are accepting of same-sex relationships and marriages.

It has also become far less brutal. It's incredible to consider that corporal punishment remained legal in British state schools until 1986. Private schools were still allowed to cane children in England until 1998, and in Scotland and Northern Ireland, it was still permissible to thrash kids into the 21st century.

I, like both my parents before me, went to a school where beatings were commonplace. My children are educated in environments where consideration and respect are core values and where they don't risk getting thrashed if they step out of line or give the wrong answer to a question.

It wasn't just schools, though – the British state was still birching young offenders and "delinquents" until 1948. On the Isle of Man, the last person to suffer judicial corporal punishment was whipped in 1976. Children as young as 15 could be condemned to a maximum of 12 strokes for minor offences like vandalism as long as the punishment "raised and did not cut the skin".

The death penalty for murder was only abolished in Britain in 1965 and in Northern Ireland in 1973. And as we saw earlier on in the book, too often this hideous and permanent act of state revenge was carried out on innocent people.

The Abortion Act was only passed in 1967 (although not in Northern Ireland), but, incredibly, it remained legal for a man to rape his wife until 1991. Homosexuality was only decriminalised in 1967 in England and Wales (followed, disgracefully late, by Scotland in 1980 and Northern Ireland in 1982), although same-sex marriages weren't permitted until 2013 and, at the time of writing, gay couples still don't have equality under the law as they are not able to marry in the nation's state churches.

Until the Race Relations Act of 1976*, it was perfectly OK to refuse to employ someone on the grounds of their colour or race. Equally, although there is still much to do, attitudes to gender, class and disability have all shifted dramatically in the last 40 years.

Standards of living for almost everyone in developed countries have improved beyond all measure in recent decades. Well into the mid-1970s, most British homes didn't have central heating; most families didn't own cars, colour televisions, telephones or many other of the array of gadgets and gizmos that now enhance our lives. The technological revolution has not only coincided with, but advanced the revolution in sexual equality.

Women fought long and hard for equality and in most European countries today the legislation is there to protect their rights. The history of our time and our immediate future will undoubtedly be dominated with significant female figures in a way that the 20th century and the long stretch of time before it, was not.

---

* The Race Relations Order came into effect in Northern Ireland in 1997

The struggle for equality is far from over. Non-binary and transgender people still fight against intolerance and, in much of the developing world, the rights of women and the LGBTQ+ community are still, for the most part, lagging by some distance behind those of the West.

The struggle for democracy and human rights is far from over too in countries like China, North Korea and the estimated 50 dictatorships in the world.

But things are, for the most part, getting better. Technology is shrinking our world and increasingly making the divisions of flags and borders more and more irrelevant.

That much lambasted word "globalisation" has done many millions of people a favour. Goods and affordable electronic products are cheaper and more freely available than ever before and so too is food. In 1973, a quarter of UK household income was spent on the weekly shop. Today that figure is 10%.

My corner of the world – Western Europe – is more peaceful than at any moment in the last 500 years. The wars that dominated the lives of my parents and grandparents have become a thing of the past. My children will not have to go and fight as pawns in some pointless war for the ambitions of others. "Fings ain't wot they used to be!" as Max Bygraves once sang and it's quite true. They are much, much better.

But we must not take any of it for granted. There are many who would have us turn back the clock. On all sides of the political spectrum in Britain, France and elsewhere, there are those who still trust and believe in a lost halcyon age when life was better and everyone happier. It's incredible to think that people hark after an era of division, isolationism and destructive nationalism, but they do. And as Brexit has shown, there are even millions willing to vote for it.

The nostalgia at the heart of fake history is bullshit but it's attractive bullshit, and it is at the root of the rise of destructive 21st-century populism and for Trump and his imitators.

The Thucydidean principle that we must not repeat the mistakes of the past but learn from them instead was at its apogee in 1945 and the generation that lived through the war gave us the UN, NHS, NATO and the EU.

Knowledge is key in overcoming and defeating the twin monsters of populism and disinformation that cause so many of contemporary political woes.

There is no path to Utopia and it is not paved with Spitfires and monuments to great men. The likes of Nigel Farage who promised such a path found their vision in misremembered history, flawed narratives, unrealistic ambitions and crucially, in the notions of a world that no longer exists and may never have done so. To embrace the present and the future, we must first understand the truth of our past.

Uncle Barry on Facebook, wallowing in phony nostalgia, likely knows as much about the facts of Churchill's long and complex life as he does about the motives of refugees. Nick the former Brexit Party candidate might have seen *Where Eagles Dare* and *Inglourious Basterds,* but it doesn't make him an expert on the causes of the First World War or the Treaty of Versailles.

The Dunning–Kruger effect and illusory superiority encourage them and many others to think otherwise. Nostalgia is no more equal to history than truth is equal to a lie.

Fake history, like fake news, poses a threat to us all. It distorts our collective worldview – it shapes our modern politics to the ultimate detriment of all. And as such we must all take responsibility to fight it, to activate our inner bullshit detectors and to query what we are told and ask these critical questions:

"Is that true?", "Did that really happen?" and "Who benefits?"

We must accept too that there's no shame in being wrong. On the contrary, mistake-making is the very path to knowledge. That willingness to learn and understand the very key to how our species has evolved from those caves in the Swabian Alps to today.

The Wright brothers did not fly on their first attempt. They spent years working out lift equations, building wind tunnels and growing from their failures along the way. And through the pursuit of understanding, through that determination and open mindedness, they succeeded.

On 17th December 1903, Orville Wright mounted an airplane made of bicycle parts, spruce and canvas and powered by a tiny 9 kW engine and, shortly afterwards, was airborne. In that first brief flight, he travelled 37 metres at a height of around 4 metres. A mere 65 years later, Neil Armstrong stepped out from the lunar capsule of *Apollo 11* and onto the surface of the Moon.

Human beings can do astonishing things when we rid ourselves of the menace of illusory superiority and embrace knowledge instead.

We would all do well to aspire to be more like Thucydides and the Wright brothers and less like Franz Reichelt or the purveyors of fake history. And in so doing we must remember too, that the best days are never, for the most part, behind us – and that, on the contrary, they are usually yet to come.

P.S. One of those stories I told you about Donald Trump in Chapter 10 is a deliberate lie – sorry

ACKNOWLEDGEMENTS

I am indebted to my agent, Doug Young, who convinced me to write this, and to Oliver Holden-Rea and the team at Welbeck for commissioning it.

The book was written during the coronavirus pandemic, so a big thank you to all those who received unsolicited calls and emails and responded so kindly. Particular thanks to Ian Kikuchi and Sean Rehling at the Imperial War Museum London for digging into the archives regarding Dunkirk and the *Tamzine*. My thanks too to Iqbal Wahhab for telling me the story of chicken tikka masala, to Neville Morley, for unwittingly giving me a crash course in Thucydides via his writings, and Dr Matthew Sweet, who first sparked my thoughts on 'Ladybird libertarians'.

I am extremely grateful to Peter and Pippa Fairbanks for their contributions on Hitler's art and for their unflinching support generally.

The *Byline Times* team – Peter Jukes, Hardeep Matharu and Stephen Colegrave – have given me almost unprecedented free range to write about the things that interest me over the last few years. Some of the ideas I first tackled on the pages of their paper have found their way into this book. Likewise, Stephan Faris and Esther King at *Politico Europe*, who first commissioned me to write about meaningless apologies. The pieces I have written for

Politico on the role of fake history in the Brexit debate played a significant part in the genesis of this work.

Enormous thanks to family, friends and academics who have acted as a sounding board for the project and who have encouraged me. Special mention to Tessa Fantoni, Dawn Beck, Per Laleng, Toby Thompson, Matt Tombs, Dr Roddy Brett, the Dalys and Team Bradley's.

None of this would have happened without great teachers in childhood. Messrs. Higham, Bromley and Pedley – wherever you may be – you inspired my fascination with history; you see, I was paying attention after all. Thanks too to Alan Beck – my university tutor – who told me I should write.

Lastly, love and gratitude to my extraordinary, long-suffering wife, Helen, and to my wonderful children, James and Sophia. My first audience, my first critics, without whom it would all be meaningless.

REFERENCES

All of the following provided useful source information:

Politico, *Spectator*, CNN, *Daily Telegraph*, *Guardian*, *Observer*, *New Statesman*, *Daily Herald*, *Daily Mail*, BBC web archive, *History Today*, *History Extra*, *Vox*, *Le Monde*, Pathé archive, First-WorldWar.com, *Quartär* (scientific journal of the Hugo Obermaier Society for Ice Age and Stone Age Research), Quote Investigator, Snopes, Margaret Thatcher Foundation archive, UK Parliamentary archive, Smithsonian, National Archive, Mass Observation Archive, International Churchill Society website and archive, *New York Times*, Association of Dunkirk Little Ships archive, World History Encyclopedia, among others.

Select bibliography

Project Gutenberg was an amazing resource during the pandemic, allowing access to dozens of original texts online, from Washington Irving's biography of Columbus to Nazi-era children's history books to Thucydides.

The following also provided key material:

Armitstead, Claire: 'The Ladybird Phenomenon' in the *Guardian* (Feb 2017)

Buckle, Richard, *U and Non-U Revisited* (Debrett's 1978)

Burgess, Anthony *A Mouthful of Air* (William Morrow and Co. 1993)

Burrows, Simon, British Propaganda for Russia in the Napoleonic Wars: the 'Courier d'Angleterre', NZ *Slavonic Journal* (1993), pp. 85–100

Chatterji, Joya and Washbrook, David (eds) *Routledge Handbook of the South Asia Diaspora* (Routledge, 2013)

Clayton, Tim *This Dark Business: The Secret War Against Napoleon* (Little, Brown, 2018)

Crystal, David, *The Stories of English* (Penguin, 2004)

Churchill, Winston *My Early Life* (1930)

Dalrymple, William, *The White Mughals* (Penguin, 2002)

Devine, Sir Tom, *The Scottish Clearances – a history of the dispossessed 160–1900* (Penguin 2018)

Grant, Oliver *Juche – How to live well the North Korean Way* (satire) (Bantam, 2020)

Graves, Robert, *Goodbye to All That* (Penguin, 1929)

Herodotus, *The Histories,* tran. Aubrey de Sélincourt (Penguin)

Hopkins, Donald R, *The Greatest Killer – Smallpox in History* (University of Chicago Press, 2002)

Irving, Washington, *A History of the Life and Voyages of Christopher Columbus* (1828)

Jenkins, Roy, *Churchill* (Pan 2001)

Johnson, Boris, *The Churchill Factor* (Hodder Stoughton, 2015)

Johnson, David *The Man Who Didn't Shoot Hitler* (History Press, 2014)

Lack, Clem, *Story of Cape York Peninsula* (archive)

Langer, Walter, *The Mind of Adolf Hitler* (Basic Books, 1972, via US OSS)

Lee, Grace, 'The Political Philosophy of Juche' (Time.com, 2014)

Marshall, H E, *Our Island Story* (Civitas, 2007) (Also *Our Empire Story* and *This Country of Ours* via Gutenberg)

McCrum, Robert, William, Cran, MacNeil Robert, *The Story of English* (Faber Faber, 2011)

Millard, Candice, *Hero of the Empire* (Doubleday, 2016)

Mitford, Nancy (ed.) *Noblesse Oblige* (Penguin 1956)

Montague-Smith, Patrick (ed.), *Debrett's Correct Form* (Debrett's, 1970)

Morgan, Scott G, Wisneski Daniel C, Skitka Linda J, 'The expulsion from Disneyland: the social psychological impact of 9/11', research at University of Illinois at Chicago (2011)

Morley, Neville, *Sphinx*, collected blogs (thesphinxblog.com)

Orwell, George, 'Notes of Nationalism' (essay) (Penguin, 1945)

Peet, John, *The Long Engagement* (Fourth Estate, 1989)

Rutherford, Adam, 'You're Descended from Royalty and So is Everyone Else' ex. from *A Brief History of Everyone Who Ever Lived* (Nautilus, 2018)

Sardar, Ziauddin, *Balti Britain* (Grantam 2009)

Scott, Harry, 'My Dear Everybody', letters (SOAS archives, London)

Silvester, Christopher (ed.) *Penguin Book of Interviews* (Penguin, 1994)

Snyder, Timothy *The Road to Unfreedom* (Vintage, 2018)

Venerable Bede; *An Ecclesiastical History of the English People*, eds. Judith McClure, Roger Collins (Oxford Classics)

Weber, Jacob, 'Patterns in British Height 1770–1845' – essay (2018)

Yeatman, R J and Sellar, W C *1066 and All That* (Methuen, 1930)

INDEX